MAXIMIZING PROJECT RESULTS

A Practical Guide to Project Selection, Scoping, Estimation and Management

J ROSS PUBLISHING

BPB PUBLICATIONS

FIRST INDIAN EDITION 2017

ISBN : 978-93-8655-148-1

REPRINTED UNDER A LICENCE FROM AGREEMENT PUBLISHER: J ROSS PUBLISHING, 300 ROAD, #305, S PINE ISLAND PLANTATION, FL 33324 (USA)

FOR SALE IN INDIA, NEPAL, BANGLADESH, SRI LANKA, PAKISTAN, BHUTAN & MALDIVES ONLY.

Distributors:

BPB PUBLICATIONS
20, Ansari Road, Darya Ganj
New Delhi-110002
Ph: 23254990/23254991

BPB BOOK CENTRE
376 Old Lajpat Rai Market,
Delhi-110006
Ph: 23861747

COMPUTER BOOK CENTRE
12, Shrungar Shopping Centre,
M.G.Road, BENGALURU–560001
Ph: 25587923/25584641

DECCAN AGENCIES
4-3-329, Bank Street,
Hyderabad-500195
Ph: 24756967/24756400

MICRO MEDIA
Shop No. 5, Mahendra Chambers, 150
DN Rd. Next to Capital Cinema, V.T.
(C.S.T.) Station, MUMBAI-400 001 Ph:
22078296/22078297

Published by Manish Jain for BPB Publications, 20, Ansari Road, Darya Ganj, New Delhi-110002 and Printed him at Repro India Pvt. Ltd, Mumbai

To my wife, Polina, who has always provided unconditional support to all of my audacious endeavors, and to my parents who have constantly served as an inexhaustible source of sobering pragmatism and common sense.

Table of Contents

Preface

What processes and capabilities does an organization need to achieve exceptional project results on a consistent basis?

Presumably, any organization that uses projects to achieve its strategic objectives would have an interest in improving the success rate or results of projects in its portfolio and every project management professional would have an interest in improving their rate of successful project delivery. As such, this book attempts to provide answers to the above question by presenting key concepts, techniques, and processes of project management, scope definition and planning, and portfolio management within a unified framework. Written in non-academic, easy-to-understand language with numerous and helpful examples, this text traces the life of projects from idea selection to closeout in order to facilitate reader comprehension and assimilation.

Readers are not required to subscribe to any specific methodology or particular brand of project management such as traditional versus Agile or weak versus strong matrix. The approach followed transcends these differences and avoids academic theories that don't really work well in real-world practice as yet. The focus is on economic principles, skills, and the hands-on practicality of tools, techniques and methodologies.

Several chapters are dedicated to the field of project scoping and elicitation of business requirements. While these topics have been explored for many years in the software engineering and development fields, they have been noticeably absent from the majority of modern project management literature. Although the author attempts to infuse the generic project management knowledge areas with the best and the greatest advances from the IT and software development industries, the concepts, tools, techniques, and methodologies presented are applicable to companies in all industries.

Each chapter of this book begins with a case example or anecdote referred to as a historical perspective. The intent is to demonstrate that humanity has been trying to address these issues for the last several centuries and to provide some fascinating and entertaining reading before delving deeply into the topics presented. For example, why did the French battleship *Magenta* receive the nickname *Le Grande Hotel,* and what does this have to do with the field of project management?

Overview of the Book

The book consists of nineteen chapters covering the key aspects of project management, portfolio management, and scope definition. The chapters are organized somewhat chronologically as one would proceed through a typical project.

Chapters 2, 3, 4, 5, 10, and 14 deal primarily with project management topics such as assessing the organizational need for project management (Chapter 2), estimation (Chapter 3), negotiations (Chapter 4), writing project charters (Chapter 5), creation of project plans (Chapter 10), and the value of lessons-learned documents (Chapter 14).

Chapters 6, 7, and 11 cover purely scope definition topics including defining high-level project scope (Chapter 6), eliciting detailed business requirements (Chapter 7), and scope troubleshooting (Chapter 11).

Chapters 8, 9, 12, and 13 embrace topics that belong to both project management and scope definition areas including the role of creativity in projects (Chapter 8), a methodology to incorporate requirements engineering into the project management process (Chapter 9), the need for peer reviews and inspections (Chapter 12), and a discussion of useful scope management techniques (Chapter 13).

Chapter 15 includes an introduction to project portfolio management and its dependence on proper project scoping and management.

Three chapters discuss the three major pillars of project portfolio management: maximizing portfolio value (Chapter 16), balancing the project mix (Chapter 17), and linking portfolio to strategy (Chapter 18).

Chapter 19 discusses some of the challenges of implementing the methodologies described in the book. See Figure P.1 for a map of the book's contents.

Who Is This Book For?

There are three categories of professionals who should find this book useful. The first group includes senior functional directors and managers, C-level executives, and senior project sponsors and stakeholders. While Chapters 1, 2, and 15–19 are most directly related to their domain of responsibilities, senior managers need to understand the issues and challenges that are faced by project managers. These managers also need to have at least a basic appreciation of the project manage-

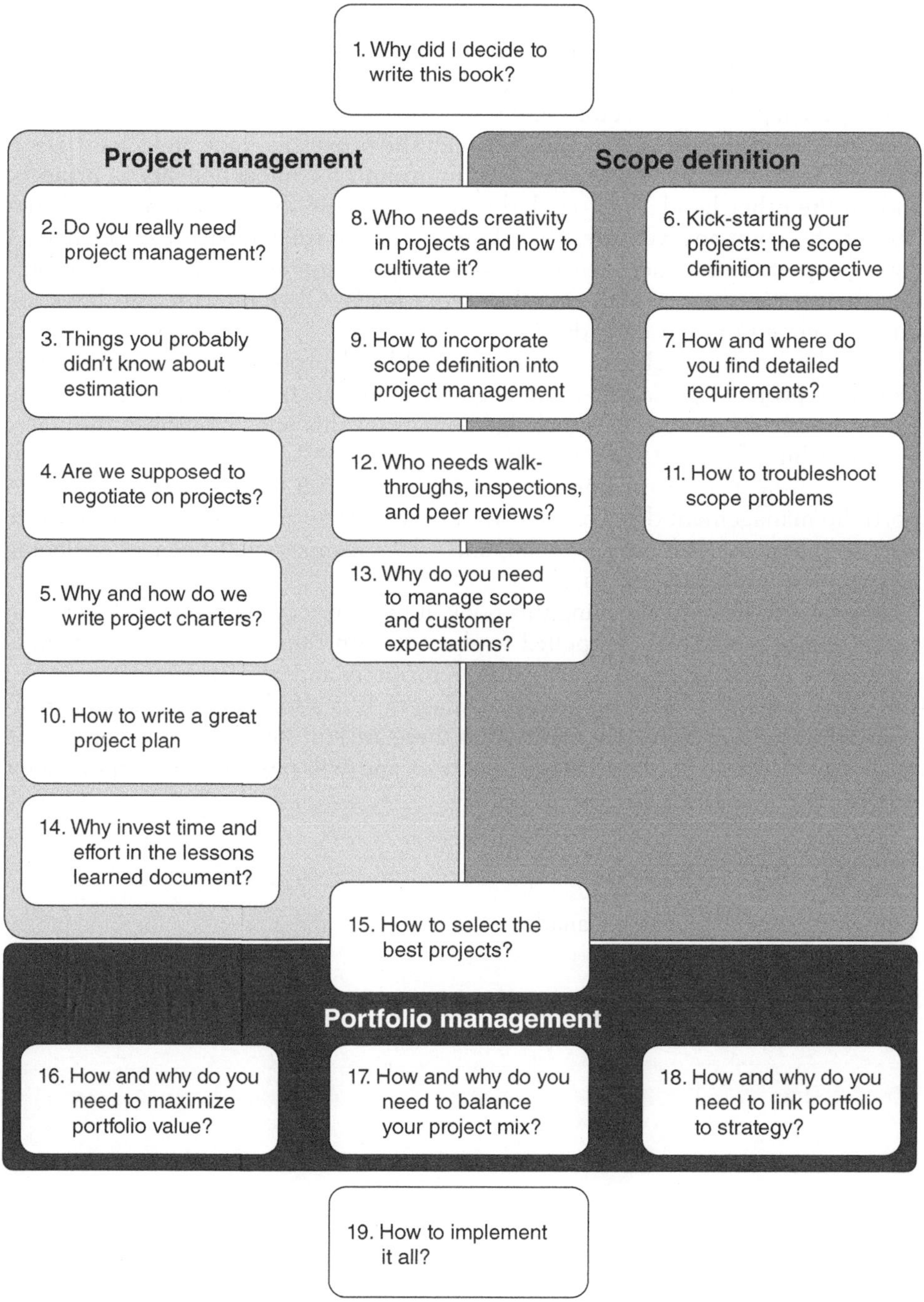

Figure P.1 Map of book's content by chapter.

ment and scope planning tactical side since portfolio selection algorithms contain such variables as scope, cost, time, and size of the project pipeline.

The second group includes program, portfolio, project management office (PMO) managers and directors, and senior project managers. Representatives of this category frequently get caught between the proverbial rock and a hard place. On one hand, they are responsible for the smooth technical delivery of projects, and on the other hand, they regularly take the blame for poor commercial success of the company ventures. In addition, these professionals need to have a good grasp of the art and science of sizing project pipelines so as not to overburden their project teams with excessive work loads. All chapters in this book are directly related to their daily duties.

The third group includes junior and mid-level project managers as well as technical project specialists (e.g., engineers, architects, developers). Chapters 3–14 directly relate to the knowledge domain of this level of project managers and of technical project team members.

These project team members frequently end up on the receiving end of bad portfolio management decisions and wonder why they are always so overworked, why so many company projects fail, and why organizational finances are being wasted on questionable ventures.

It is hoped that, after reading this book, junior project managers and technical team members will feel compelled to share it with their superiors so that these superiors can learn how to select projects properly and gain an understanding of the daily challenges faced by project managers. It is also hoped that senior managers who read this book will realize that there are still some improvements to be made to their project management practices and will pass this book on to their subordinates.

Enjoy!
Jamal Moustafaev
Burnaby, British Columbia,Canada

Prologue

I really enjoyed reading this book. It is well written and the author, Jamal Moustafaev, has a charming and sometimes subtle sense of humor delivered in a chatty, simple style. The chapters, full of valuable insights well beyond the typical project management presentations, are introduced with diverse and engaging historic case examples. These are presented to illustrate the advice that follows and to drive home key points.

And the advice that follows is based primarily on the author's own working experience together with the experiences he has culled from the executives, business analysts, portfolio managers and project managers that he has taught in his classes. At times, Jamal's advice and recommendations as to why you should use this or that technique are reduced to a simple cost example to demonstrate the relative economics. At other times, the text is laced with short anecdotes to demonstrate the consequences of false moves.

The author also provides tables of practical and probing questions to ask those difficult people reluctant to give the time to the thoughtful answers necessary to deal with difficult project management situations. Interestingly, the book is as much about organizational attitudes and behavior as it is about project planning and procedures.

Executives faced with project portfolio management, or who are venturing into the area for the first time, will find the latter part of the book particularly valuable. New solutions are offered for those seemingly intractable problems of project portfolio management. Examples include how best to display complex data to busy executives for optimum decision making, or how best to manage "pipeline capacity" for maximum throughput.

For those in a hurry, each chapter concludes with a summary that can lead readers back to the solutions they will inevitably need at some time in their future management careers. Enjoy.

R. Max Wideman, P.Eng
FCSCE, FEIC, FICE, FPMI
Vancouver, British Columbia, Canada

About the Author

Jamal Moustafaev, BBA, MBA, PMP—president and founder of Thinktank Consulting, is an internationally acclaimed expert in the areas of project/portfolio management, project scoping, process improvement and corporate training. He has done work for private-sector companies and government organizations in Canada and the United States including Port Metro Vancouver, Accenture, Best Buy, Central1, Wolters Kluwer Financial Group, Kaiser Permanente, HSBC Bank, Standard Life Insurance, Kodak, and many others.

Mr. Moustafaev is a certified Project Management Professional (PMP®). He holds an MBA in Finance and a BBA in Finance and Management Science from Simon Fraser University. In addition to teaching project management courses at British Columbia Institute of Technology, Jamal also offers the following corporate seminars through his company:

- Practical Portfolio Management—Selecting and Managing the Right Projects
- Successful Hands-on Management of IT and Software Projects
- Successful Hands-on Management of Modern-day Projects
- From Waterfall to Agile—Practical Requirements Engineering

Mr. Moustafaev is a published author who contributes to various project management publications, and he is a frequent speaker at various project management conferences and events such as Project World, Business Analyst World, and many others. His presentations have consistently received a very high rating from conference attendees.

For further information, feel free to contact Mr. Moustafaev at:

Jamal Moustafaev BBA, MBA, PMP
President and CEO
Thinktank Consulting
E-mail: info@thinktankconsulting.ca
Website: www.thinktankconsulting.ca

Foreword

For almost half a century, project managers were brought on board projects merely to facilitate the execution of the project plan. Project managers neither participated in the selection of the project (and the accompanying portfolio management process) nor were they involved in the establishment of the project plan. It was not uncommon for the marketing and sales force to make unrealistic promises to the client to win their business, accept perhaps impossible deadlines and budgets, develop a high-level plan based upon extreme optimism, and then bring the project manager on board and say, "Execute." To make matters worse, project managers were not informed as to the sometimes unrealistic assumptions that were made in the decision to bid on a contract. If the project was successful, sales and marketing would be at the head of the line looking for their bonus. If the project was to fail, then the *let's blame the project manager* and try to convince the customer that a more experienced project manager is now available to take over the project tactic was a common practice.

Today, all of that has changed. Project managers are now expected to have a much better understanding of the business than their predecessors. In addition, project managers are being brought on board the project at the beginning of the initiation phase rather than at the end of the phase. Leading companies that are positioning themselves for the future rather than the present are asking the project managers to participate in project selection, scoping, and estimation as well as management.

Jamal Moustafaev's book, *Delivering Exceptional Project Results: A Practical Guide to Project Selection, Scoping, Estimating and Management* gives us a glimpse into the future role of the project manager as mentioned above. While some project managers may be doing some of these things now, most project managers are simply viewed as being responsible for project execution. This picture will change.

The book is easy reading in a cursory format with numerous examples explaining why and how the role must change, and it discusses the ill-fated results of not doing these things. The author cites numerous military examples which are interesting, since project managers often consider themselves conducting a battle with senior management for project management improvements. If your company believes that project failure is an option, then perhaps you should not read this book. But if you want the ratio of successes to failure to improve significantly, you must begin with a good understanding of the role of the project manager. This book will guide you from there into the future.

Harold Kerzner, Ph.D.
Professor Emeritus
Baldwin-Wallace College

This book has free material available for download from the Web Added Value™ resource center at *www.jrosspub.com*

At J. Ross Publishing we are committed to providing today's professional with practical, hands-on tools that enhance the learning experience and give readers an opportunity to apply what they have learned. That is why we offer free ancillary materials available for download on this book and all participating Web Added Value™ publications. These online resources may include interactive versions of material that appears in the book or supplemental templates, worksheets, models, plans, case studies, proposals, spreadsheets, and assessment tools, among other things. Whenever you see the WAV™ symbol in any of our publications, it means bonus materials accompany the book and are available from the Web Added Value™ Download Resource Center at www.jrosspub.com.

Downloads for *Delivering Exceptional Project Results* include templates for documenting project charters, plans, meeting minutes, change requests, status reports, and summary/lessons learned reports.

Strategy without tactics is the slowest route to victory.
Tactics without strategy is the noise before defeat.
Sun Tzu, Art of War (490 BC)

1

Introduction

Historical Perspective

Look on My Works, Ye Mighty, and Despair!

The idea for building a colossal dam in the southern part of Egypt had been considered by the country's president Gamal Abdel Nasser since the mid-fifties. There were a number of reasons why he and the rest of the Egyptian government thought it would be a great benefit to their country: the desire to come up with an impressive deed after defeats in the war with Israel and the Suez crisis, the need to maintain steady levels of the Nile throughout the year, and the aspiration to produce more electricity to support the increase in the production of cane sugar, cottons, maize, fertilizer, steel, and textiles.

After the Western powers withdrew their promise of aid for the dam, the Egyptians turned to the Soviet Union for financing and expertise. The Soviet government, for its own political reasons, duly obliged and the project got underway.

While managing to capture the technical scope of the project fairly well, the planners somehow completely neglected to talk to the real customers: the people who would be most affected by this venture. As a result, a multitude of issues, both tactical and strategic in nature, surfaced soon after the completion of the dam in 1971 (see Illustration 1.1).

First, the construction of the power plant led to the flooding of the temples of Abu Simbel which eventually had to be lifted above the water and repositioned at a great cost to the government of Egypt.

The second disappointment was the realization that the hydro plant associated with the dam would not produce sufficient amounts of electricity for Egypt's growing economy. The situation was made worse by the ironic fact that, because

Illustration 1.1 Aswan Dam—satellite photo

the Nile was no longer flooding the valley and depositing rich alluvial silt on the agricultural fields, the country was faced with an increased demand for fertilizer production.

And finally, the construction of the Aswan Dam led to a significant increase in the population of snails, the carriers of a dangerous and debilitating disease—*bilhazria*. It has been estimated that a third of the Egyptian population is now suffering from this ailment.

It is quite fascinating to analyze this project from three different angles: project management, portfolio management, and requirements engineering (scope definition). Let us start with scope definition. As mentioned previously, the planners of the Aswan Dam neglected to consider the needs of the real customers of the project—the people living in the valley of the Nile. A simple fact taught to school-age children around the world is that the ancient Egyptian civilization flourished thanks to the Nile flooding the valley and depositing its fertile silt on the shores of the great river. How this little detail somehow eluded the planners of this project is mind-boggling, to say the least.

It is also quite obvious that the risk management area of project management was also completely lost on the planners. For example, it is surprising that they managed to completely ignore the possibility of flooding of the Abu Simbel temples. The catastrophic rise in the occurrence of bilhazria, although not so easily predicted, should have also been foreseen.

The issues on the portfolio management side are therefore deeply rooted in the failures in the areas of project and scope management. Had the requirements-elicitation stage been conducted properly, the additional costs associated with the soil depletion could have been avoided. Had there been better project risk management, the cost of Abu Simbel's relocation could have been reduced. The impact of the disease is difficult to assess, but it is safe to assume that the fact that one-third of the population suffers from a serious disease is devastating.

Therefore, it is not surprising that when considering all of these blunders, the financial costs alone of the Aswan Dam, both short-term and long-term, by far outweighed any benefits to the Egyptian people.

Why Did I Decide to Write This Book? The Manifesto

Like most project management professionals, I was trained to think that there are several distinct and independent project-related disciplines or sciences out there: project portfolio management, project management, and requirements engineering (see Figure 1.1). Just to clarify, requirements engineering, although considered to be a part of scope definition, frequently falls into the hands of business analysts in the software development industry, architects in the construction industry, and engineers in the technology sector.

During my career as a project manager, requirements analyst, process improvement consultant, and especially as a course instructor, I have relied on my

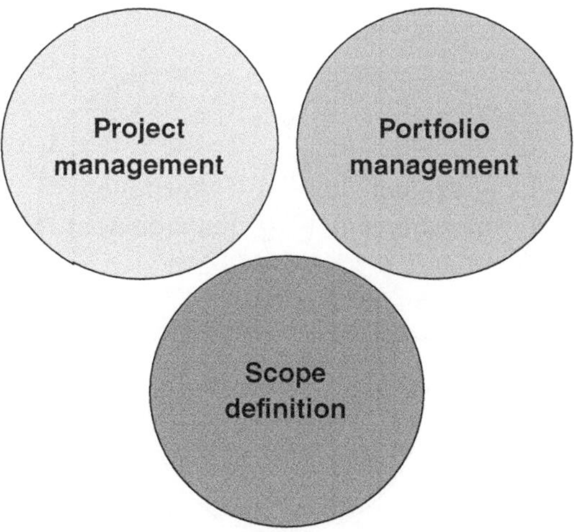

Figure 1.1 Project management, portfolio management, and scope definition—separate

own experience as well as the multitude of great books, schools of thought, and methodologies developed in portfolio management, project management, and scope definition.

In recent years however, I have found myself in a number of peculiar situations (to be described later) that led me to the following observations:

1. Project management, portfolio management, and scope definition are strongly interrelated (see Figure 1.2), and while it has so far been acceptable to study and develop them separately at the academic level, the desire to deliver successful projects will nearly always necessitate consideration of all three of these disciplines. Failure to recognize this complete three-dimensional picture leads companies to wasted efforts and disappointments when attempting to control their project pipeline.
2. The business requirements elicitation (i.e., the initial phase of project scope definition) is underdeveloped (for good reasons to be explained later) in today's project management science with the exception of IT and software development where scope definition (aka business analysis) is relatively advanced but excluded from the project manager's domain of responsibilities. As a result, most industries have a prominent knowledge gap in project-scope planning—a gap that starts sometime after the project charter has been completed and approved and ends somewhere around the point when the work commences on the detailed blueprints, technical drawings, and bills of materials.
3. Few companies have a good grasp of these three disciplines or understand their interdependence, which is one of the major reasons so many projects fail or underperform. According to the Project Management

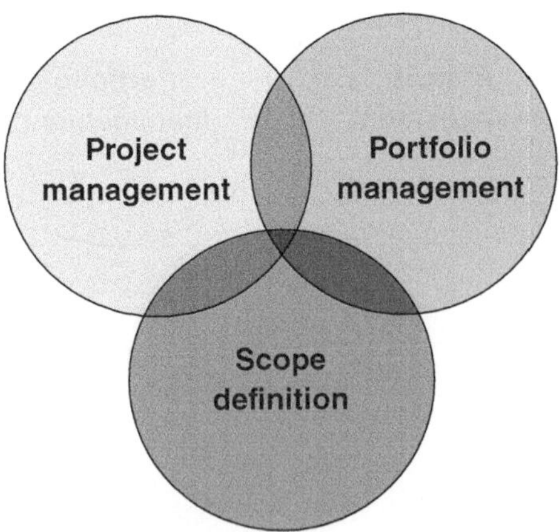

Figure 1.2 Project management, portfolio management, and scope definition—overlapping

Institute[1] (PMI®), out of the $2.3 trillion that is spent annually on projects, $1 trillion ends up in underperforming ventures.

4. While there are many great books devoted to each one of these disciplines, there is a distinct lack of works dedicated to unifying project management, portfolio management, and requirements engineering into one easily understood, user-friendly, best practices platform. This implies that a professional or a senior manager interested in learning and understanding how to run projects efficiently in order to deliver great products or services has to purchase several books of various complexity and written by different authors, examine them all, and integrate all of the different methodologies into one coherent and functioning strategy.

In my experience this is something that almost never happens and is one of the major reasons I decided to write this book.

Is It All Really Interconnected?

Studies have shown that how people perceive things can vary greatly based on their personal experiences and, consequently, can cause them to draw different conclusions. This phenomenon proved to be true when trying to explain this interconnected concept prior to using a few extremely simple business case scenarios in seminars with experienced project managers and executives. As was the case with these students, it is hoped that anyone reading the scenarios will perceive each one with the same understanding and will agree with the suggested conclusions.

Case Scenario 1

> The CEO of a company hires a contract project manager to lead his team in the development and successful delivery of a specific product. He calls the project manager into his office and proceeds to tell her that the product in question is the best typewriter ever built by mankind. She is told, in no uncertain terms, to get to it right away. Assume that internal company stakeholders are eager to cooperate with the project manager and to readily provide her with all the high-level features and detailed requirements for the device. She is given a reasonable budget and a deadline in order to deliver the final product. After several months of work, while meticulously following all of the applicable project management rules and methodologies, the project team indeed delivers the best typewriter in the world, on budget, and even a little bit ahead of schedule.

Did she do a good or a bad job as a project manager? Obviously she did a good job at delivering precisely what the client ordered.

Do you think this product would sell successfully on today's market? Since the target audience has been using word processing software on computers for twenty years or more, the typewriter likely would be a complete commercial failure.

Whose fault is it that the project has little or no chance of being successful? It is the fault of the client CEO who ordered it.

The lesson here is *a company can only deliver successful projects if it selects good projects to implement*, which falls under the executive-level portfolio management domain.

Case Scenario 2

> Dave, a successful entrepreneur, owns a piece of land on an exotic island, and he decides to build a luxury family home there as a short-term investment. He estimates that the sale price of the home will be $500,000 and the building contractor assures Dave that his company can accomplish the job in one year for a budget of $400,000. A study of the cost of similar homes built in the area confirms that this number is reasonable. As such, Dave estimates his return on investment (ROI) for this deal to be 25 percent [($500,000 – $400,000)/$400,000]. Since a 25 percent ROI on a short-term investment is a respectable number, Dave agrees to proceed with the project.
>
> Due to other demands on Dave's time, he is unable to fly to the island throughout the year to check on the work being done. The construction project manager assures him during informal chats, on the occasions that Dave calls him for an update, that everything is going great. Dave learns at the end of the year, however, that the ad hoc approach to project scoping and scheduling that other key project management methods used by the project manager causes the project cost to balloon to $600,000 and that he is legally obligated to pay that amount. This new cost figure drives his initial project ROI from a respectable 25 percent to a disastrous minus 16.7 percent [($500,000 – $600,000)/$600,000].

Was this project a good idea overall? Obviously the answer is yes according to the cost estimates confirmed as being reasonable for the area and the projected ROI.

What factors prevented this venture from becoming a successful project? Dave contracted with a construction company that had poor project management expertise and that was unable to scope, plan, and properly deliver the project on budget. The wrong type of project contract was used. Dave should have insisted on a fixed-price agreement. There were serious issues with project monitoring and control as the contractor did not provide Dave with honest and reliable status reports.

The lesson here is that *to deliver a successful project a company must have a good understanding of the tactical side of project delivery (project scoping, planning, monitoring, and control mechanisms), which falls under the project management domain,* in order to ensure that the good ideas are properly converted into great products or services.

Case Scenario 3

> You are a student in a project management course and the average number of questions on a two-hour final exam for this type of course is five. How well would you realistically expect to do on the two-hour exam if the instructor decided to include 100 questions of the same size and complexity on the final test?

Obviously, no matter how smart and well-prepared you had been for the exam, you would have undoubtedly failed.

The lesson is that *a company must have an appreciation of its own throughput capacity and be able to ensure that the total size of its ventures corresponds to the size of its project pipeline*. This means the number of projects your employees can handle and deliver successfully is a finite number, which falls under the executive-level portfolio management domain.

It is hoped that now you are open to the idea that these distinct disciplines are interconnected.

The Origin of This Interconnected Concept

Let me now share some of my experiences and conversations that first led to the belief that project management, portfolio management, and requirements engineering are interconnected. Real world experiences are discussed in the following examples.

Project Management and Requirements Engineering

> **Example 1.** Early in my career while teaching a project management course in both corporate and university environments, I would eventually get to the project scope definition part of the course and say that the project manager, with the help of other technical team members and with input from customers, should define the project scope. Project scope is captured in the project plan or in a separate document called software requirements specifications, statement of work, or some other term, depending on the industry.

This statement was typically greeted by complete silence in the room with about twenty pairs of eyes looking out in utter confusion and bewilderment. Finally, one brave student in the room would raise a hand and say, "This is all very informative, but exactly how do you do that?"

Not surprisingly, this topic was beyond the scope of this course and was not addressed in any of the general project management books. It was taught in a best-practices course in requirements engineering. To address the gap, I used the great advances in requirements elicitation achieved in software development and transferred them to a two- to three-hour module on project scope definition in my course. However, there were still a number of important topics that I did not have time to cover because I had only a three-hour lecture at my disposal.

> **Example 2.** Another key overlap of project management and scope definition was best illustrated when a business analyst who was attending my requirements engineering course asked, "Okay, so what you are saying is that there is a project management triangle with scope, time, and budget at the top of each corner. The project manager is in charge of time and budget, and I am responsible for documenting the scope since I am the only one qualified to gather and record the requirements. Let's assume that we are capable of communicating really well back and forth about these three dimensions (which is rare). But what if we need to negotiate the triangle (different options) with the customer? Who should be doing that? How do we reconcile the fact that the project manager is in charge of two dimensions and I am in charge of another?"

Project Management and Portfolio Management

Consider a shift in focus to the higher levels of the organizational pyramid in order to describe several interesting interactions with senior managers.

> **Example 3.** I had the following conversation after presenting project cost and budget estimation to a group of executives of a large construction company:
>
> EXECUTIVE: My department heads have always been telling me that we need more people to accomplish all of our projects. I have a bit of an issue with that stance since I don't know whether:
>
> 1. They are lying to me, and I just have to continue pressuring them to be more efficient and creative.
> 2. They are telling the truth, and I have to provide them with additional resources and cut some projects
>
> In addition, if I decide to cut some projects, how do I know which projects should be killed? And to complicate things even more, if I provide them with additional resources, how do I convince a board of directors that an increase in head count is a worthwhile investment?
>
> AUTHOR: What we are discussing today is project management, and your questions fall into the domain of portfolio management. I simply can't answer those questions during a 15-minute break.
>
> EXECUTIVE: I wish we had more time to talk about it.

> **Example 4.** Likewise, I was teaching a project portfolio management course to a group of high-ranking executives, and as I was wrapping up the first module of the course, the following conversation between one of the managers and me took place:
>
> AUTHOR: Once you have selected the initial grouping of projects to include in your portfolio, you will have to manage them and monitor their performance.

MANAGER: Hey, wait a second there. Tracking and monitoring are in the domain of project management, aren't they?

AUTHOR: Yes, they are.

MANAGER: So, what you are saying is that unless I have a reasonable level of project management, I can't do this portfolio stuff?

AUTHOR: Unfortunately, this would be very challenging. By the way, you will also need a good grasp on scoping as well. Otherwise, how would you be able to make a go/kill decision on project proposals if you don't know what you are trying to build?

These conversations reminded me of the infamous rock-paper-scissors game where one domain is dependent on a second knowledge area, and the second area, in turn, is correlated with a third methodology.

Applying the Scientific Approach

The types of experiences previously discussed presented themselves time and again, which led me to re-examine the classical portfolio management model (see Figure 1.3).

Essentially, this diagram demonstrates that in order to run a successful portfolio of projects, the company has to start with an idea that should be encapsulated in a business case document. The document is submitted for a review (gate), and the management team makes a go/kill decision at that time. If the idea receives management's blessing, the project charter is written, and another review takes

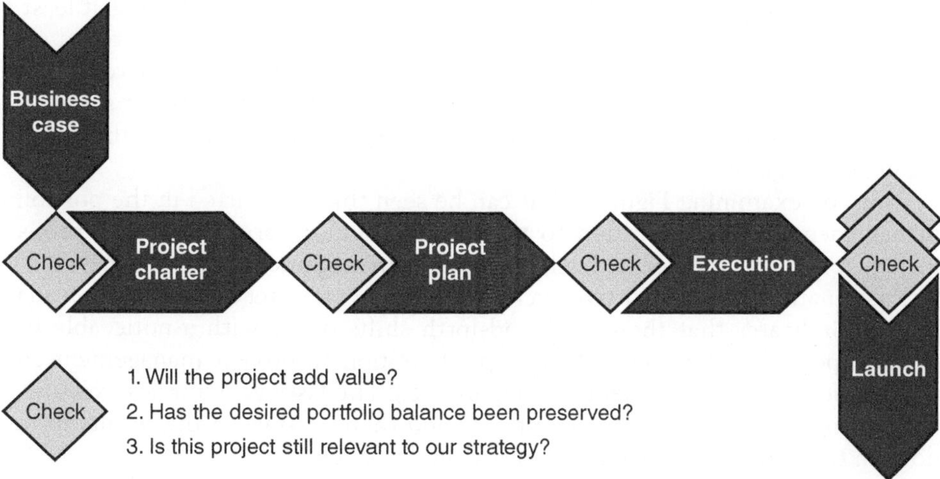

Figure 1.3 High-level view of the project portfolio management process

place. If the project is still considered to be valuable to the organization, the project charter is approved and the project moves to the planning stage where the project plan is created. It then progresses to the execution phase with go/kill reviews at regular intervals. At each one of these reviews, the following three questions have to be answered by the executives:

1. Will the project add value to the organization?
2. Has the desired portfolio balance been preserved?
3. Is this project still relevant to our strategy?

But here is an important question: what are the uniting characteristics of the first three steps in Figure 1.3, namely, creation of the business case, project charter and the project plan? In all of the first three steps someone has to scope the project and estimate the project with progressive degrees of accuracy as we move from the business case to the project plan. This is where requirements engineering and project management come into play.

In addition, once the project moves into the execution stage of the portfolio cycle, the organization needs a sound project management framework to control and monitor it in order to provide senior management with meaningful information for go/kill decisions at later stages.

Let's examine the expanded, zoomed-in version of the processes shown in Figure 1.3 (see Figures 1.4 and 1.5).

As seen in Figure 1.4, once the idea for a new venture is generated, someone, typically the person responsible for the idea, has to write a business case document. The business case should enable the executives of the company to answer the three key project portfolio management questions mentioned previously. But how can an executive assess the value of the project (typically financial because most of the companies are in business to make money) without having at least a ballpark estimate of the project cost? And how can we arrive at the project cost if we do not know, at least at a high level, what we are building? Therefore, it is obvious that in order to write the business case document, the author should be able to first scope the project (at a high level) and, second, estimate the project (again, at a high level).

Thus, by examining Figure 1.4, it can be seen that we started in the portfolio management's domain, shifted to the scope definition area, moved to project management, and then came back to portfolio management.

Examination of the next two cycles—the project charter and the project plan phases—indicates that these back-and-forth shifts occur with a noticeable frequency: portfolio management to scope definition to project management and back to portfolio management (see Figure 1.5). The last cycle implies executing, monitoring, and reporting on the project and then passing on the results to the domain of portfolio management for go/kill decisions.

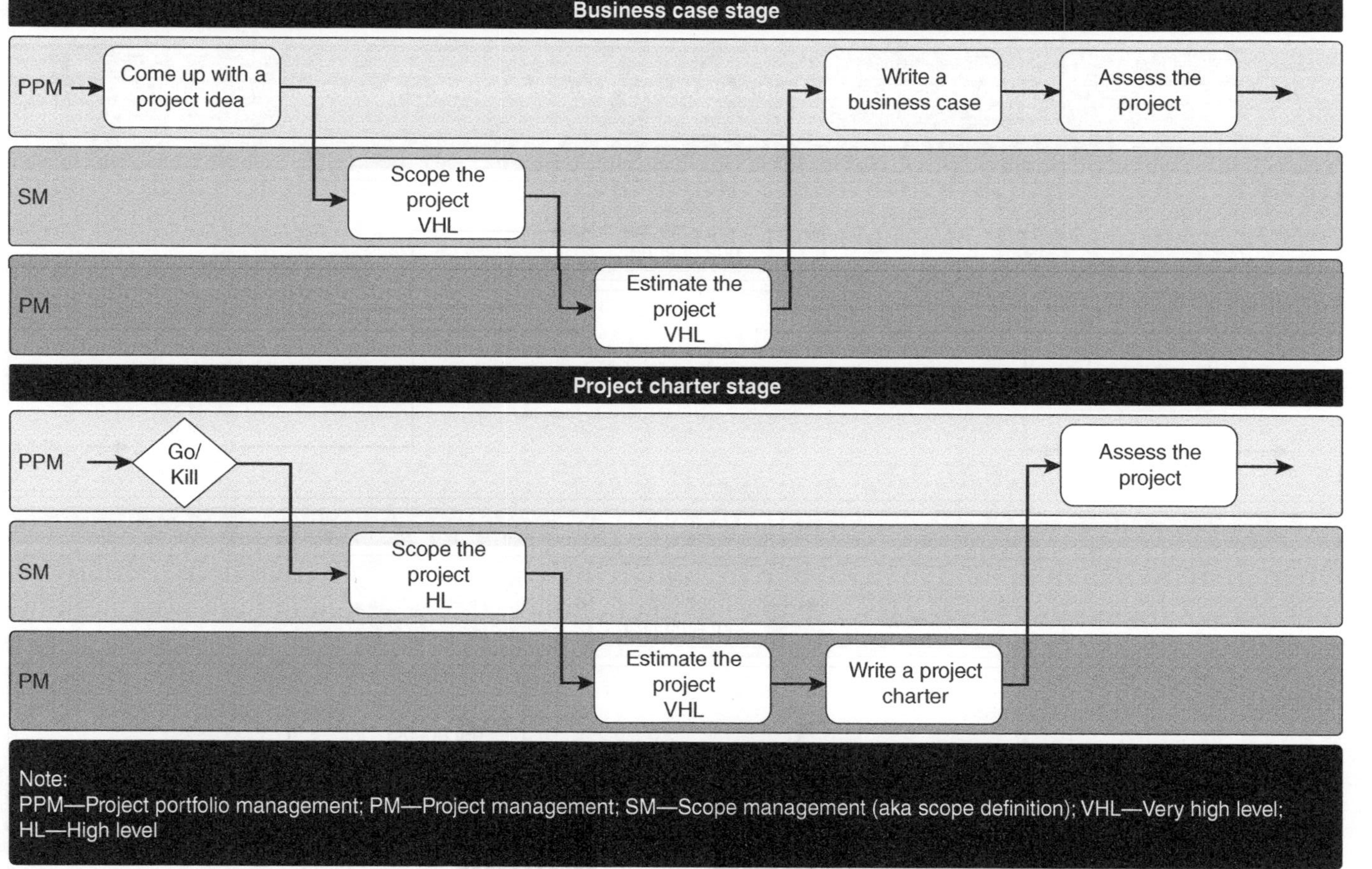

Figure 1.4 Detailed view of the project portfolio management process (part 1)

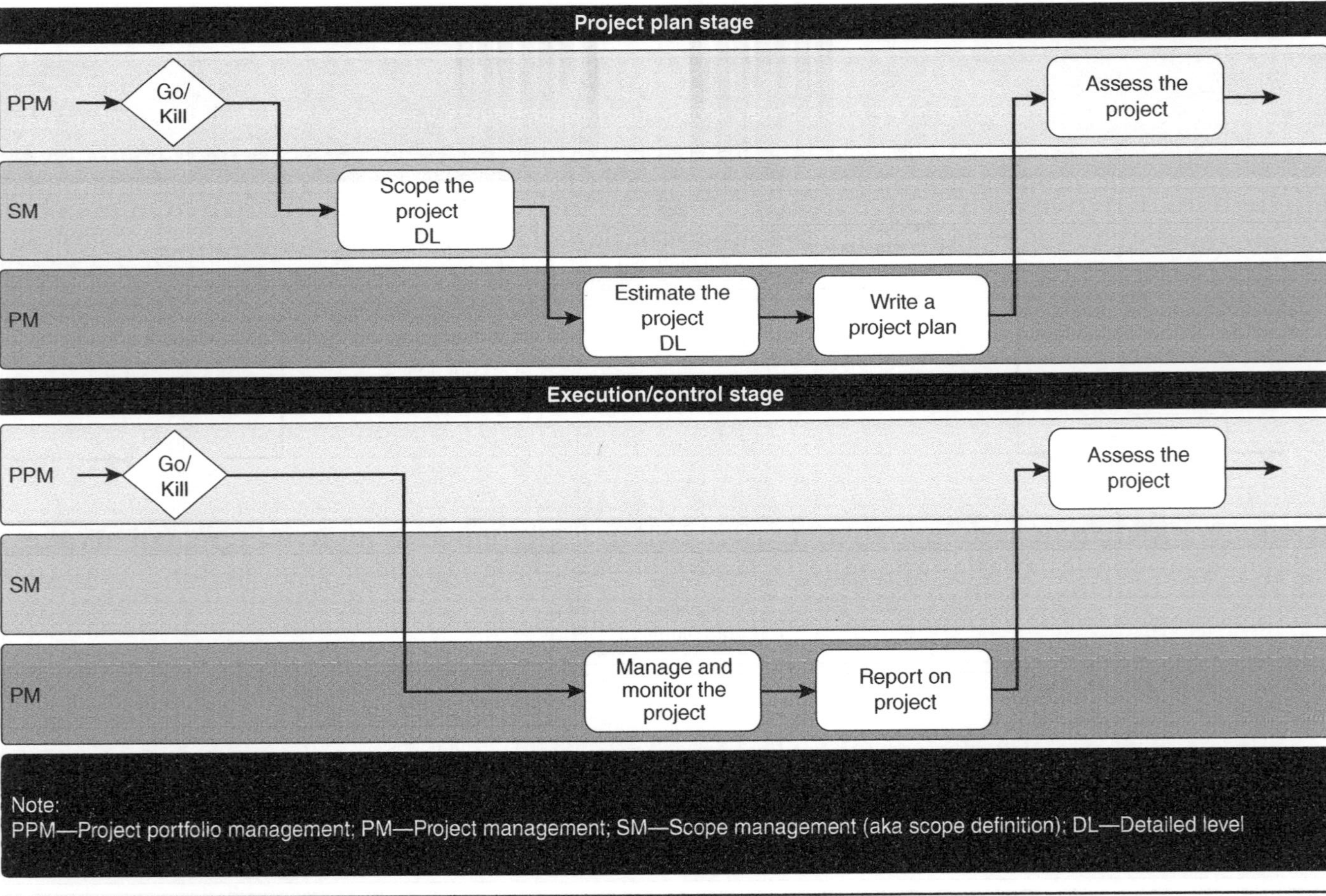

Figure 1.5 Detailed view of the project portfolio management process (part 2)

Do We Know How to Gather Business Requirements?

As mentioned earlier, none of the generic, nonindustry specific project management textbooks, including the *PMBOK® Guide*, provide the proper methodologies for project scope definition. These books tell you a lot about budgeting, scheduling, and communications with a multitude of supporting tools and techniques like program evaluation review technique (PERT), network diagrams, fast-tracking, crashing, meeting minutes, etc., but when it comes to project scoping, you are on your own.

While attending a project management conference, I decided to ask one of my highly experienced colleagues why none of the generic project management books cover project scope. He seemed puzzled at first but finally managed to shed some light on the topic: "Project scope definition is so different in, say, software development from scoping in construction that it would be very difficult to generalize and institutionalize that particular knowledge area."

The reality is, we are quite proficient at developing detailed scope documents that typically emerge at the end of the planning stage, including stacks of blueprints, bills of materials, detailed lists, as well as design and architecture documents. But when it comes to the initial stages of projects, there is no universal framework available for us to perform the elicitation of high-level initial sets of customer problems, issues, and needs to help us develop proposals for potential solutions.

Do Companies Need Help?

American researchers employed by PMI® found (based on data released by the Bureau of Economic Analysis) that in 2001, the U.S. public and private sectors combined spend approximately $2.3 trillion on projects every year. This number accounts for a quarter of U.S. gross domestic product (GDP). If you extrapolate this number to the global level, you will arrive at a staggering $10 trillion worldwide being spent on projects in 2001.

Despite this grandiose shift in the nature of the work we do, Standish Group[2], in its *Chaos Report*, asserts that only 35 percent of the projects started in 2006 could be considered a success, meaning they were completed on time, on budget, and met user requirements. Nineteen percent of projects were outright failures, and the remaining 46 percent constituted troubled projects.

Furthermore, according to Standish Group, five out of the top eight reasons why projects fail are related to requirements. They include:

- Incomplete requirements
- Lack of user involvement
- Unrealistic customer expectations
- Changing requirements and specifications
- Customers no longer need the features provided

On the project portfolio management side, Robert Cooper claims in his book, *Portfolio Management for New Products*[3], that:

- Eighty-four percent of companies either do not conduct business cases for their projects or perform them on select key projects
- Eighty-nine percent of companies are flying blind with no metrics in place except for financial data
- Eighty-four percent of companies are unable to adjust and realign their budgets with their business needs

Based on the percentages researched and reported by Cooper, out of the $2.3 trillion spent annually on projects, $1 trillion ends up in underperforming projects.

Despite all the advances within the project management field over the past several decades, the statistics shown in this section clearly imply that we are a long way from perfection when it comes to selection, scoping, and managing our projects.

Interactions with my academic and professional peers; feedback from many company executives, directors, portfolio managers, and project managers who have attended my university courses or my training classes; and communication with professionals for whom I've acted as a consultant have all carried a common theme. This common theme is the expressed need for a resource that pulls project management, portfolio management, and requirements engineering together into a unified framework that is understandable to project managers, portfolio managers, and executives alike. This resource also needs to be a practical how-to reference and not just academic theory. With the goal of satisfying this need and of playing some small part to improve reported statistical results from the practice of project management, I made the decision to write this book.

Some of the detailed questions that will be addressed in this book are:

- How can executives determine the value of a project candidate if project value is frequently a function of project cost?
- How can the cost of a project be estimated early in its life if the company does not have a good scoping methodology at the business requirements level?
- How can senior managers reconcile the fact that they need to know precise project sizes with respect to cost, effort, and duration, yet no project of significant size or complexity can be predicted with any reasonable degree of accuracy?
- How can the balance of a portfolio be assessed if the sizes and durations of the projects are exceedingly volatile (i.e., almost unknown)?
- How can executives assess project pipeline capacity if they don't know project candidate sizes or the throughput capacity of their organizations?
- How can regular reviews of projects in the portfolio mix be conducted if the company does not possess a clear iterative approach to refining project estimates with respect to scope, cost, effort, and duration?

- How are organizational leaders expected to conduct regular portfolio reviews if they do not receive accurate project updates stemming from proper project monitoring and control processes?

Summary

The fields of project management, portfolio management, and requirements engineering are strongly interconnected. In order for companies to succeed with managing their project pipelines, management should be aware of all three areas of knowledge and appreciate their interdependence.

Scope definition is, by itself, another weak area of modern project management. For some reason the advances made in the fields of requirements engineering in IT and software development industries have not migrated to other industries.

If we examine the classical portfolio management model, it becomes fairly obvious that portfolio management is impossible without project scoping, project estimation (including budgets, duration, and resource needs), and project monitoring and control.

Unfortunately, the vast majority of organizations are still facing major challenges with their project portfolios both at the tactical and strategic levels.

References

1. Cooper, Robert G., Scott J. Edgett, and Elko J. Kleinschmidt, *Portfolio Management for New Products* (Basic Books, 2002).
2. Project Management Institute, *The PMI® Project Management Fact Book*, 2nd ed. (Project Management Institute, 2001).
3. Standish Group, *CHAOS Report* (Standish Group International, 2006).

Summary

References

2

What Is Project Management, and Do You Really Need It?

Historical Perspective

The Curious Case of Arthur Wellesley

This is a story about a very peculiar human resource management system that existed in British and several other European armies up to the end of the nineteenth century. The ranks in the army were not awarded based on education, valor or even years of service. Basically, anyone with enough money could march into the War Office (Department of Defense) and purchase officers' commissions ranging from junior lieutenant to colonel. These commissions also were freely sold via newspaper ads that were placed by retiring officers.

The interesting part, however, did not stop there. Once the patent was purchased, the candidate had to finance recruitment, ammunition, weapons, and uniforms out of his own pocket. To make matters even worse, the new officers were not paid large salaries; they were expected to generate their income from the spoils of war. Even then, a significant percentage had to be shared with the War Office. This doesn't sound like a good deal now, does it? Nevertheless, people paid enormous amounts of money for such commissions. There is a recorded sale of a colonel's patent in 1840 for a mind-boggling sum of £30,000 (approximately US$3,000,000 in 2005, adjusted for inflation).

If you still find these facts questionable, let me tell you a story of one Arthur Wellesley, a young man of aristocratic kin whose parents, unhappy with his lack of direction in life bought him a lieutenant's patent in 1787. Arthur was 18 years old at the time and decided that he did not feel like reporting to duty. His caring relatives responded by buying him progressively higher ranks, until in 1794 at the age of 25, he gracefully agreed to accept the rank of colonel in the British army.

After several setbacks at the hands of Napoleon Bonaparte, Arthur finally managed to beat the French emperor in Spain and later at Waterloo. For his military feats, Arthur Wellesley was granted the title Duke of Wellington and Peerage; in 1828, he was elected to be the prime minister of England (see Illustration 2.1).

Illustration 2.1 Duke of Wellington

The question asked after telling this story is, "Why do you think the British army had this system in place?" If you are not sure where to start, try to think of this policy in terms of an economic principle known as *cost of failure*. In other words, what did the War Office stand to lose in the case of the officer's failure? The answer is: absolutely nothing. Remember, the new officer had to pay for all the expenses in the first place. If the candidate were a bad leader, he would first lose several battles and would probably get killed. However, if the candidate were a good commander, he quickly would win several battles and earn a lot of money by capturing enemy goods. This would allow him to purchase new and higher commissions to get even higher percentages of captured booty.

Here is an interesting aspect: this policy was never implemented in the British navy. Can you explain this from a cost of failure point of view? The answer is quite obvious: the ships were expensive. Admiral Nelson's *HMS Victory* cost the British taxpayers £7 million in 2009 pounds; the original price tag was £63,176 and 3 shillings. Who in his right mind would entrust a $10.5-million-dollar piece of equipment to an uneducated, inexperienced person?

This example is often used when interacting with senior managers and executives of various companies who still are unsure about project management. Admittedly, their curiosity is quite genuine. Some of their questions have included:

- We have typically assigned our functional managers to run projects on a part-time basis. Why should we change this model?
- I keep hearing that project management is very important; however, there are a lot of organizations that don't have project managers and are quite successful. How do you explain that?
- How do I know when to switch to the project management model with appropriate methodology and project managers in place?

The reply was, "If you don't have much to lose in the event your projects fail—similar to the War Office example—then you probably don't need to invest too much of your company resources into project management. However, if your projects are important ventures, and their failures would have significant negative impacts on your organization—similar to the British navy example—you may want to give project management your full consideration."

Project management is not a one-size-fits-all proposition and benefits will vary. Most all organizations will gain intangible benefits from their investment in project management such as more effective use of human resources; improved attainment of strategic objectives, regulatory compliance, and competitiveness; and better overall management. Some organizations will gain more tangible benefits from their investment in project management such as significant cost savings, increased revenues, and improvements in market share and customer retention.

How Are We Doing with Projects Today?

Some Sad Examples

As cited in Chapter 1, the success rate of projects in general is quite low. The 35 percent success rate reported by Standish Group[1] clearly demonstrates that there are still a lot of opportunities to improve our handling of projects.

To reinforce this point, one may recall such recent fiascos as the Denver airport baggage handling system which required an additional 50 percent of the original budget to complete—nearly $200 million. The Channel Tunnel project between continental Europe and Great Britain was more than 100 percent over budget (£4.9 billion versus £10 billion), which drove the company involved into bankruptcy. The Virtual Case File initiative by the FBI in 2000 was abandoned after the cost overrun for the project reached either $100 million or $200 million—depending on whom you chose to believe—and delivered only 10 percent of the promised scope.

Interestingly enough, Standish Group decided to take an additional step beyond simply reporting miserable results. They went back to the employees of the companies they surveyed and asked them a very simple question: "why do your projects fail?" The answers are presented in Table 2.1.

At first glance, it all makes sense: users who are not being involved will not bode well for the project's success, lack of executive management support will likely preclude you from getting the right resources, and if you are not sure what exactly you are supposed to build, you are not likely to deliver it.

An interesting phenomenon happens, however, if these root causes are organized by type and items 2-6, 8 and 9 are highlighted (see Table 2.2). These issues

Table 2.1 Why projects fail

Item	Category	Percent
1	User involvement	19
2	Executive management support	16
3	Clear statement of requirements	15
4	Proper planning	11
5	Realistic expectations	10
6	Smaller project milestones	9
7	Lack of competent staff	8
8	Lack of ownership	6
9	Clear vision and objectives	3
10	Lack of hard-working, focused staff	3
TOTAL		**100**

Table 2.2 Why projects fail—categorized view

Item	Category	Percent
1	User involvement	19
2	Executive management support	16
3	Clear statement of requirements	15
4	Proper planning	11
5	Realistic expectations	10
6	Smaller project milestones	9
7	Lack of competent staff	8
8	Lack of ownership	6
9	Clear vision and objectives	3
10	Lack of hard-working, focused staff	3
TOTAL		**100**

are directly related to the domain of management whereas issues 1, 7 and 10 relate to human factors. This table illustrates that 70 percent of a project's success is dependent on leadership and proper management while only 30 percent is dependent on the people involved.

In other words, if Team A has a group of average technical experts but a good project manager, they are approximately 2.33 times more likely to deliver a successful project than Team B, which has extraordinary technical gurus but no leader.

Is Managing Projects Easy?

People at the top of company hierarchies need to understand that managing projects is a tough process. It is argued by some that real requirements (scope definition) for any given project are never complete because it would be very difficult for a group of people, let alone one person, to account for all alternative flows and various interdependencies of the scope items.

Changes always happen whether the changes are scope, time, budget, resourcing or any other myriad of things that can change because time has passed, and the world today is not the same as it was at project initiation.

Priorities can and will most definitely shift. Resources that the project manager was promised will magically disappear in order to be applied to other strategic initiatives. Various risks, ranging from a key resource becoming ill to political turmoil within a country, can materialize. Estimates, especially if they were imposed from the top, will turn out to be unrealistic.

All of these tendencies lead to a very interesting question: why does project management, which is deeply rooted in some industries (typically construction, the military, and engineering), have difficulties gaining acceptance in other industries? To paraphrase James Carville, "It is about economics!"

Think about this question in terms of cost of failure. Consider the following:

- A company builds a high-rise condo structure, but it collapses one week after the residents move in
- A defense contractor constructs a fighter jet, but it explodes as soon as it takes off
- An organization builds a nuclear reactor, but it melts down and poisons everything within a radius of 100 km

It is obvious that the repercussions against the companies involved in any of these scenarios will be pretty severe.

On the other hand, a lot of companies, until recently, managed to get away with poor project management practices and with delivery of poor products. A favorite example is the first release of Windows 95. Those who are old enough may remember all of the time spent sitting in front of a computer, staring at the *blue screen of death*, restarting the system numerous times, and hoping that this time the computer would work fine and that the important file would not be lost.

One also may recall numerous occasions when projects were over budget and late, but no one really suffered. Sometimes the product was delivered, but no one ever used it.

Problems start to emerge, especially for company executives, when it is discovered that the projects have become larger, more sophisticated, and more important.

Is the Reality Changing?

There is change in the air. Projects are becoming more complex. One executive described his experience with this growing trend: "The projects we used to handle in years past were contained to one specific department. We always referred to them as the marketing department's project or the engineering department's project. Currently it seems almost all of our projects involve at least five or six departments concurrently. Some of our flagship projects involve all departments. All of them!"

Speaking of flagship projects, because of the general increase in project size and scope, projects are naturally becoming more mission critical than in the past. A CIO of a very large bank commented after a long day, "It seems only 10 years ago [that] we had maybe one or two IT projects that were on the board of directors' radar. Now we have 20 of them. And, guess what? Even the smallest one out of these 20 is twice the size of our entire portfolio 10 years ago."

There is also pressure coming from top management to decrease project-related costs and to drastically improve quality. Recent economic difficulties in

2008–2010 have definitely added to the pressure. Remember the Windows 95 example? Microsoft tried the same trick with Windows Vista. This time the results were quite different according to the press and feedback from clients, colleagues and students. Quality is no longer a customer desire; it's a demand. The negative reaction from users and particularly the corporate world reportedly had a lot to do with the recent release of Windows 7. Reports of quality issues today can have serious ramifications.

The interest in project management practices, tools, techniques, and standards has been growing at warp speed. Evidence of this change in reality is not difficult to find. The Project Management Institute (PMI®), a non-profit association, has experienced phenomenal growth over the past 15 years. In 1995, PMI had approximately 26,000 members. In 2002, PMI's membership stood at around 93,000 with the vast majority in the United States and Canada. Just five years later in 2007, membership grew to more than 253,000 members with much of the growth coming from countries outside North America. As of February 2010, PMI reported having more than 500,000 members worldwide. As of December 2009, on-line project management communities such as gantthead.com grew to include more than 430,000 senior IT management members, and projectsatwork.com grew to over 110,000 program and portfolio management members. These are just a few among the many examples showing the huge growth in the practice of project management worldwide.

Chapter 1 discussed some results reported a few years ago by the Standish Group. A review of its CHAOS 2009[2] report shows the failure of software projects at the highest rate in over a decade. Only 32 percent were reported to be successful. Approximately 44 percent were reported as troubled, which means late, over budget, or failed to meet all requirements, and 24 percent were reported as having failed or were never used. An analysis of this data also showed that about 21 percent of large companies' IT budgets are wasted.

Obviously, statistics can be misleading when variables or certain conditions change. It is not unusual to learn of project managers or software development staff in Europe or North America training people in Mexico or India, for example, as their replacements due to the pressure to cut costs. This likely explains some of the reasons for the recent increase in project failures and huge membership growth in groups such as the PMI. Project management isn't easy; training and education are a must.

The Standish Group's CHAOS Report[3] suggests that project management is getting worse. In reality, there are a significant number of leading organizations that fully embraced project management a decade or more ago. These organizations obtained professionals who were formally trained in project, program, and portfolio management, or they invested in their professionals' training and education through groups such as the PMI or one of the many engineering associations. Some of these organizations were already leaders, and others have more recently become leaders. These organizations are gaining the intangible and tangible benefits mentioned previously and are achieving increasing maturity levels of project management. These leaders took it upon themselves to gain an understanding of the interdependencies between project management, portfolio management and requirements engineering. A larger number of organizations, called followers, have embraced project management but lack an understanding of the important interdependencies that have been discussed. A third group is called the stragglers. The stragglers are the largest group and are those organizations that may have invested in project management at some level but did not fully embrace the concept. Within this group are those that believe that technical engineering or IT-skilled staffs are enough or that functional managers can run projects on a part-time basis.

Reality is definitely changing. With today's rapid technological advancements, thriving IT industries, and globalization, project management solutions are in demand throughout the world as the fundamental forces that are necessary to complete projects within defined scope, time, and cost constraints.

What Is Project Management?

What Is a Project?

Before launching into the discussion of project management, it's important to define what a project is. There are various definitions that can be found in textbooks and in on-line dictionaries, but the following provides the best explanation:

> A *project* is a temporary endeavor with a defined start and finish undertaken to create or deliver a unique product or service.

Since projects are temporary ventures with a defined start and finish, mass production of paper plates, cars, or furniture cannot be defined as projects. If the mass production of cars, for example, had a defined start and finish, it still would fail to meet the second criteria of creating or delivering a unique product or service. These are ongoing operations or business as usual. The creation of the first prototype of a specific SUV for mass production, however, is a project because the new SUV is, by definition, a unique product, and it is a temporary endeavor with a defined start and finish. Constructing a building, launching a military operation, or cooking an omelet would fall under the category of projects. These events have a well-defined start and finish, more or less.

Programs are closely related to the concept of projects. A program is a grouping of interdependent projects united by the same theme or topic. Note that the relative size of projects and programs can vary vastly from organization to organization. For instance, preparation for the Olympic Games in any given city would be considered a program. By the same token, building a stadium to host some of the events would be considered a project—one of many—by the Olympic Organizing Committee. Construction of the same stadium, however, probably would be considered a program (with several subprojects) by the construction company responsible for building this venue.

Project portfolios are a collection of projects and programs in an organization that are often classified by the type, objective, or goal that they are expected to achieve. Project portfolio management (PPM) is a grouping of methods for analyzing and collectively managing a group of current or proposed projects based on numerous key characteristics. The fundamental objective of the PPM process is to determine the optimal mix and sequencing of proposed projects to best achieve the organization's overall goals—typically expressed in terms of hard economic measures, business strategy goals, or technical strategy goals—while honoring constraints imposed by management or external real-world factors. For more on portfolio management please see Chapters 15–19.

What Is Project Management?

There are a multitude of project management definitions available in textbooks and on the web. Two popular definitions are:

1. *Project management* is the discipline of planning, organizing, and managing resources to bring about the successful completion of specific project goals and objectives
2. *Project management* is the application of knowledge, skills, tools, and techniques to project activities to meet project requirements

A preferred and slightly different project management definition is:

> *Project management* is the science and the art of delivering a project by maintaining cost, schedule, and technical performance that satisfies stakeholder expectations while honoring internal and external constraints.

Table 2.3 demonstrates the project management matrix consisting of nine knowledge areas and five process groups informally referred to as project phases. Each one of the cells contains the description of activities that have to be undertaken by the project manager in order to ensure successful delivery of a project.

The Project Manager's Responsibilities

A project manager is a professional in the field of project management who has the responsibility of planning, executing, controlling, and closing any project assigned to him or her. Table 2.4 demonstrates some of the responsibilities of the project manager broken down by knowledge areas.

Table 2.3 Project knowledge areas by process group

	Process groups or phases				
Knowledge areas	**Initiation**	**Planning**	**Execution**	**Control**	**Close-Out**
Integration	Develop a charter with high-level scope definition	Develop a project management plan	Direct and manage execution	Monitor and control work and change control	Close project
Scope		Plan and define scope Create WBS		Scope verification and control	
Time		Task duration estimation and development of a schedule		Schedule control	
Cost		Cost estimation and budget creation		Cost control	
Quality		Quality planning	Perform quality assurance	Quality control	
Human resources		Human resources planning	Acquire and develop a project team	Manage project team, resolve conflicts	
Communications		Communications planning	Information distribution	Performance reporting and stakeholder management	Create a lessons learned document
Risk		Risk identification, analysis and response planning	Monitor risks	Risk control	
Procurement		Creation of outsourcing plans	Request vendor responses and select a vendor	Contract administration	Contract closure

Table 2.4 Project manager's responsibilities

Knowledge areas	Project manager's responsibilities
Integration	• Develop the project management plan and get it approved • Ensure the project executes in accordance with its approved project management plan • Ensure an overall change control process is followed
Scope	• Ensure the project has a signed business requirements document • Ensure the project constraints, assumptions, and dependencies are documented and agreed upon
Time	• Ensure the project schedule is decomposed to a sufficient level of detail that allows accurate effort estimation • Ensure the project is an accurate and defined activity sequence (network of dependencies)
Cost	• Estimate project costs • Create project budget • Track budget (capital, operating expense) and report on status
Quality	• Ensure documents are properly reviewed and approved • Any testing activities are planned for and executed • Get customer acceptance
Human resources	• Ensure roles and responsibilities for all project team members are clearly understood, followed, and communicated • Ensure role assignments are filled with qualified staff
Communications	• Ensure that a communications plan exists for the project • Ensure project records (i.e., project plan, project status, open issues list, meeting agendas and recaps, etc.) are kept up to date and reported in a timely manner • Ensure that project closure occurs when the project completes • Ensure lessons learned sessions are conducted, documented, and analyzed for ongoing process improvement
Risk	• Identify and quantify risks • Develop risk mitigation strategies for each risk • Communicate risks in a timely manner • Complete periodic reviews of project risks and adjust approach strategies where necessary • Identify, quantify, communicate, and resolve project risks
Procurement	• Create outsourcing plans • Request vendor responses and select a vendor • Conduct contract administration and contract closure

The Project Manager's Dual Personality Disorder

In addition to the previously mentioned difficult and somewhat technical responsibilities, there are quite a few intangibles that accompany every project manager throughout his or her career. The project management profession may be described, perhaps jokingly, as having a dual personality disorder. There are indeed several aspects or dimensions where a good project manager has to be able to balance, or turn the volume up or down, on their feelings and urges.

Good project managers have a high emotional investment in any project they are responsible for. Treating a project like their own baby and protecting it from external forces is a natural instinct or behavior. These very positive and useful instincts, if left unchecked, unfortunately can lead to a reluctance to share accolades with the entire team—the ego aspect.

Every project manager has to be an autocrat and a delegator at the same time. On one hand, a manager's life is full of situations where quick decisions are absolutely essential to project success. On the other hand, getting into a habit of making all the decisions without collaborative input from project team members and stakeholders is one of the surest recipes for disaster.

Unfortunately, no project is 100 percent scoped and defined until the very end. There is always uncertainty in the requirements, time and cost estimates, risks, etc. The ability to tolerate ambiguity and convince all project stakeholders to do the same is a very important skill for any project manager. That said, the inability or reluctance to pursue perfection while using the ambiguity argument as an excuse definitely will have a negative impact on the quality side of the product or service being delivered.

A project manager has to be extremely adept at both written and oral communication. According to PMI, an average project manager spends approximately 90 percent of his or her time communicating to various project stakeholders. The ability to communicate is not, however, the only variable in this equation. Knowing which communication method to use depending on the audience and the situation at hand is also one of the indispensable project management skills.

Furthermore, project managers have to be able to combine and harness both patience and impatience in their characters. Project managers always need to encourage their team members to focus and to act on delivering results and yet allow them enough time to analyze and to assess the myriad of problems that emerge almost daily on every project.

Do You Need Project Management?

How to Find the Optimal Level

Recall the British army and British navy examples at the beginning of this chapter. Why bother with a story that is based on events taking place more than 200 years ago? The reason is that executives who are contemplating the value of project management for their companies have to decide whether their companies are more like the British army of the nineteenth century or more like the British navy at that same time. If projects are small and insignificant to the company's overall success, reading *Project Management for Dummies* can save money. This is not meant to be sarcastic. There are plenty of organizations that typically do pretty well without project management: accounting and law firms, restaurants and bars, small manufacturing companies, and doctors' offices. The overall success of these organizations is not dependent on the success of the projects they run because the projects may be small or insignificant. Economically, it does not make sense to hire a $100,000-a-year project manager if the value of your projects is not worth substantially more.

On the other hand, if a review of a company's portfolio shows that the number or the size of projects has increased dramatically over the last decade or so, and if the projects are no longer cheap regiments but are very expensive war ships, then it is time to reconsider project management.

It is impossible to define the exact values for cheap, small, expensive, large, significant, or important. These values will vary widely from company to company. There have been situations at both ends of the spectrum. A student mentioned how an overzealous implementation of project management methodology at a telecom company mandated completion of a project charter and a project plan for a five man-day project. On the other end of the spectrum, a group of executives claimed, "Yes, we know it was a $500 million venture, but how were we supposed to know we needed a dedicated project manager to oversee it?"

The following test was presented to executives who were asked to consider the value that project management might bring to their organization: a table was shown that described the changing project characteristic as one moves from being functional (i.e., with silos) to being a *projectized* (almost fully concentrated on projects) organization. What wasn't revealed was that the matrix shown was incomplete; it was missing one final row (see Table 2.5).

It is fairly obvious from this table that the authority of the project manager and the overall importance of project management increase gradually as one moves from the functional to the projectized model.

The next question to executives was, "Where do you think your organization is with respect to this matrix?" Their answers typically indicated that they were somewhere between the functional and the weak matrix columns. Then they were asked to estimate what percentage of their employees is involved in their organization's projects, either full or part time. The information these executives provided was cross-checked with the data obtained from interviews with the company employees and, at last, the final number, or range of numbers, was recorded. Finally, the complete table showing an additional row containing ranges indicating the percentages of employees involved on projects was unveiled (see Table 2.6).

Table 2.5 Organizational structure versus project management—Version 1

Project characteristics	Organizational structure				
	Functional	Matrix			Projectized
		Weak matrix	Balanced matrix	Strong matrix	
Project manager authority	Little or none	Limited	Low to moderate	Moderate to high	High to almost total
Project manager role	Part time	Part time	Full time	Full time	Full time
Project manager titles	Project coordinator, project leader	Project coordinator, project leader	Project manager, project officer	Project manager, program manager	Project manager, program manager
Administrative staff assigned to projects	Part time	Part time	Part time	Full time	Full time

Table 2.6 Organizational structure vs. project management—Version 2

Project characteristics	Organizational structure				
	Functional	Matrix			Projectized
		Weak matrix	Balanced matrix	Strong matrix	
Project manager authority	Little or none	Limited	Low to moderate	Moderate to high	High to almost total
Project manager role	Part time	Part time	Full time	Full time	Full time
Project manager titles	Project coordinator, project leader	Project coordinator, project leader	Project manager, project officer	Project manager, program manager	Project manager, program manager
Administrative staff assigned to projects	Part time	Part time	Part time	Full time	Full time
Percent of employees involved on projects	Almost none	0 to 25%	15 to 60%	50 to 95%	85 to100%

Table 2.5 was shown to a group of executives from a government organization involved in a number of projects ranging in size from several hundred million to several billion dollars. They were asked to what structure they thought their organization belonged. Most of them agreed that they were somewhere around the functional or weak matrix structures. One or two of the executives mentioned that that was exactly where they should be due to the nature of their business.

When asked what percentage of their employees was involved on projects, the team of executives estimated the number to be 10 to 20 percent. However, a survey of approximately one hundred employees conducted earlier put this figure closer to 60 to 70 percent, which theoretically would have placed them in the strong matrix column. The executives then were asked whether there was a discrepancy between where they were now and where they should be. The organization suddenly discovered itself in the strong matrix needs zone while they were still in functional reality.

This is one of the most reliable tests as it allows executives to quickly assess what their project management needs are. The logic here is that the more employees they have involved in projects, the more attention they should pay to the project management methodology and the project manager's authority.

This discussion is not about, however, the deficiencies of the siloed company versus the advantages of the fully projectized organization. As mentioned previously, there are a number of organizations that do not need professional project management help. However, companies should reassess their project management approach once they progress from small and simple ventures to larger, more sophisticated projects.

Things to Beware of in a Functional Organization

What happens if a company whose project portfolio has grown and has become more sophisticated decides to stay in functional reality? There are several aspects that may have a negative impact on the successful and timely delivery of that company's projects (see Table 2.7).

Table 2.7 Potential problems in a functional organization

Potential problem	Explanation
Fiefdom War Lords	• Resource allocation problems • Communication problems • Decisions favor strongest functional groups • Control of functional specialists requires top-level coordination • Day-to-day functional thinking instead of ongoing project thinking
No one individual responsible for the total project	• Responsibility for project difficult to pinpoint • No focal point with customer • Response to rapidly changing environment is slow • Lack of technical interchange between functional groups
Project management is secondary to the main organizational objectives	• Coordination complex and approval lead times lengthy • Lack of career continuity and opportunities for project personnel • Less motivation and innovation

The projects in this functional organization will likely take longer to complete than in their more projectized counterparts. It takes extra time to coordinate between functional groups in order to get the resources needed for a project. Also, the lack of interchange between groups in a project may result in problems either being missed or taking a long time to solve.

Summary

The ability to handle projects is still far from perfect. One of the reasons is that many members of the corporate world do not have a full appreciation of how unpredictable, sophisticated, and difficult project management is. The reality is changing, however, at a fairly rapid pace—projects are becoming larger, more complicated, and more mission-critical for organizations. Therefore, it is very important that more people start to understand what project management is and what project managers are expected to do.

As the projects of any given company start to grow in size and in number, the organization may need to consider a shift toward a more disciplined project management approach and toward dedicated project managers with higher levels of authority. If an organization continues to neglect new project realities, it will have to cope with longer project time lines and a proportionally higher number of problems, omissions, and quality defects when compared to their more projectized counterparts or competitors.

References

1. Standish Group, *CHAOS Report* (Standish Group International, 2006).
2. Standish Group, *CHAOS Report* (Standish Group International, 2009).
3. Ibid

3

Things You Probably Didn't Know About Estimation

Historical Perspective

You Are Not an American, Are You?

In 1942, the Red Army suffered several disastrous defeats at the hands of the Germans and lost close to five million soldiers. Around that time Soviet dictator Joseph Stalin summoned one of the country's leading military airplane designers and his personal senior weapons adviser, General Alexander Yakovlev, to his office in the Kremlin (see Illustration 3.1).

"Comrade Yakovlev," said Stalin, "the situation at the fronts is very tough. Our army is experiencing a critical shortage of airplanes. Furthermore, the ones we still have at our service are not very good when compared to their German counterparts. They are inferior in speed, maneuverability, and firepower. Your assignment is to come up with a design of a new airplane, and put it in full production. Of course, it has to be the best fighter plane in the world. You have three months."

After overcoming his initial shock, Yakovlev tried to explain the reality of designing and building fighter planes to the dictator. He had to choose his words carefully because Stalin was notoriously intolerant of words like *order* and *impossible* being used in the same sentence. Arguing with the tyrant was the surest way to get a one-way ticket to a prison camp in Siberia or to an execution chamber in the basement of the KGB headquarters, located not too far from the Kremlin.

"Comrade Stalin," said Yakovlev, while trying to suppress his anxiety and force a polite smile on his face. "Designing a new fighter plane is a very complicated

Illustration 3.1 General A. S. Yakovlev

project. For example, it takes the Americans on average two to three years to put a new plane in full production."

Stalin stopped pacing the room and gave the general one of his famous menacing stares. "But you are not an American, are you, Comrade Yakovlev?" replied Stalin sarcastically.

"No, Comrade Stalin, I'm definitely not an American."

"In that case, three months should be sufficient," stated Stalin, ending the meeting.

Incidentally, the Yak-3 was indeed designed and was put into full production in three months (see Illustration 3.2). It became one of the most feared Soviet airplanes during World War II. In his memoirs, however, Yakovlev remembers a very difficult moment almost three years later when he was again summoned to Stalin's office in the Kremlin. The dictator proceeded to tell him that there were some serious problems with the airplane design and with bad-quality paint, items overlooked during the initial development. Stalin accused the general of being the saboteur and promised to prosecute him to the fullest extent of the law, which once more meant a one-way ticket to a prison camp in Siberia.

According to Yakovlev, it took the Soviets several more weeks working 24/7 to address the issues and thereby avoid prison.

Illustration 3.2 Yak-3 Fighter

This story illustrates what happens when common sense is ignored and unrealistic estimates are imposed on employees. No matter how much pressure is applied on people, no matter how afraid they are, if it takes two to three years to deliver a quality product, it is practically impossible to do it in three months without running into some quality issues.

Are We Good at Estimating?

The Estimation Exercise

How naturally adept at estimating are you? Table 3.1 contains five questions that are designed in such a way that an average person would not typically know the exact answers. However, the average person should possess some general knowledge in these areas or be able to use logic to guess the right answer. This exercise

Table 3.1 Estimation quiz questions

Question	Min	Max
What is the distance between New York and Paris?		
What is the area of Australia?		
In what year was Alexander the Great born?		
What is the weight of the largest elephant on record?		
What is the surface temperature of the sun?		

does not require exact answers; a range of answers—a minimum and a maximum—is preferred. The average person must choose a range that includes the right answer within a probability of 90 percent. Try to answer these questions independently using knowledge and logical thinking. Avoid using Google for the answers.

Now, compare your results with the correct answers (see Table 3.2). How did you do after having been asked to provide ranges rather than single numbers? How many answers did you get right? Historical results from numerous others who have tackled this exercise were very depressing indeed. The typical result was between 5 to 25 percent of correct answers. The requested 90 percent confidence level for estimates, therefore, translates into 5 to 25 percent probability of hitting the target. Let's face it, few are good at estimating.

Historically, when asked why they thought they missed their estimates, respondents usually replied that the range they chose was too narrow. When asked why they picked a range that was too narrow, respondents could have said that the distance between New York and Paris is more than zero but less than 40,000 kilometers (the circumference of the earth), but the typical reply was that there was some kind of inner pressure to narrow the estimation range as much as possible, which is a common phenomenon.

The intent of this chapter is to analyze the key root causes for our estimation failures and to provide project managers with tips that should make their lives easier.

What Are the Root Causes?

We Are Bad at Estimating

It has been proven by numerous studies that humans invariably tend to underestimate the time and the effort required to accomplish certain tasks. This phenomenon is applicable even in situations when the person providing the estimate is an expert in the technical field.

Another factor contributing to the issue is that the estimation process, no matter how sophisticated, is a guessing exercise similar to weather forecasting or

Table 3.2 Estimation quiz answers

Question	Answer
Distance between New York and Paris?	5,839km (3,628 mi)
Area of Australia?	7,686,850 km^2 (2,967,909 mi^2)
What year was "Alexander the Great" born?	356 BC
What is the weight of the largest elephant on record?	12,000 kg (26,000 lb)
What is the surface temperature of the Sun?	6000°C (10,800°F)

stock market predictions. Our everyday experiences confirm the fact that forecasts, predictions, and estimates are prone to wild variations and inaccuracies.

We Ignore All Available Degrees of Freedom

Projects in the technology world are frequently measured (sometimes for the purpose of false simplification) on a one-dimensional scale—time. Many projects start with a supervisor or a customer who approaches the project manager and says, "I have a project for you. It needs to be completed in six months. Can you do it?" For the rest of the journey the only variable that exists in the project is the deadline. It either can or cannot be moved along the time axis to the right or to the left of the desired completion date. Needless to say, the more it is moved to the right of the desired milestone, the higher the rate of customer dissatisfaction. All other dimensions of the project, including effort (manpower), scope, and quality, are usually ignored, thus removing additional (and valuable) degrees of freedom.

We Are Not Good at Understanding Our Counterparts or at Negotiating

There is another key obstacle that both IT and the business side find very difficult to overcome. On one hand, business people usually do not have much expertise in technology, requirements gathering, or project management. While it would be fairly obvious to an average business person that a new customized Ferrari cannot be sold by the dealership for $5,000, they will often have a very hard time understanding why a simple web development project can cost $100,000. On the other hand, some technical people are either too intimidated or too lazy to explore different options allowing them to properly align the technological capabilities of their departments with the business needs of their customers.

What Can We Do?

What is an Estimate?

One common definition of *estimate* is: an approximate judgment or calculation as of the value, amount, time, size, or weight of something; an assessment of a likely quantitative result that should include some indication of accuracy (+/− x percent).

The latter part of this definition typically surprises most people. People have been programmed to think about estimates as single numbers, e.g., 30 days, 3 months, $50,000, or 53 man-days. Estimates, however, always contain a degree of uncertainty that is reflected in plus-minus qualifiers or ranges. This will be discussed later.

Estimates, Targets, Commitments: What Is the Difference?

Examine this typical situation: a project manager, with the help of a technical team, comes up with an estimate for a project and presents it to the customer or the company's management. Typically there is a discrepancy between the desired target and the technical estimate (see Figure 3.1).

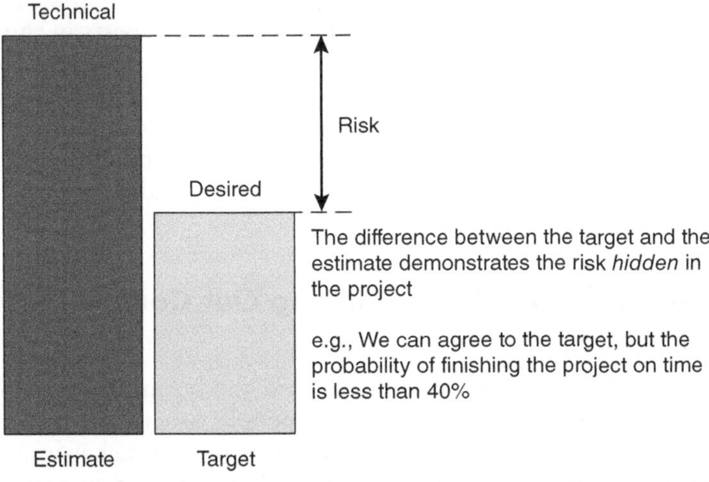

Figure 3.1 Technical estimate vs. desired target

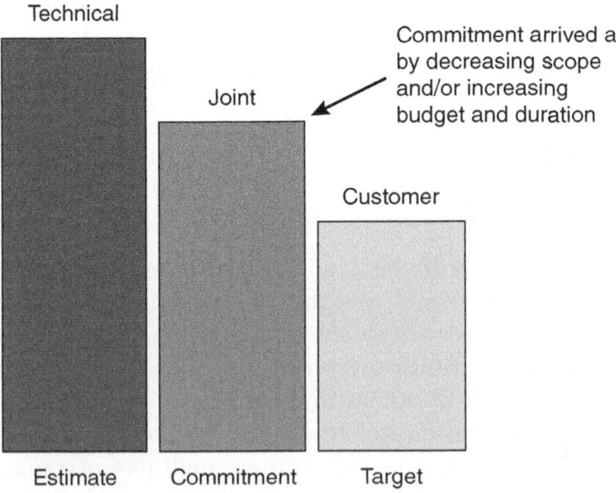

Figure 3.2 Joint commitment

The gap between the estimate and the target represents the amount of risk inherent in the project. If the bars were to represent durations of the project, the risk may have a negative impact on the areas of scope, quality, budget, and time or any combination of these dimensions. In other words, there is a chance that the project will fail to deliver the full scope, deliver a poor quality product, go over the budget, or be late.

Hence, we need to introduce the third component into this equation—the joint commitment arrived at by reducing the scope or increasing the budget or extending the deadline (see Figure 3.2). It also pays to gain an understanding of the subtle differences between various questions asked by the project manager (see Table 3.3).

There Is Uncertainty in the Estimation Process

Another key concept already mentioned in this chapter is the acceptance of uncertainty in the estimation process. Here are just a few questions that can rarely be answered at the very beginning of a project:

- Will the customer want Feature X?
- Will the customer want the Honda Civic or Ferrari version of Feature X?
- If the Honda Civic version of Feature X is implemented, will the customer later change his or her mind and demand the Ferrari version after all?
- How will Feature X be designed and built?
- How long will it take to address all the mistakes that are made while building Feature X?

Since these kinds of inquiries can rarely be clarified at the very beginning of a project, they add considerable white noise to all of the estimates.

The Cone of Uncertainty

Figure 3.3 demonstrates the concept of uncertainty from two distinct points of view: project management industry benchmarks for all types of projects and historical data from the software development industry.

Table 3.3 Estimating, targeting, and committing

Types of questions	Examples
When you are estimating, you are answering questions like:	• How much will it cost us to do Task A? • How long will it take?
When you are targeting, you are answering questions like:	• Can we do Project Y in 12 months for $650,000? • Can we build these features by 12 Nov 2008?
When you are committing, you are making statements like:	• We will deliver the project for $500,000 and by 5 Apr 2007.

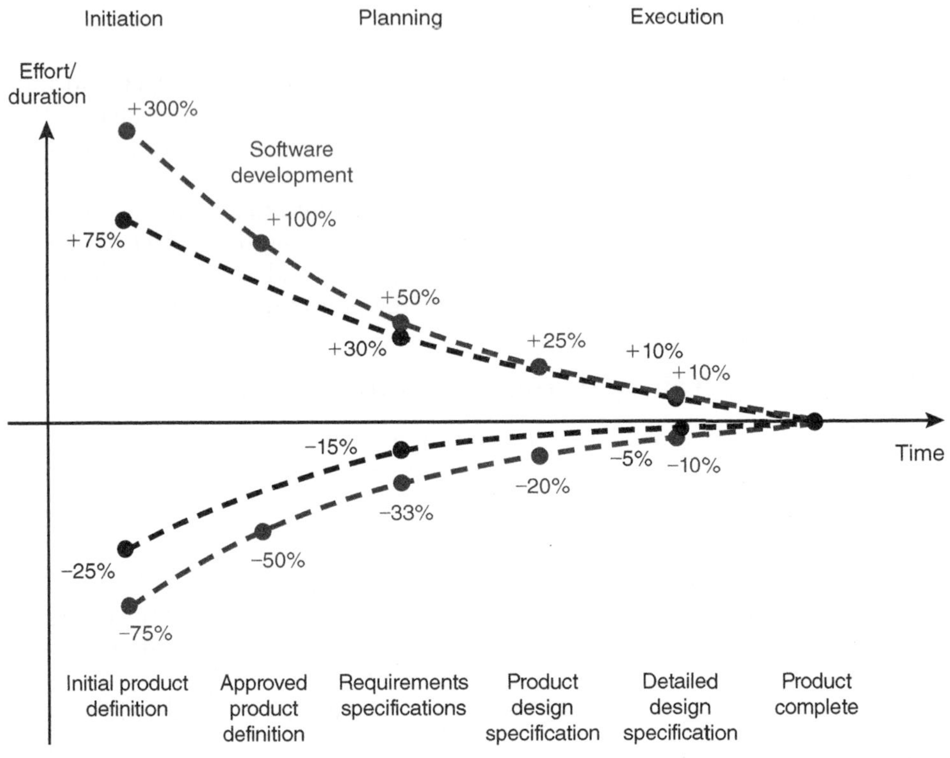

Figure 3.3 Cone of uncertainty

In the project management industry, the generally accepted estimate ranges are:

- +75 to −25 percent for the initiation stage
- +30 to −15 percent for the planning stage
- +10 to −5 percent for the execution and control stages

In other words, if the actual cost of the project turns out to be $100,000, it is absolutely acceptable for the project manager to provide the customer with an initial estimate ranging from $75,000 to $175,000.

The study of IT and software companies described by Steve McConnell[1], a guru of software estimation, demonstrated that the funnel for software development projects was even wider. Among other things, it showed that even good software development companies were in a +300 to −75 percent accuracy range when estimating early in the project life.

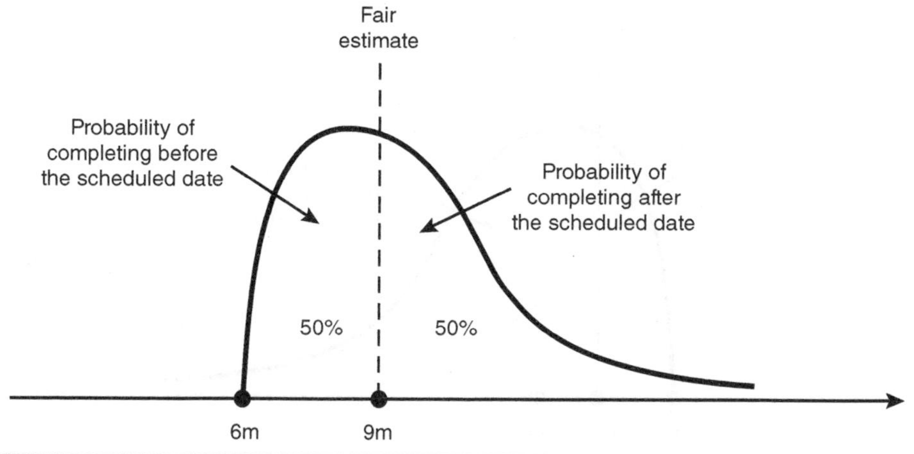

Figure 3.4 Fifty percent probability of success

Do Not Set Yourself up for Failure

If you were to assign the same project to identical teams, repeat the experiment an infinite number of times, and plot the cumulative frequency of project durations of the XY plot, it would probably look like Figure 3.4.

Note that the area under the curve shows the probability of finishing the project on or before the specific date, and in this particular example, six months is an absolute minimal time needed to accomplish the project.

For the purposes of our exercise let's assume that the expected duration of the project is nine months, (i.e., there is a 50 percent chance of finishing the project before the nine-month mark and a 50 percent chance of finishing after. This point is marked as "Fair estimate" in Figure 3.4.

What happens if you succumb to a customer's pressure and agree to deliver the project in, say, seven months (see Figure 3.5)? Suddenly, the chances of delivering the product on time decreases from a relatively comfortable 50 percent to approximately 20 percent.

What would happen if you were to come under even more pressure and agree to a four-month deadline? It is obvious that the chances of finishing the project on time would become zero. The ironic aspect of this situation is that you haven't even started the project yet.

In some cases, project managers cheat by padding their estimates. Examine what happens in those cases (see Figure 3.6).

It is obvious that by padding their estimates, project managers can increase the chances of finishing their projects on or ahead of schedule. Typically, while somewhat effective in the short run, this technique usually backfires in the long run. Eventually management or customers will notice that, for some reason, projects

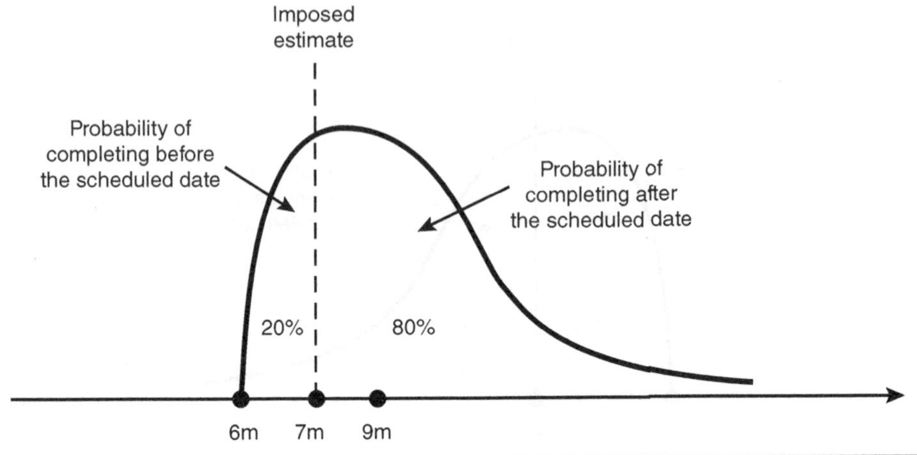

Figure 3.5 Twenty percent probability of success

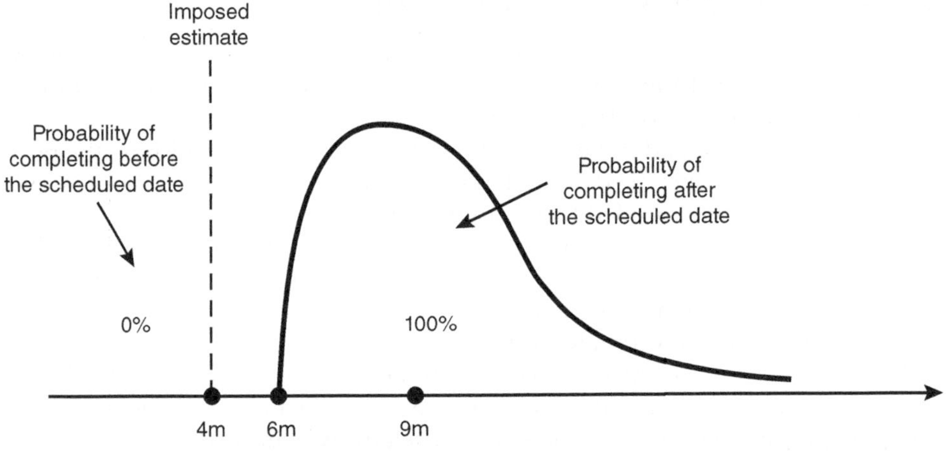

Figure 3.6 Zero percent probability of success

are taking longer and are costing more money than similar projects that had been handled by peers.

There is at least one scenario, however, where padding is justified provided that it has been communicated to the customer. What happens if a project manager is responsible for a regulatory project that has to be completed by a specific date? Would a 50 percent probability of finishing on time be sufficient to the customer? Probably not. In such cases, giving a team 12 months to deliver the project would be more appropriate than allowing 9 months (see Figure 3.7).

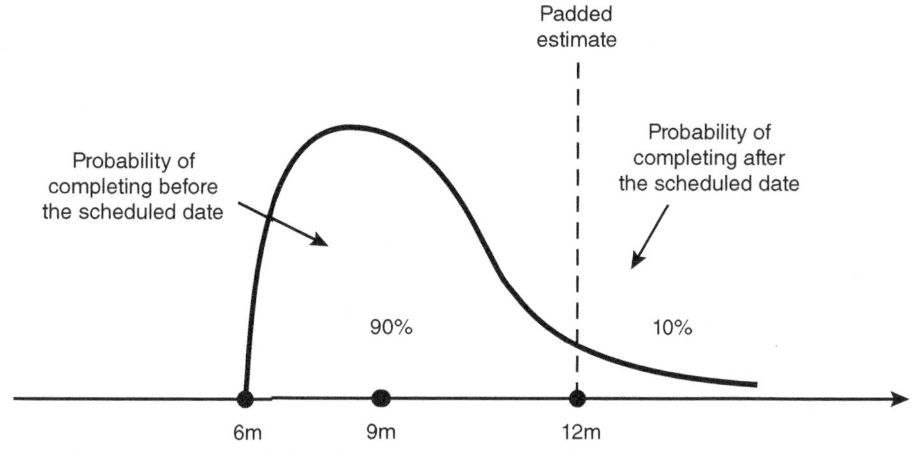

Figure 3.7 Ninety percent probability of success

Accuracy Versus Precision Versus Reliability

Managers and technical project team members frequently confuse terms like accuracy, precision and reliability when it comes to estimates. An accurate estimate (no matter how wide it is) describes a range that includes the actual outcome. For example, *the distance between New York and Paris is between 0 and 40,000 kilometers* is an absolutely accurate estimate since the range actually contains the true value (5,839 km).

Precision of the estimate is, on the other hand, the exactness of the number provided. For instance, if you claim that the distance between New York and Paris is 14,563 kilometers, you are providing a precise estimate but not an accurate one.

Finally, a reliable estimate implies that you are confident enough to make project commitments based on its accuracy. For example, reliable time estimates are typically associated with high probabilities of hitting the target on or before the date provided in the forecast. An example of a reliable cost estimate would be: "We are 95 percent sure that we can build the home on a budget of less than or equal to $500,000."

Efforts and Duration

The following example, which is derived from personal consulting experiences, involves an amusing dialogue with the senior vice president of sales (SVP) of a very important client company. The project manager had to provide an estimate for a project, and the following exchange took place:

> SVP: Have you spoken to the technical guys? How long will the project take, and how much will it cost?
>
> PM: Yes, we had a couple of group discussions, and it looks like we are looking at a 12 man-month effort.
>
> SVP: What? Twelve months? The customer will not wait a year!
>
> PM: No, what I meant is that the total effort of all the people involved will be around 12 man-months. Because we have three team members, we can accomplish this project in about four months. Three people working full time on this venture for four months equals 12 man-months.
>
> SVP: I see.
>
> PM: And since we charge a flat rate of $200 per hour, the total cost should be around $432,000 (40 hours/week × 4.5 weeks/month × 12 months × $200/hour). Obviously, these are preliminary estimates, but I would feel fairly comfortable quoting a duration of four to six months and a budget of $400K–500K.

Effort is the total amount of hours (days, weeks, months, years) that the project team will log in order to complete the project. It is measured in man-hours, man-days, man-months and man-years. Effort should not be confused with duration—something that happened in the dialogue above—because duration is the total length of the project from initiation to closure.

There is an inverse relationship between effort and duration. Generally, within reasonable limits, the more people one throws at the project, the less the project duration will be. Having said that, the relationship between duration and effort is not really linear; it is rather a convex curve. A former boss once explained this concept in the following manner: if it takes one woman nine months to deliver a baby, it does not mean nine women can do the job in one month.

Work With All the Degrees of Freedom

One of the most important notions of project management is the project management triangle concept (see Figure 3.8). According to this concept, every project has at least three dimensions: scope, time, and budget. Furthermore, the golden rule of project management states that a customer can have any two of the dimensions, within reasonable limits of course, but never all three.

For example, if a customer is shopping for a luxury car with custom features, and she wants it as soon as possible, she had better be prepared to spend a lot of money. On the other hand, if a student with a budget of $5,000 is looking for a vehicle to drive to and from college, and she needs it by Monday, she will probably have to settle for a used, lower-priced vehicle such as a Honda Civic.

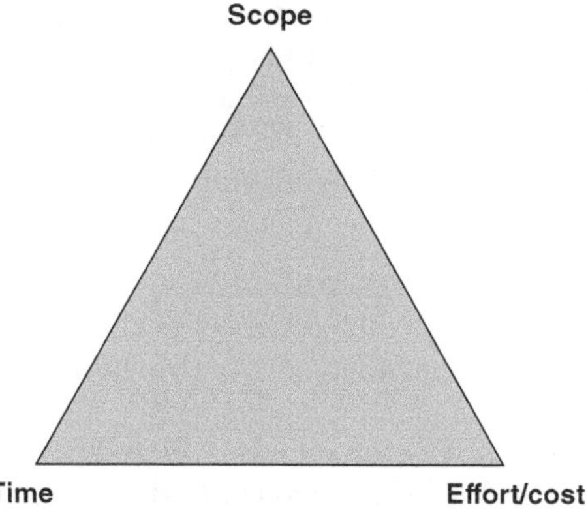

Figure 3.8 Project management triangle

Trying to break the triangle is a dangerous game to play, indeed, as was illustrated by the story about the creation of the Yak-3 at the beginning of this chapter. Inevitably, one or more of the corners will suffer, thus endangering the results of the entire project.

Another more recent concept is called the project management pentagon. While it is similar in its concept to the project management triangle, the pentagon differentiates between the concepts of cost and effort and between scope and quality (see Figure 3.9).

The first differentiation is explained by the fact that some companies (especially government agencies) usually have a fixed head count (effort) but frequently have enough funds to outsource work to contractors. The second differentiation is more

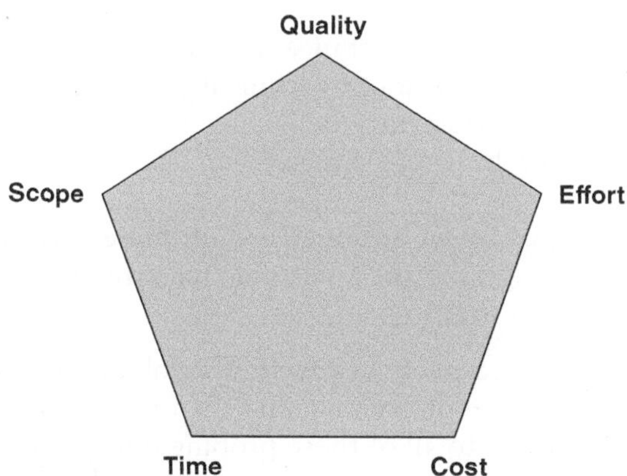

Figure 3.9 Project management pentagon

important for project managers because it acknowledges the fact that the number of features produced and their quality do not necessarily go hand in hand.

Transitioning from the one-dimensional approach described earlier to a five-dimensional approach provides project managers with more flexibility and opens more options. Once a project is assigned, start analyzing alternatives and asking questions such as:

1. Is there a fixed or a flexible deadline? Can it be moved?
2. What is the size of the team assigned to this project? If it is discovered that a larger team is needed, can extra bodies be obtained relatively easily?
3. If extra bodies cannot be obtained, is there enough money to outsource some of the work? Will this be permitted?
4. How flexible is the scope? Which features are must-haves, and which ones are nice-to-haves?
5. What about quality? Will all of the bugs or will just 95 percent of the key ones have to be fixed?

This is a game of How Badly Do You Want This Project to Succeed? With proper preparation, this is one of the most exciting things a project manager gets to do on any project. Once an initial opinion on the project has been formed, and the responses have been analyzed according to these questions, try channeling curiosity toward the customer and company management. Sample questions that can be used to improve the chances of successful delivery of a project are:

- Can only the must-have features be delivered? (scope)
- Can the project be split into two phases and certain features be delivered later? (scope)
- Is it possible to cut some of the features? (scope)
- Do all requirements have to perfect? Can certain design attributes be relaxed? (scope)
- Can the boss provide more technical people? (resources)
- If the boss can't provide more technical people, can more experienced ones be assigned? (resources)
- Can the customer be more involved in the scope definition process? (resources)
- Can a schedule goal be set but not as an ultimate deadline? (time)
- Can estimation ranges be used with an agreement to refine them as the project progresses? (time)

There are two entertaining aspects to this methodology. First, it may be surprising to learn how many different doors open when proper probing questions are asked. Second, if the answer to all of these probing questions is an emphatic, "no, I can't do that," then one can draw his or her own conclusions about how much the customer or boss is interested in the successful delivery of the project. See Chapter 4 for a detailed discussion on the negotiation of project estimates.

Presenting Your Estimates Properly

As was discussed earlier, an estimate is not usually a single number but is a range that typically includes a minimum and a maximum. Here is a list of other options for effective estimation presentation:

- Plus-or-minus qualifiers (6 months ± 2 months)
- Ranges (4 months to 8 months)
- Cases (best case—4 months, most likely—6 months, worst case—8 months)
- Course dates and time periods (3 quarters instead of 270 days)
- Confidence factors (95 percent sure that the project will be completed within 90 to 118 days)

Beware of These Difficulties

What are the drawbacks of these methods? There are a couple of aspects associated with this approach that can make life a tad more complicated. First, be more courageous. Bosses and customers could be somewhat surprised if they are suddenly grilled with the questions outlined in the Degrees of Freedom section. Actually, customers' and management's reactions to such questions could range from surprise to utter outrage. The good news is, however, that it takes only one successful run through the project to completely win these individuals over and to have them convinced of the effectiveness of this technique. Second, when meeting with the customer, do the homework every time. Become armed with historical data or program evaluation review technique (PERT) estimates to prove the case. This implies dedicating a certain amount of time for going through what-if scenarios and having enough knowledge of the estimation methodologies. Finally, put on a businessperson's thinking hat. Manipulations with the project management pentagon have to make business sense, otherwise the entire effort will be wasted.

Summary

We—as a species—are not very good at estimation. We tend to underestimate the effort and the time required to accomplish a venture successfully.

An estimate should be defined using a range of minimum and maximum numbers that will include the actual result. It is important to accept the fact that every estimate, by definition, contains inherent uncertainty. A 100 percent certainty can only be achieved at the completion of a project. Estimate ranges typically decrease as the project progresses from initiation to the close-out stage.

It is important to understand the difference between accuracy, precision, and reliability and the difference between effort and duration. When discussing estimated work, try using all available degrees of freedom: time, budget, scope, quality, and effort.

Finally, know how to present estimates properly by using ranges, plus-minus qualifiers, and course dates. These concepts and tips should help the businessperson develop better estimates on projects—one of the keys to project success.

References

1. McConnell, Steve. *Software Estimation: Demystifying the Black Art*, (Microsoft Press, 2006).

4

Are We Supposed to Negotiate on Projects?

Historical Perspective

Operation Husky—Allied Forces and Don Calo

Operation Husky, the Allied invasion of Sicily started on July 9, 1943. It was a large-scale amphibious and airborne operation, followed by six weeks of land combat. The Anglo-Canadian Forces landed on the east cost of the island and had a seemingly simple task in front of them. The resistance was known to be poorly equipped with weapons and ammunition; in some cases, their positions were defended by captured Russian artillery that nobody could operate because the Italian army forgot to translate the operating manuals. And yet, despite all of the planning shortcomings, the Italians fought well. English and Canadian forces spent five weeks and incurred thousands of casualties to reach their objective—the town of Messina.

American troops, on the other hand, had a much tougher challenge: the occupation of the mountainous center and the western half of the island. Nevertheless, the American Seventh Army was able to reach the north coast of Sicily in only seven days and with hardly a shot fired. What allowed the U.S. troops to accomplish "the fastest blitzkrieg in history," as General Patton once described this campaign?

According to some historians, the American government managed to strike a deal with the most powerful man on the island, the *capo di tutti capi* of the Sicilian Mafia—Don Calogero Vizzini (see Illustration 4.1). The U.S. Office of Strategic Services (OSS), the wartime predecessor of the Central Intelligence Agency (CIA),

Illustration 4.1 Don Calogero Vizzini

recruited Charles "Lucky" Luciano to act as an intermediary between the advancing U.S. Army and *La Cosa Nostra*. As a result of these negotiations, the Mafia protected the roads from snipers, arranged enthusiastic welcomes for the advancing troops, encouraged mass desertions from the Italian army, and provided guides through the confusing mountain terrain.

One might wonder what events lead to such an unlikely alliance between the Allied forces and the Mafia chieftain? A negotiating expert would call this situation a value-creation exercise in negotiations. This was a classic case of proverbial synergy, where two sides stood to benefit immensely from one shared goal—the liberation of Sicily from fascists. The benefits derived from this partnership, however, were quite different but surprisingly congruent. The Americans were obviously interested in achieving their goal of liberating the island as quickly as possible and in avoiding large casualties. In addition, the Americans and the British were seriously concerned about the spread of communism in Italy in general, and in Sicily in particular.

The situation with the Mafia was not quite as simple. The Mussolini regime took a heavy toll on *La Cosa Nostra*; many of the best Mafia members had been converted to fascism. Others were still in jails in 1943 and were just about to be released. As a result, the honored society had lost most of its power in Sicily and was desperately looking for ways to recapture its former glory. The Mafia was also concerned about the rise of communism among the Italian population and viewed them as their natural enemies who jeopardized the traditional ways of the country.

Hence, the unlikely alliance was struck: the Americans got a free pass to Palermo, thereby accomplishing their mission in the shortest time possible with negligible losses. The Mafia candidates were promoted quickly to positions of power by the grateful American forces, hence regaining much of the Mafia's former power within a matter of weeks. Additionally, the common goal of impeding the advance of communist ideology in Italy and in Sicily was achieved.

What Is Negotiation?

What is the first thing that comes to mind when the word *negotiation* is mentioned? The responses from high-ranking executives, project managers, and academics varied somewhat in form but essentially came down to:

> Negotiations are a type of haggling process akin to something that takes place at a Middle East bazaar. Alternatively, it is a discussion where one's sole purpose is to get as much of the pie as possible by being tough, secretive, and cold-blooded.

These impressions likely come from Hollywood's portrayal of the negotiations processes, for example: veins bulging, fists striking the tables, people yelling and sometimes brandishing heavy weapons. Consider one of the most famous dialogues in movie history—the conversation between young Michael Corleone and his future wife:

> MICHAEL: My father went to see the bandleader and offered him $10,000 to let Johnny go, but the bandleader said no. So the next day, my father went to see the bandleader again, only this time with Luca Brasi. Within an hour, the bandleader signed the release with a certified check of $1000.
>
> KAY: How did he do that?
>
> MICHAEL: My father made him an offer he couldn't refuse.
>
> KAY: What was that?
>
> MICHAEL: Luca Brasi held a gun to his head, and my father assured him that either his brains or his signature would be on the contract.

Although Hollywood stories bear little resemblance to the real world, many people probably have wished for their own Luca Brasi when dealing with some stakeholders. In reality, negotiation is a dialogue intended to produce an agreement upon courses of action, not only by actively selling one's position, but also by focusing on the other side's interests, needs, priorities, constraints, and perspective.

How to Negotiate on Projects

Use Investigative Negotiations

When negotiating on projects, both parties involved default to a discussion of their respective demands or try to state their positions in the clearest ways possible. Perhaps some of the following statements have been heard from clients or managers:

- This project must be delivered by October 30 of this year.
- This project is limited to ten resources.
- The budget is capped at $100,000. This number is not negotiable.
- The scope items outlined in the Statement of Work must be delivered.
- Outsourcing is not allowed on any parts of the project.

Project managers are also prone to uttering statements such as:

- We can't hit this deadline even if we work sixteen hours a day.
- If we don't get the resources we asked for, we are not going to deliver this project.
- The budget is too small. If it is not revised, we will not deliver the entire scope by the deadline.

The problem with this approach is that the focus is on the demands of both parties rather than on trying to understand each side's underlying interests and reasons. It is assumed that the key to a successful negotiation lies in understanding *what* the counterpart actually wants. While this is true, it is not the end of the process but rather a beginning. Focusing on what their customers want frequently distracts even the most experienced project managers from *why* they want it in the first place.

Therefore, questions like why and why not become the project manager's best friends during any negotiation process. Keep in mind that, while project managers are typically experienced professionals who can plan, scope, budget, and control their project, they cannot know all of the constraints and details associated with the project as seen by the customer. On the other hand, while the customers may know in detail what they want and why they want it, they are typically not trained project managers who can appreciate all the potential difficulties related to a successful project delivery. As a result, an inherent awareness gap exists on every project, especially in the earlier stages. Unfortunately, the job of bridging that gap falls on the shoulders of the project manager.

A colleague who is an experienced project manager recently shared a relevant discussion regarding a newly assigned project that involved a fairly difficult vice president of risk management at a large international bank:

> VP: This is one of the most important projects in our portfolio. Unfortunately, there isn't much flexibility on the scope nor the deadline because this is a regulatory government-mandated project.
>
> PM: I understand. I have done some preliminary assessments of the scope of work involved, and it looks like I'll need a team of 10 people (resources) assigned to this project on a full-time basis.
>
> VP: That is not an option. You can only have seven technical people assigned to your team. Besides, I may need one or two of them from time to time.
>
> PM: May I ask why you can only provide seven people?
>
> VP: Because the people in my department will be generating a lot of reports and conducting analyses at the quarter end. That would be around the same time when your resource needs will reach their peak. You have to understand, I wouldn't even consider giving you all seven of my team members if it were not for the importance of this project.
>
> PM: You mean I can't have all 10 resources from your department? That is not exactly what I had in mind. Remember Bill, John, and Stacy, the external consultants who worked on the BASEL 2 project?
>
> VP: Yes, I most certainly do. They have done a great job.
>
> PM: If you can provide me with additional budget, I could involve them on our project. That would take the number of resources from seven to the required ten people. What do you think?
>
> VP: Yes, I believe I have some flexibility in my budget. Why don't you contact them and see if they are available?

What happened in this dialogue? The project manager believed that he needed 10 people to ensure a successful delivery of the project. The vice president, on the other hand, could only provide seven (or less) of his people. These were the starting positions in the example provided. Had the project manager neglected to probe further regarding the VP's reluctance to increase the project team to 10 members, the negotiations would have gone nowhere. Because he investigated, however, the underlying interests of the executive—to have his people available to work on their regular tasks during the peak season—he discovered that the VP hadn't even considered the possibility of hiring a group of external consultants.

Invent Options for Mutual Gain

One of the prevailing superstitions in project management is the fixed-pie assumption. In other words, both sides assume that the project results, speaking mathematically, are binary—either the team delivers the project on time or it doesn't; either the project is on budget or over, and so on. Fortunately, negotiations are typically not like the NBA finals when team A meets team B in a seven-game series where the winner gets the Larry O'Brien Championship Trophy, and the loser goes home empty handed.

Situations on most projects are similar to the fable involving two kids quarrelling over the ownership of an orange. Finally, their father enters the room and, operating under the fixed-pie assumption, cuts the orange into two halves and distributes the fruit between the brother and the sister. Interestingly enough, the brother eats the orange and throws away the peel. The sister uses the peel from her half as an ingredient in pastry while disposing of the fruit.

The situations between customers and project teams are often similar to the fable described previously: the underlying interests, constraints, and risk tolerances of both parties are rarely identical. The proverbial pie usually looks quite different to each party. Hence, a good project manager can increase the size of the pie by looking for things that are of low cost to him and his team and high value to the customers (and vice versa). Consider the following interaction between an experienced construction project manager and a customer:

> CUSTOMER: I would like to add another clause to our contract. If the work on the new mall is not finished by the deadline in the contract, I want your company to pay a penalty of $5,000,000.
>
> PM: Hmm, we have already signed the contract without the late penalty clause. I am not sure how our management would react to that.
>
> CUSTOMER: I am sorry, but I have been instructed by my boss not to proceed without this modification to the contract.
>
> PM: And may I ask you why you feel the need to add this clause?
>
> CUSTOMER: Our CEO is really anxious about hitting the deadline outlined in the contract. He had some bad experiences with construction subcontractors before and wants to ensure a timely completion.
>
> PM: I just had an idea. You are very concerned about us finishing the construction on time, and we are fairly confident in our ability to do so. Would you be open to the idea of adding (in addition to the penalty clause) a bonus provision to the contract if we finish ahead of schedule? How does $3,000,000 sound? This way, if we are late, we pay the penalty of five million, and if we finish ahead of schedule, you give us an additional three million.

What happened in this conversation? The hopeless situation was defused by the project manager who honed in on the difference in underlying interests. The customer's interests were deeply rooted in their extreme risk aversion; ensuring that the project be completed on time was paramount. The construction company, on the other hand, was more concerned about generating additional profit. Since they were fairly confident in their ability to finish this project on time, they willingly accepted the penalty clause with the addition of the bonus clause.

The Need for Objective Criteria

While trying to understand the underlying interests and constraints of counterparts is one of the cornerstones of successful negotiations, there is one area that has little flexibility: the fairness of the objective criteria used when assessing various dimensions of the deal. All of the inputs to the negotiations process should be reasonable and fair; otherwise, there won't be good outputs. The garbage in, garbage out principle, so famous among statisticians, applies strongly to the negotiations game. Most project managers no doubt have witnessed biased standards used in project negotiations such as:

- Imposed duration and budget estimates
- Insufficient numbers of resources allocated to the project team
- High-risk ventures treated as low-risk ventures
- Draconian penalty clauses in contracts

From time to time, a manager may be subjected to pressure that can take many forms. There could be a threat (if she doesn't do this, she will be fired), a fake appeal to trust (why doesn't he believe that this could be done in only six months?) or a veiled bribe (the boss will seriously consider promoting him to senior program manager if he agrees to this). Succumbing to the use of these unfair yardsticks is a dangerous technique to employ during negotiations. Just because the customer has heard that a similar project was delivered in half the time and with a quarter of the budget does not mean that the project manager should instantaneously agree to use this yardstick to assess his own projects.

Table 4.1 lists some of the questions the project manager could ask when dealing with unreasonable stakeholders insisting on using irrational criteria.

Table 4.1 Challenging irrational criteria

Question	Example
What is your theory?	How did you arrive at this estimate?
What standards should we use?	Should we use our own historical data in trying to assess the potential cost of the project?
Are these standards reasonable?	Can we really apply the data from the previous smaller project to this particular one?
What criteria have been used before?	What estimation techniques did we use on a previous venture?
Were we even successful?	Did we finish the project on time and on budget?

Don't Lie!

The following dialogue between a project manager and the director of a company magnifies some of the issues we have with honesty on our projects:

> DIRECTOR: I am going to assign you to this new regulatory project. Keep in mind, this is a high-profile endeavor; our main client is the senior VP of our company.
>
> PM: Yes, I have heard about this project. I have spoken to some of our technical people, and they have estimated that the project will take about nine months.
>
> DIRECTOR: Yes, that is another problem. I have personally promised that we would deliver the product in three months.
>
> PM: What? Three months? When he finds out the truth, he will be mad.
>
> DIRECTOR: Don't worry about that. I have a plan. We will proceed by breaking the news to him gradually.
>
> PM: (after a very long pause): Are you counting on him not noticing the difference between a three-month project and nine-month project?

On a more serious note, lies in the world of project management are encountered almost on a daily basis. Customers hide their actual budgets while project managers, as a colleague eloquently said, "Think of a random number, double it, then, just in case, double it again." Lying in negotiations is a frequent phenomenon. It is assumed that it's easier to inflate the project budget requirements than to obtain the resources.

Alternatively, managers are sometimes pressured into decreasing their forecasts in order to please clients or superiors. Such behavior is justified by convincing oneself that everyone lies during negotiations; being honest creates a distinct disadvantage. This could be true in the short term. A bit of breathing room can be obtained by inflating a forecast. But what is forgotten while under the pressure of negotiations is that, in the long term, the reputations of managers and their relationships with customers suffer. It takes months, sometimes years, to establish a trusting relationship with stakeholders. But if, for whatever reason, one is caught in a lie, the trust and the bond disappear in a flash. For the sake of one's reputation, it is very important to consider the long-term impacts of lying.

Thus, the obvious question that arises from this discussion is: if managers are not supposed to lie, how do they overcome the potential difficulties in project negotiations? Table 4.2 provides the reader with some of the techniques that should always be at the project manager's disposal when negotiating with project stakeholders.

Don't Dismiss Anything as Their Problem

When managing projects in general and negotiating in particular, managers are all acutely aware of their own interests, constraints and risks. They know the

Table 4.2 Overcoming difficulties in negotiations

Advice	Explanation
Prepare to answer difficult questions.	Make sure that you have done your homework. Familiarize yourself with project scope. Be able to explain how you arrived at time, resource, and budget estimates. Be aware of all key risks.
Do not respond to questions under time pressure.	Refuse to provide an immediate answer to the questions you are not prepared to respond to.
Build trust by asking questions.	Ask lots of questions such as: What do you plan to do with our product? Who are your customers? What do you plan to do if we can't provide you with the services you need? Can you tell us more about your organization?
Build trust by giving away some information.	Start a difficult discussion by saying: I know we have a lot to talk about, so let me start by talking about the issues that are most important to us. Once we are done, you can do the same.
Educate your stakeholders.	The best time to do this is when you are not working on specific projects. This will free the customers of all the suspicions about any hidden agenda or subjectivity at your end.

chances of finishing the project on time and on budget and how many people are needed to accomplish a critical task. Unfortunately, in many cases, they are not very interested in understanding the customer's issues and problems. An attitude such as *my plate is full and I don't have time to care about the customer's interests* is prevalent among many project management professionals. As a colleague said, "I am in charge of nine knowledge areas spread over five project phases with all the inputs, outputs, tools and techniques. And you really expect me to analyze a customer's hidden worries and concerns?"

Consider a scenario that took place between a project manager and a senior vice president of sales. Both were working on a first-person shooter video game.

> SVP: Listen, a decision was made to move up a deadline for the Operation Alpha project. We need it finished by the beginning of June.
>
> PM: Well, this could be a bit difficult since we were projecting an October completion for the Christmas season.
>
> SVP: The decision to move the deadline comes directly from the top. We don't have any flexibility on that.

PM: Okay, let me try to understand the situation. If I may ask, what caused the shift in the release date?

SVP: Well, that's the point. We are not shifting the official release date; it is still in October. But there is an exhibition on the West Coast that we need to be prepared for. The CEO wants to showcase this product at this trade fair.

PM: I understand. Well, we aren't likely to finish the entire product by June, but we can provide you with one working level of the game. We were just putting the finishing touches on the *Jungle Battle* section. It is one of the action-filled parts of the game. What do you think?

SVP: You know what? This may actually work!

What happened in this example? The vice president dropped unpleasant news on the project manager. What options did the project manager have in this situation?

- Reject the VP's request outright
- Ask for more money
- Ask for more people
- Threaten that the quality of the product would suffer
- Make a false promise and work his team to death

What the project manager did, however, was to understand the real problems the vice president had. The key issue, as it turned out, was that the CEO wanted to demonstrate a functioning product at the exhibition. The question of whether it should be a full game or just a part of it had never been discussed. Only the project manager, with his technical expertise, could propose that alternative.

What If They are Irrational?

A project management student at the British Columbia Institute of Technology where I teach once exclaimed after completing the section on project negotiations, "This is all great and whatnot, but some of my customers are really crazy. I have difficulty talking to them, let alone negotiating. How would this theory apply in those situations?"

Crazy or difficult customers are a curse every project manager faces. The interactions between the project managers and the clients, especially during the initiation and planning stages, should be frequent and fairly vigorous events. Defining scope, understanding their problems, fidgeting with budget, scheduling, and dealing with constrained resources—all of these activities are fairly challenging even with cooperating and friendly stakeholders. If, however, the customers and management are being unreasonable and are not willing to weigh different options by sitting down with the project manager, the experience can become a nightmare.

What are the reasons behind such unreasonable behavior? One of the key motives behind such an attitude is the fact that most stakeholders are probably uninformed about the possibilities that negotiations can provide for them. Unfortunately, the only alternative for the project manager is to educate the customer about the negotiation process, which typically means leading by example.

Another possibility is that counterparts may not have sufficient authority to address the issues being raised. In other words, while the project manager is sitting with the customer trying various approaches, the stakeholder is rejecting one proposal after another because he has not been provided with enough decision-making power but is unwilling to admit to that.

The following section, Targeting Different Corners, will provide the reader with several hands-on approaches that should help in addressing this problem.

Negotiations in the Real World: Where To Start

Targeting Different Corners

Although the concept of the project management pentagon has already been covered extensively in Chapter 3, it needs to be revisited because this theory is used extensively in project-related negotiations as well. The idea behind the pentagon is that every project has five potentially flexible dimensions: scope, quality, time, effort, and cost (see Figure 4.1). In this model, scope and quality are positively correlated with time, effort, and cost. In other words, the more features or the more quality the customer wishes to see in the final product, the more money and people should be working on the project for a longer time.

What are the options available to the project manager during negotiations using the project management pentagon concept? The project management pentagon can be used as a cheat sheet when discussing the various options available. One approach is to draw the pentagon on a whiteboard with scope, time, cost, effort, and quality at the top of each corner, then attack each one of the five corners

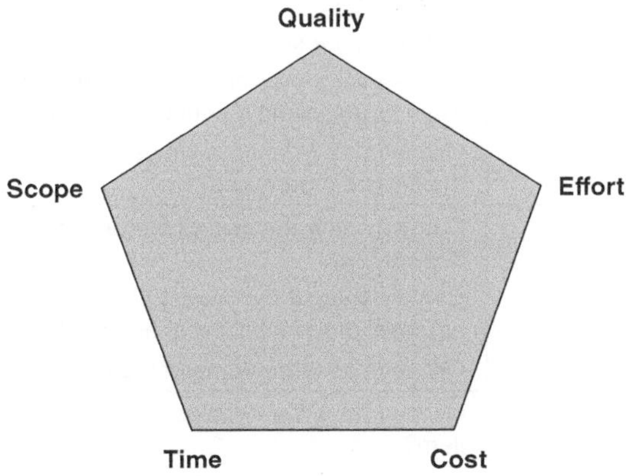

Figure 4.1 Project management pentagon

to see if an agreeable and fair approach to the project can be worked out. Table 4.3 contains some of the questions a project manager may ask during negotiations in order to obtain the degrees of freedom. Keep in mind that the questions in Table 4.3 represent only the starting points in the search for the degrees of freedom. Each one of these inquiries has a potential to unravel into a series of new discussions and, more importantly, concession points from the stakeholders.

Try looking at another example. This project is a government-mandated regulatory project at a large international bank. Like most regulatory projects, it has very few degrees of freedom available: rigidly defined scope, no flexibility on

Table 4.3 Focusing on the degrees of freedom

Category	Questions to ask
Scope degrees of freedom	Can we move some of the desired functionality into the next phase? Can we deliver the product or service in stages? Can we cut some scope items altogether? Can we polish some features less? Can we relax the detailed requirements for each scope item?
Resource degrees of freedom	Can we add more technical resources? Can we add more experienced resources? Can we provide our resources with proper training? Can we add more administrative support? Can we increase the degree of technical resource support? Can we eliminate company red tape? Can we increase the level of customer involvement? Can we increase the level of executive involvement?
Schedule degrees of freedom	Can we set a schedule goal but not an ultimate deadline? Can we set a project goal of short schedule, and look for ways to reduce time planning and execution stages? Can we use estimation ranges, and agree to refine them as the project progresses?
Cost degrees of freedom	Can we share the cost of the project between several departments? Can we exceed the project budget by x% without getting the approval of the senior management? Can we capitalize some of the project expenses?
Quality degrees of freedom	Can we relax the detailed requirements for each scope item? Do all the scope items have to be of the highest quality possible?

quality, and a strict deadline. To make matters even worse, the IT department of the bank tells the project manager that his team is limited to five people, and even if the risk management department was willing to spend some money for outsourcing, which they most definitely weren't willing to do, this would not be allowed because of confidentiality laws.

There was, however, one nuance. The essence of the project was to provide the government agency with a series of electronic reports with approximately 500 fields in total. The project manager was provided with a list of the required fields, but there was a problem. The names of the fields did not always correspond to the names in the database. In addition, some of the fields required complicated calculations and manipulations. As a result, the following conversation took place between the PM and the SVP of risk management:

> PM: This project could be a bit of a challenge for us. The deadline, scope, and quality are fixed and not subject to negotiations with the government. We are not able to get additional internal resources and can't outsource.
>
> SVP: So, what other options do we have? Looks like we have exhausted all of the corners of your project management pentagon.
>
> PM: There is one possibility still. You know how the fields in the government document do not correspond directly to the field names in our database?
>
> SVP: Yes, my people have informed me about that.
>
> PM: Here is how we can save some time. Our IT guys are not financial experts. They know all of the fields in the database, but they can't easily map them to the ones mentioned in the government's documents. No doubt, they can use phones and e-mail to uncover all of the details, but that would take a lot of time. Would you be able to assign a couple of your senior financial experts to help us out with the mapping process? I think we can easily shave a couple of months off the project duration.
>
> SVP: Yes, I can see how this could be a problem for the developers. I think I can assign a couple of my senior managers to help you out.

Present Multiple Offers

A good project manager can take negotiation methodology one step further and really impress management and clients. Consider a project that should take approximately nine months to deliver according to the team's objective estimates. The boss, of course, expects delivery of the project in seven months. After engaging management and other project stakeholders in a fact-finding discussion, prepare a list of possible scenarios that may look something like those outlined in Table 4.4.

Why is it a good idea to put several offers on the table? First, it demonstrates professionalism; the stakeholders would definitely appreciate that the project manager had listened to their concerns and constraints and had prepared not one

Table 4.4 Providing several options

<table>
<tr><th>Offers</th><th colspan="2">Parameters</th></tr>
<tr><td rowspan="3">Option 1</td><td>Scope:</td><td>Remains the same</td></tr>
<tr><td>Time:</td><td>Seven months</td></tr>
<tr><td>Effort:</td><td>Add two engineers and replace the designer with a more experienced one</td></tr>
<tr><td rowspan="3">Option 2</td><td>Scope:</td><td>Decrease number of features by 30%</td></tr>
<tr><td>Time:</td><td>Seven months</td></tr>
<tr><td>Effort:</td><td>Remains the same</td></tr>
<tr><td rowspan="3">Option 3</td><td>Scope:</td><td>Decrease number of features by 15%</td></tr>
<tr><td>Time:</td><td>Seven months</td></tr>
<tr><td>Effort:</td><td>Replace the designer with a more experienced one and outsource some work to a sub-contractor</td></tr>
</table>

but several potentially acceptable options for them. Second, in this particular example it opens three possible doors to a successful project completion.

What if Project Managers Choose Not to Negotiate?

When discussing project management negotiations with all the useful do's and don'ts, it is important to touch upon a more strategic topic: what happens if it is not possible to negotiate?

First examine some of the reasons why project managers prefer to bypass the options provided to them by the negotiation process:

- The corporate culture does not endorse negotiations
- Management is intimidating
- Negotiating with customers is unprofessional
- Negotiating with customers will hurt the company image

While all of these arguments are understandable, it would be worthwhile to examine the alternatives to negotiations on projects.

What Happens if There Are No Negotiations?

What happens if the project team, for whatever reason, chose not to negotiate? Most project managers would agree that having both parties—the customers and the project team—wholeheartedly agree on all aspects of a project would be very rare. There are always some differences with respect to scope, deadlines, budgets, and so on. Thus, if the project team chose not to negotiate, the team has only two options.

The first option is to be inflexible and tough and keep rejecting one customer request after another until they agree with all of the team's conditions. Since there are multiple providers of similar services, it doesn't take a genius to realize that the customers would simply walk away from the table and start talking to competitors as soon as they could locate a fresh copy of the *Yellow Pages*.

The other option is to agree to whatever demands—usually unreasonable—that customers make, cross your fingers, and hope to deliver the project on time and on budget. Needless to say, doing this before the project has even started is a recipe for a disaster. Therefore, having proper negotiations on projects is an absolutely essential ingredient for project success.

Summary

Effective negotiations involve not only actively selling a position but also focusing on the other side's interests, needs, priorities, constraints, and perspectives. When negotiating on projects, use investigative techniques and questions as much as possible in order to understand the position of a counterpart. Once their situation is understood, try to invent options for mutual gain so that both parties can benefit from the agreement. Insist on using objective criteria for topics of discussion by relying on objective standards, historical data, and previous experience.

Never lie during project negotiations because a little tactical gain will nearly always lead to a strategic loss of trust and will damage the relationship with the other party. Also, do not dismiss a counterpart's issues as being their problem since you may be in possession of a very cheap solution for their expensive problem.

Understand that people tend to be irrational in negotiations for a reason. Typically, it is a lack of proper negotiations-related training or lack of decision-making authority. Good project managers educate their customers between projects when waters are calm rather than during active negotiations.

Use the project management pentagon to full advantage. Ask questions targeting each one of the five corners, and new doors will start to open. In addition, remember that it is always better to present customers with several potentially acceptable offers rather than with just one.

Finally, bear in mind that although there are two alternatives to negotiating (rejecting all of the unreasonable requests outright or agreeing to whatever the clients demand), both of these alternatives are inferior when compared to a calm, analytical discussion with project stakeholders.

This book has free material available for download from the Web Added Value™ resource center at *www.jrosspub.com*

Summary

5

How and Why Do We Write Project Charters?

Historical Perspective

Initiation Barbarossa

Late in 1940, the Soviet government was starting to get concerned that the country was in danger of German invasion despite the signing of a peace treaty with the Nazis in 1939. The suspicions were initially aroused because Hitler began to accumulate a significant number of motorized infantry and tank divisions in the vicinity of the Soviet-German border. German Foreign Minister Ribbentrop continued to insist, however, that those troops were simply preparing for Operation Sealion—the invasion of England.

Joseph Stalin, the dictatorial leader of the Soviet Union (see Illustration 5.1), who was not known to be an overly trusting individual, needed reliable information regarding German plans and intentions. He delegated this task to Filipp Golikov (see Illustration 5.2), the chief intelligence directorate of a powerful and highly secretive organization called the GRU (military intelligence). The GRU was an organization similar to Russia's KGB only more powerful and more secretive. Golikov concluded that he required certain indicators that would tip him off about the impending invasion. As a result, all GRU operatives in Europe were ordered to keep a watchful eye on the sheep farming industry. Golikov ordered operatives to create a file on every large sheep operation and on every market where sheep were sold. From that point on he would receive a daily report with prices of sheepskins and mutton from all major European livestock breeding centers.

Illustration 5.1 Joseph Stalin

Furthermore, Soviet spies started paying a lot of attention to oiled rags discarded by German soldiers after cleaning off their weapons. These rags were gathered all over Europe (wherever German troops were stationed) and dispatched to Moscow via diplomatic channels. Upon arrival in Moscow, the rags were transferred to the leading research centers for analysis.

Based on the sheep memos and the results of the chemical studies, General Golikov regularly reported to Stalin that the Germans were in no way ready to attack the Soviet Union. Golikov also insisted, and Stalin agreed, that warnings from all other intelligence sources, including British Prime Minister Winston Churchill, should be ignored.

When examining Golikov's reasoning, it becomes apparent that he was convinced any country that was considering invading Russia had to undergo a rigor-

Illustration 5.2 General F. Golikov

ous planning and preparation stage. For example, he contended that since the winters in Russia were extremely cold, the invading army would have to be supplied with warm overcoats. At that time the only overcoats that could withstand Russian winters were made from sheepskins. Hence, argued the general, if the entire German army of six million was to be provided with sheepskin coats, a lot of sheep would have to be slaughtered. This, in turn, would have a dual impact: the sheepskin prices would skyrocket and the price of mutton on the world markets would plummet.

Golikov also knew that German gun oil would freeze at temperatures below 14°F (−10°C). Hence, by the same token, he assumed that the German high command (OKW) would have to replace the type of gun lubricant used by their army. In the meantime, as long as Soviet experts were reporting that the Germans were still using the same old oil, there was no serious threat of invasion.

The dual irony of this situation is that Hitler decided to attack the Soviet Union without any preliminary preparations for cold weather. Initially, Soviets suffered several disastrous defeats and were able to stop the Germans only near

Moscow. However, by the time German troops reached the Soviet capital in the winter of 1941, the German soldiers were suffering from bitter cold and their weapons (including tanks, artillery, and airplanes) were refusing to function properly because freezing gun oil would jam all the equipment.

One can identify several project management lessons from this story, including project scoping and risk planning, but it is important to concentrate on the initiation stage of this project, especially the questions that hadn't been asked and the answers that had not been provided at the earlier stages of Operation Barbarossa.

One of the key parts of a project charter is the objectives section where the planner is supposed to explain, at least at a high level, how the project goals will be met. If the goal of Operation Barbarossa was to conquer the western part of the Soviet Union by the end of 1941, the objectives section should have provided broad-stroke details of how to achieve the goal. While the direction of strategic army thrusts, stockpiled material, and accumulated troops, tanks, and artillery was planned more or less properly, the simple inquiry along the lines of, "Oh, and by the way, how cold does it get in this vast country we are going to invade?" somehow completely evaded the OKW. And upon discovering that the temperatures in some regions can drop to a mind-boggling −49°F (−45°C), at least one of the German generals might have realized that woolen overcoats would not protect their soldiers from the bitter cold. In addition, building fires under the tanks to liquefy the oil (a task that many Wehrmacht soldiers had to perform on a daily basis) was not the best way to run a successful military campaign.

Who Needs Project Charters?

Introduction

"Hey, you know what you have to do; why waste time?" This question has been heard countless times from managers and customers. One boss went so far as to say, "What do you mean you need a week to write a project charter? We are late already with this project, and you are telling me that you plan on wasting five full man-days on writing a charter? You know what you have to do, I know what has to be done, and your team members understand the scope of work. Why do you insist on writing that document anyway?"

Comments like these have inspired this journey to write a book that can explain why project charters are needed and how they can be properly written.

The Role of Project Charters

There are two different underlying needs for project charters: the micro (project) need and the macro (portfolio) need. The micro view will be examined first.

Basically, the project charter is a list of several questions that have to be answered, at least at a high level, before proceeding with a project. The rule is that no matter how small a project is, if a manager can't provide the answers to the questions outlined in this section, maybe she is not entirely ready to proceed, or maybe she does not have a project at all. A project charter does not have to be written when planning to renovate a bathroom, but the answers to these questions still must be known at either a conscious or an unconscious level. Some of these questions include:

- What problem needs solving?
- Where is the project going and when will it get there?
- How much money is needed?
- How long will it take?
- What kind of resources and materials are needed?

The reason for committing this useful information to paper is pretty straightforward. With the amount of information being exchanged in today's business environments, it is simply unfathomable that any given person, no matter how superior his or her memory is, can remember all the minute details that should be outlined in the project charter. For example, a man leaves a shopping list on the kitchen counter and only discovers its absence once he arrives at the supermarket. How well does he do with remembering all of the items on that list? Here is an important question: why would anyone consider the time spent compiling a 20- or 30-item shopping list of items totaling around $100 a good investment but would neglect to write a project charter for a $100,000 project?

Having said that, the rule that quantity does not equal quality applies very strongly when it comes to creating project charters. Keep in mind that some of the greatest documents produced in the course of human history were extremely succinct:

- U.S. Constitution (including the Bill of Rights)—7,000 words
- Ten Commandments—300 words
- Magna Carta—5,000 words

Two or three pages are more than enough for any project charter, especially considering the fact that executives and senior managers are typically the primary target audience for the project charters.

And now to the macro level. From the portfolio point of view, after reading the project charter senior management should be able to make a go/kill decision with respect to the project. One of their key concerns is whether the idea for this project that was initiated in the business case stage still adds value—financial, strategic or any other—to the organization. The project charter with its refined (but still high level) estimates for project cost, duration, manpower, and revenue projections should provide executives with enough data to assess the project's value to the firm (more about the portfolio view in Chapters 15–18).

Who Should Write Them?

Project Management Institute (PMI®) insists that project charters must be written by one of the project sponsors, typically a senior executive. (For anyone sitting for the Project Management Professional (PMP®) exam, this is the right answer.) In a perfect world, this would be ideal. In reality, few executives have the time and, more importantly, the expertise to write a coherent project charter document. If a project manager doesn't write it, nobody will.

The Project Charter Contents

Problem/Opportunity Statement

The purpose of the problem/opportunity statement is to identify the real reasons for initiating the project. The expectation is that a company is either trying to address a problem (e.g., a regulatory project) or capitalize on a value-adding opportunity (e.g., increase in revenues). Failure to identify a project as belonging to one of these categories will likely cause a project to be perceived as a waste of company resources. It is usually easier to identify the problem or the opportunity by answering the following question:

> *What problem is being solved, or what opportunity should be seized?*

Table 5.1 provides some examples of how this question may be answered in different environments and for various projects. Table 5.2 demonstrates some of the improper, but unfortunately popular ways of capturing reasons for project initiation.

Table 5.1 Problem and opportunity statement examples

Statement example	Type
The implementation of the ABC project will ensure the bank's compliance with BASEL 2 Accord	**Problem**
To prevent a decline in the market share, our company must develop a web-based stock trading platform that will offer reduced trading commissions	**Problem**
A new and high-growth market potential exists for cellular phones with built-in high-quality cameras	**Opportunity**
The construction of a supermarket in the Oakmount area will provide our company with additional revenues from the affluent residents of the neighborhood	**Opportunity**

Table 5.2 Improper ways of defining the scope

Improper way	Sample statement	Issue
We will do whatever we built last time.	Phase 2 will be very similar to Phase 1, only much better.	The world has changed since Phase 1. Was it even successful?
We will do whatever we forgot to do or did not have enough time to do in the previous phase.	Scope features dropped from Release 1 will be at the heart of Release 2.	Features were probably cut for a good reason. Is it important to concentrate on nice-to-have scope items?
We will build whatever is hot and trendy.	The new cell phone will be capable of storing 1000 songs, taking high-resolution photos, and recording movies.	Shouldn't the focus be on real customer needs rather than trendy fads?

Goals

The goal statement has a dual role. It is supposed to describe at a very high level what the project will deliver and by when. Basically, when filling out the goals section of the project charter, the following question should be answered:

Where does the project need to go and by when?

A few examples of goal statements are:

- Prepare and launch the space shuttle *Atlantis* on March 4, 2002, from Cape Kennedy, Florida
- Design and build a Victorian-style, three-bedroom, two-bathroom home by June 4, 2008
- Begin the company website development project on January 20, 2008, and complete it by March 15, 2008

Objectives

Objectives describe how the goals of the project will be achieved. Consider the following question when completing this section of the project charter:

How will the project get there?

It is very useful to employ the SMART methodology to improve the quality of the objectives. The SMART methodology implies that all objectives should be:

- Specific—Identify the expected result. Be as precise as possible on the desired outcome or outcomes

- Measurable—Quantify the results where possible, and ensure that there is a reliable system for measuring it
- Assignable—Ensure that objectives outlined in the charter are indeed achievable
- Realistic—Clearly connect the objectives of the project to the overall company strategy
- Time-related—Mention the time frame including the deadline (with plus/minus qualifiers) and, where possible, with key milestones

A few examples of well-written project objectives are:

- Design and build a prototype of a universal bottle corkscrew opener that complies with department store specifications by June 2008 (SMART)
- Complete the registration process for the first year of the ABC University's Business Administration program by May 2010 (SMART)
- Bob will save $5000 by the end of August 2010 in order to pay XYZ Training the required tuition fees for the PMP preparation course (SMART)

Now compare them to this statement:

> *The feasibility of installing new high-definition color security cameras will be calculated by the department's representative (SMART).*

This statement is not specific because it is not clear to what kind of feasibility the author is referring. Is it financial, strategic, security, etc.? The objective is not measurable because there is no quantification in it. It is also impossible to assess whether the objective is assignable because it is not known who specifically will be responsible for undertaking it. Based on the information provided, it is impossible to say whether the statement is realistic. And finally, there is no duration, date, or deadline of any kind mentioned in the objective.

High-Level Budget and Schedule

Before discussing the budget and the high-level schedule of the project, it is worthwhile to revisit the project management triangle (or pentagon), and establish relative priorities between scope, time, and budget. Priorities or importance factors are basically percentage weights that should add up to 100 percent:

- Scope and Quality Importance Factor—60 percent
- Duration Importance Factor—30 percent
- Budget Importance Factor—10 percent

This importance weighting will allow for the establishment of project priorities from the initiation stage and will guide future decision making.

At this point in the project the estimates should be presented with the following plus/minus qualifiers:

- +300 to −75 percent for new or unique projects (e.g., R&D, new product development)
- +75 to −25 percent for familiar projects (e.g., new feature development for an existing system)

(Note: A detailed discussion of generating and presenting the estimates was discussed in Chapter 3.)

Project Feasibility

Project feasibility is rooted in a simple concept that a company that borrows at 10 percent and invests at five percent will not be around for long. While financial measures are not the only measure of whether the project should be added to the company portfolio, starting to assess the financial value of the ventures is the first great step forward that very few companies seem to be taking.

The key concept in the net present value (NPV) and internal rate of return (IRR) methods is the time value of money; the concept that one dollar today is not the same as one dollar one year from now.

Net Present Value

The NPV formula implies that one has to take the cost of implementing the project and add all the future incremental cash flows discounted to today's value.

$$NPV = -Inv + \frac{CF_1}{(1+r)} + \frac{CF_2}{(1+r)^2} + \frac{CF_3}{(1+r)^3} + \cdots + \frac{CF_n}{(1+r)^n}$$

Where:

- *Inv* is the cost of the project
- CF_n is the incremental increase in the cash flow
- *r* is the internal discount rate, typically the weighted average cost of capital (WACC)

The decision criterion is pretty simple: if the NPV is positive, the project should be accepted; if it is negative, the project should be rejected. Note that NPV has a negative relationship with the discount rate (i.e., the higher the discount rate, the lower the NPV will be). See Table 5.3 for a sample NPV calculation.

Discount rates act as a risk measurement ingredient. Low-risk projects are typically evaluated with a WACC in the range of 5 to12 percent; most company projects fall into the 15 to 20 percent range. New ventures are typically evaluated with discount rates in the 25 to 40 percent range because of their extreme levels of risk.

Table 5.3 Net present value calculation example

Year	Cash inflows/outflows	Present value
0	−$100,000	−$100,000
1	$50,000	$44,643
2	$45,000	$35,874
3	$40,000	$28,471
NPV		**$8988**
Accept this project since the NPV > 0		

Note: Discount rate = 12% per annum

IRR

The IRR concept is similar to NPV, only instead of solving for the value of NPV, the NPV is set to zero, and the equation is solved for the discount rate. This way, instead of assessing the dollar value of an investment, the percentage return on investment is measured and compared to the required benchmark return on investment (ROI) value. See Table 5.4 for an IRR calculation example.

Practical Application

Some common attitudes among project managers regarding the financial analysis methodology are that these formulas are too complicated, the forecast data is notoriously unreliable, there are too many intangibles, etc. The following mini-case studies demonstrate how considering financial aspects from an accountant's point of view can weed out wasteful projects or shortsighted decisions in an organization.

Table 5.4 Internal rate of return calculation example

Year	Project A	Project B
0	−$100,000	−$100,000
1	$50,000	$10,000
2	$45,000	$20,000
3	$40,000	$50,000
4	$35,000	$70,000
IRR	**27%**	**14%**
Decision	**Accept**	**Reject**
Required IRR	**18%**	**18%**

Case Study 1—A conversation between the VP of finance and the project manager

VP: I need to automate certain reports that we are supposed to submit to the government.

PM: The estimate for this project is $100,000.

VP: My people are wasting a lot of their time each year on them. I have a large budget and money is not a significant constraint in this project.

PM: How many times a year are you supposed to submit these reports?

VP: Twice a year.

PM: How much time do your people spend on these reports?

VP: I have two people working on these reports for five days each time.

PM: Okay, let's do the math. Two people times five days times two times per year times $400 per man-day equals $8000 per year savings.

VP: That's correct.

PM: And we are spending $100,000 to save $8000 per year. I don't think the NPV will look very good. Do you still want to go ahead with this project?

Case Study 2—A conversation between the VP of risk management and the project manager

VP: We have to finish this regulatory project in six months by December 31. (Today is June 30.)

PM: Here is the deal. We can do this in nine months and it will cost us $100,000, or we can crash the project by adding more resources and finish it in six months. But this would cost us $300,000.

VP: I told you it was a regulatory project mandated by the government. We *have* to finish it in six months.

PM: What happens if we are late?

VP: Don't even think about it!

PM: No, really, what happens then?

VP: We will have to pay heavy fines.

PM: How much?

VP: Around $20,000 per month for every month we are late.

PM: Okay, let's do the math (see Figure 5.1).

PM: It looks to me that it would be more beneficial for us to go with the nine month version of the project.

These examples demonstrate that one doesn't need to conduct a complicated financial analysis of the project cost and benefits. Resorting to complicated for-

	Option 1	*Option 2*
Project Cost	*$ 300,000*	*$ 100,000*
Penalties	*0*	*$ 60,000*
Total Cost	*$ 300,000*	*$ 160,000*

Figure 5.1 Project cost calculations

mulas and spreadsheet modules early in the project initiation stages does not make sense if one remembers that all forecasts are made with, at best, a +75 to −25 percent confidence range. A significant number of project proposals have been weeded out by performing simple back-of-the-envelope calculations like the ones in these examples. These examples aren't meant to suggest that the financial analysis formulas are not useful or not necessary in some situations. Their purpose is to help managers make good decisions. However, probing questions, logic, common sense and some fairly simple calculations such as ROI and NPV often work just as well.

Other feasibility measures may include consistency with values, consistency with strategy, regulatory/government-mandated projects, competitive advantage, market attractiveness, etc. (More information on this topic is in the portfolio management chapters of this book.)

Risk Management

A lot of confusion exists in project management circles regarding assumptions, constraints, and risks. This section defines each one of these important risk management categories and provides several examples of each.

Constraints

Constraints are the things that limit one's options with respect to the successful delivery of project products or services. They typically, but not exclusively, include deadlines, budgets, and availability of resources.

The budget of the project was capped at $100,000.

The final product must be delivered by October 31, 2009, for the Christmas shopping season.

The product must receive a rating of 90 percent from the focus group of users.

Risks

Risks are the uncertain things that can jeopardize the project's success (i.e., bad things that may happen on a project, but the manager is not entirely sure they will).

> *There is a possibility of a major contractor's employees going on strike.*
>
> *There is a distinct possibility that the regulatory agency may change the scope of the requirements necessary for the successful delivery of the project.*

Note that when the probability of risk reaches 100 percent, it becomes either a constraint or a scope item.

Assumptions

Assumptions are typically good things that are supposed to happen on a project, but the manager is not entirely sure they will happen.

> *The manager assumes that all the resources required for the successful delivery of this project will be available.*
>
> *The manager assumes a timely delivery of the product blueprints outsourced to the external design company.*

Typically, it is beneficial to start first with constraints since they are definite, well-known aspects of the project, and then move on to risks. Items that do not fall into the constraints or risks categories can fall into the assumptions bucket. Needless to say, if an item is mentioned in one of the groups, then it should not be duplicated in other ones.

How Big Should the Project Be to Warrant a Project Charter?

How big should the endeavor be in order to be considered a full-scale project? How can a manager distinguish between business-as-usual tasks (that could have a definite start and finish and be fairly unique in nature) and real projects? When does one need to apply the project management methodology?

These questions are among the most hotly contested topics at companies considering implementing project management methodologies. The correct answer to this question can determine whether project management will be viewed as a helpful tool or just another bureaucratic layer in an organization.

Some organizations implement a business-as-usual ceiling at some fixed amount. For example, if the endeavor's projected budget exceeds $10,000, it should be considered a project; if it doesn't, business as usual. This is a fairly easy and straightforward approach that, unfortunately, has at least two drawbacks. First, what should happen if a budget that was initially forecasted to be around $7500 is later increased to $12,000? This is a completely plausible scenario that has perplexed more than one manager. Second, what happens if the project cost exceeds the imposed threshold but only requires a few days of work? A manager of a real estate department of a large construction and development company once remarked, "Sometimes we make purchases of land costing millions of dollars, but it only takes us a couple of weeks to accomplish the deal with one person working about 30 percent of the time (i.e., ten days times 30 percent equals three man-days of effort). Do we have to write a project charter for that too?"

Using an effort threshold has been by far the most successful methodology of distinguishing between a business-as-usual classification and projects. For example, a large international banking institution uses an upper limit of one man-month in order to qualify a job as a project. If the total resources required exceed approximately 20 man-days, it is a project; if less, it is business as usual. This approach would allow for the cases when expenditures on a particular undertaking were fairly large (e.g., the purchase of a $2,000,000 server), but human effort was fairly minimal.

Summary

Project charters play a dual role in the life of projects. They represent a list of questions that need to be answered before moving into the planning phase, and they play a strategic role for the organization's executives who need to make go/kill decisions based on the information in the document.

Although it is not officially the direct responsibility of the project manager to write the project charter, practical experience in the field of project management indicates that it is in the best interest of project managers to make sure a project charter is indeed written, and written properly. When writing a project charter, try to be succinct, but make sure all of the questions are answered fully. Remember the concept of the project management triangle or pentagon and the degrees of freedom associated with them.

When discussing project feasibility, always try to provide at least back-of-the-envelope calculations of NPV or ROI. While financial forecasting is notoriously unreliable (for both revenue and cost projections), the financial models can be great tools for weeding out projects with a definite negative value.

Try to establish a company-wide definition of what exactly constitutes a project in the organization. Use either a project budget (less reliable) or a project effort (more appropriate) that is measured in either man-months or man-days as a yardstick.

6

Kick-Starting Your Projects—The Scope Definition Perspective

Historical Perspective

M247 Sergeant York Story

In the late seventies, the U.S. Department of Defense (DoD) outsourced to Ford Aerospace the development of a self-propelled anti-aircraft (AA) weapon, which featured twin radar-directed, 40-mm rapid-fire guns. The project was assigned the name *Sergeant York,* after the World War I U.S. Army hero who undoubtedly would not have appreciated this dubious honor had he been alive in 1979. The weapon was intended to replace the M163 Vulcan air defense system and to fly alongside the M1 Abrams and M2 Bradley fighting vehicles in the U.S. Army. This aircraft was similar in concept to the successful Soviet and European systems such as the *ZSU-23-4* and the *Gepard.* In essence, it was an air defense weapon mounted on a surplus M48 Patton tank chassis provided by the army, which held large quantities of these tanks in their depots. The main job of the weapon was to sit on the front lines and automatically shoot down enemy aircraft, especially helicopters. As a result, it was designed to hone in on metal parts rotating in the air (i.e., propeller blades).

The final test of the AA weapon involved a demonstration involving a prototype weapon that could shoot down a hovering helicopter on one of the U.S. DOD proving grounds in the desert somewhere in the southern United States (see Illustration 6.1). The cost of the project at that time was approximately $1 billion.

According to a legend cultivated in the aerospace and defense industries, there was a portable toilet installed not far away from the testing grounds. Because of the hot climate, the toilet cabin had a small electric fan in it. It's probably easy to imagine the rest of this legend—the $1 billion piece of equipment ignored the much larger target (the helicopter) and targeted the unique signature of the portable toilet's electric fan.

Further tests revealed that the AA gun had the following deficiencies:

- The radar could not track low flying targets due to excessive ground clutter
- The radar could not distinguish a hovering helicopter from a clump of trees
- Turret traverse was too slow to track a fast crossing target
- The radar could be jammed easily

As a result, the project that began in 1975 was finally cancelled by then Secretary of Defense Caspar Weinberger in 1985.

Illustration 6.1 M247 AA Gun

This story is a perfect example of a botched scope definition exercise as most of the DoD requirements, both obvious (i.e., the ability to track low flying targets and fast moving targets, the resistance to radar jamming) and implied (i.e., not confusing the helicopter with a clump of trees or a portable toilet) had been left unfulfilled.

What is the State of the Industry?

As previously mentioned, five out of the top eight reasons why projects fail are related to scope definition according to the Standish Group.[1] These include:

- Incomplete requirements
- Lack of user involvement
- Unrealistic customer expectations
- Changing requirements and specifications
- Customers no longer needing the features provided

Further analysis of the causes of bad requirements yielded the following results (see Table 6.1).

A study conducted by Barry Boehm[2] (one of the leading thinkers in the field of software development) involved an analysis of 63 software development projects at companies such as IBM, GTE, and TRW and determined the relative costs of fixing an error at various stages of a project. Results from the study demonstrated a phenomenal increase in the cost of a mistake from one dollar at the initiation stage of the project to a \$40–\$1000 range at the closeout (see Figure 6.1). While this information is based on the software development industry, this trend, to a certain extent, holds true for most of the other industries.

Imagine that a mistake is made at the very beginning of a project. Someone forgets to include a requirement for an underground parking garage for a condo building that a company is about to erect. How much will this mistake cost at the end of the project once the company realizes that the only way to insert the garage is to completely destroy the tower and to start over? Obviously this mistake would have been very inexpensive to fix at the initiation stage of the project.

Table 6.1 Root causes of bad requirements

Root causes	Percent
Incorrect fact	49
Omission	29
Inconsistency	13
Misplaced requirements	5
Ambiguity	2

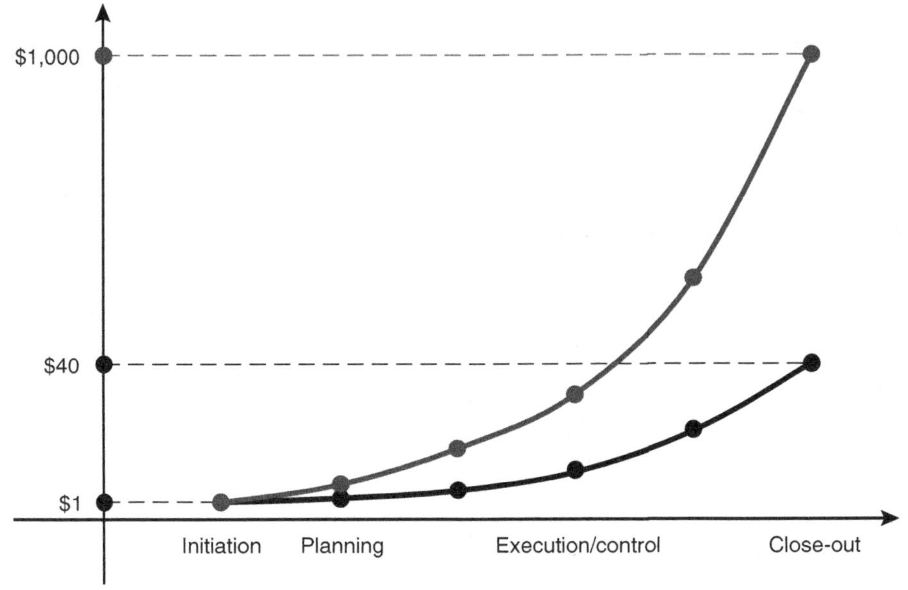

Figure 6.1 Cost of a mistake

Many managers are probably thinking that this could not happen in the real world. In reality, it happens a lot more often than one might think. For example, a real estate development company acquired a 100-year-old heritage building with the intent of converting it into a luxury condominium complex. There was one little requirement that was somehow overlooked—heritage buildings do not have underground parking. The problem was finally solved by acquiring (at great cost) the rights to a portion of several dozen parking spots in a new high-rise located nearby. The developer was fortunate to have had this option despite the high cost.

This scope problem is not rooted in the inability to come up with detailed blueprints, bills of materials, or design and architecture documents. The predicament lies in the initial stages of the projects, when there is a need to elicit a high-level initial set of customer problems, issues, and needs in order to propose potential solutions.

Defining the Initial Scope

What Is a Business Requirement?

To answer what a business requirement is, it's important to first determine what a business requirement is not. A business requirement is not a combination of emails, voicemails, sticky notes, and annotations in a notebook; it is not verbal instructions from customers or superiors; and it is not drawings on a napkin. A business requirement (aka high-level project scope item) is:

> Something the product or service must do or a quality it must have. A requirement exists either because the type of product or service demands certain qualities or functions or because the client wants that requirement to be a part of the delivered product or service.

Business requirements should be documented either in a stand-alone business requirements document or, at least, captured in the project charter.

Asking the Right Questions

The first step in every project should be to determine what is going to be built, or what will be done for the customers, either internally or externally. Getting started in the right direction depends to a large degree on the type of questions that team members ask. For example, assume that the first question posed by management is:

> *Is there a way to protect a group of people from the unpleasant elements of the surrounding environment?*

Results from an exchange of possible solutions could be:

- Shack
- Typical family home
- Buckingham Palace

But what is being built? This is by far not the only question that should be asked at the beginning of the project. Table 6.2 lists the mandatory high-level questions that project managers should be prepared to ask once a project is handed down to them.

Once the ballpark scope of the project has been determined, one can proceed to more detailed questions. These also could fall into the category of project charter-level questions:

- How big will the house be?
- Is it going to be a one-, two-, or three-level home?
- What square footage is preferred?
- What style is preferred (e.g., Victorian, Tuscan, Contemporary)?
- How many bedrooms are needed?
- How many bathrooms are preferred?

Keep in mind that all of the questions directed at the entire project in Table 6.2 should now apply to every scope item under discussion. For example, review

Table 6.2 Questions to ask when defining scope

Question you should ask	Why should you ask this question?	What happens if you don't ask it?
Why are we doing this?	To make sure there is a clear understanding of the needs and benefits for the project.	You may end up working on a project that will deliver little or no value to your company or the customer.
What happens if we don't do this project?	Just another way of ensuring that the management thought through the potential penalties of not doing the project.	Your company may end up with low-priority, soon-to-be-cancelled projects while the high-value projects remain on the backburner.
Who is the client?	You have to know who the original source of the requirement is.	You may end up receiving requirements that have been distorted by going through the chain of command.
What problem are we trying to solve?	As a representative of the technical team, you may have a much better (cheaper, faster) solution that the customer is not aware of.	You may end up delivering a Ferrari when a bicycle solution will do (or vice versa). As a result you may: a. Waste company resources b. Disappoint your customers
If you don't know this, then who does?	You need to make sure you are getting the correct information.	You may end up talking to the messengers instead of real project champions. As a result, you may end up with bad information.
Who else could be impacted by this feature?	There could be hidden interdependencies between this feature and other ones that you are not aware of.	You can miss important interdependencies or even contradictions between various scope items.
How much money are you ready to spend?	High-level understanding of the project budget (or duration).	There could be a significant discrepancy between what the customer wants and what you can deliver with the budget he has in mind.
How much time do we have?	High-level understanding of the project budget (or duration).	There could be a significant discrepancy between what the customer wants and what you can deliver regarding the time she is willing to provide you.

some of these questions a project manager could ask with respect to the number of bedrooms:

- Why are five bedrooms needed?
- Are four bedrooms adequate?

- The budget allows only for a four-bedroom home. Which is preferable: downgrading the scope or allocating more money to the budget?

Assigning Priorities

Typically, because customers want significantly more features than the project budget and timeline will allow, it is important also to assign priorities to the scope items or features discovered at this stage. The suggested categories for the priorities are:

- Priority 1 (must have)
- Priority 2 (should have)
- Priority 3 (nice to have)

Unfortunately, the concept of assigning priorities is frequently misunderstood by the project stakeholders. Usually, the lion's share of features gets stamped with the must-have priority label at the beginning of the process, thus eliminating any potential flexibility in future scope-related decisions. It is in the project manager's best interest to help stakeholders understand priority categories that are developed early in the process and, if need be, present them with some simple examples.

Imagine that the company is designing the first-ever car. The scope items falling into the must-have category would likely be:

- Frame
- Four tires (or maybe even three, depending on design)
- Engine
- Driver-side seat
- Steering wheel
- Brakes

Things like passenger-side seat, seat belts, windows, and roof would likely fall into the should-have bucket. Car stereo with speakers and navigational system would likely fall into the nice-to-have category.

Now, how would the scope items of this project break out within these three categories? The point here is if the stakeholder is provided with a simple example, there is a better chance that the stakeholder will not tag everything as a must-have and will thereby build some potential flexibility into future scope-related decisions.

Getting Rid of the Ambiguity

Another important and very frequently overlooked aspect of the scope definition is the ambiguous language one can encounter in the project and portfolio documentation. These include words like *fast*, *pretty*, *big*, *small*, *cutting-edge*, *usable*, etc.

The danger of these words is that psychologically one is trained to accept them as normal, everyday concepts. However, when it comes to project management, words like these can act as deadly time-bombs. For example, the term *cutting-edge* seems like a normal, even a cool word, to describe a product. And while it looks fine in marketing materials or TV ads, introducing this word to scope documentation can cause a lot of issues down the road. The reason is that, while everyone understands, more or less, what cutting-edge means, no two people have an identical understanding of the concept. These differences in understanding can lead to very expensive and time-consuming scope adjustments once the project moves into planning and execution stages.

In training programs, many executives have provided relevant examples of their own. One such example is: "We had a construction project budgeted at $500 million. Because we allowed the term *cutting-edge* to sneak into the business case, our final bill for the project ballooned to $700 million. There always was at least one key stakeholder in the room for whom a given feature was not revolutionary enough. And because we initially made a commitment to being cutting edge, there was no way for us to back away from that."

The Problem Versus Solution Discussion

When gathering the requirements, project managers frequently come across stakeholders' ideas for a solution rather than the description of the underlying problem. Always strive to interpret what is said in order to uncover the essence. For example, the manager of a large downtown office building has contacted a security company expert. The offices of the companies located there have experienced a string of thefts and break-ins. There are two possible scenarios for how this conversation might go:

> Scenario A
>
> BUILDING MANAGER: Your company has to install card readers at all the entrances to the building, and we need all the employees in this building to have an access card.
>
> SECURITY EXPERT: Okay, no problem. Let's determine the number of entrance points into the building and the number of people requiring the card. Then I can probably provide you with an estimate for the project.
>
> Scenario B
>
> BUILDING MANAGER: Your company has to install card readers at all the entrances to the building, and we need all the employees in this building to have an access card.
>
> SECURITY EXPERT: So what you are really saying is that we need to make sure that only authorized people have access to your building, right?
>
> BUILDING MANAGER: Yes, that is exactly the problem we have.

SECURITY EXPERT: Well, our company has a variety of alternatives for you depending on your budget, time, and how state-of-the-art you want the solution to be. Here is a list of options we can offer:

- Retina scan
- Fingerprint scan
- Palm scan
- Voice recognition
- Card and card readers
- Remote controls
- Chips implanted under the skin
- Hiring a security guard
- Neighborhood Watch program

BUILDING MANAGER: Oh, I didn't realize we had so many options. Let me talk to my colleagues and get back to you.

In which scenario would the customer be left with a better impression and, more importantly, in which scenario would the solution chosen address the customer's needs better? If this scenario seems a bit cheesy, especially considering the option where a chip is implanted under the skin, then the following example, which is based on personal experience while working in an IT department of a large international financial institution, will illustrate how this essence principle works.

BOSS: Risk management is having problems with their desktop statistical analysis software. They are asking for an Enterprise edition of the software and a dedicated server. Our initial ballpark estimates for this project are at $500,000, and we have neither the money in our budget nor the resources to accomplish that. Your mission is to explain to them that they are not getting this stuff in the next couple of years.

AUTHOR: [*entering the risk management department*] What is the problem?

RISK MANAGEMENT PERSON: We have to store files on the shared server because of privacy laws and access them through our desktops. Processing times are very slow. We have to upgrade to the Enterprise Server edition and get a new server.

AUTHOR: [*calling network and infrastructure people*] Why is the processing slow? Is it the network or the overloaded server?

NETWORK PERSON: We checked the network and it does not appear to be overloaded.

INFRASTRUCTURE PERSON: Are you kidding me? The entire building is using this server. Of course it's overloaded and slow.

AUTHOR: So, what can we do?

INFRASTRUCTURE PERSON: We will give them a dedicated NT server; we have one laying around here somewhere.

Result: The $500,000 project was diminished to a $2000 server and 3 man-days of work. Problem solved.

Table 6.3 Examples of tilt avoidance

When the manager says . . .	Our response . . .
This information is classified, and I can't share it with the project team.	We stop exploring that particular avenue.
That violates our company policy.	We let go of a promising idea.
Our president would never approve of that solution.	We become intimidated and change the subject.

Constraints, Preferences, and the Tilt Concept

The tilt concept comes from the game of pinball. Some pinball players tilt their machines all of the time. These are not very good players because they can't restrain themselves. Some players never tilt the pinball machines; they are the worst players because they always follow the rules. The best players do tilt the machines, but they never overdo it—hence, the tilt concept. If one never tilts, he is not using all of his resources.

Some examples of being afraid to tilt are shown in Table 6.3. Tilting also means unnecessarily constraining design options. Here is an example of what bold-versus-timid designers would do in similar situations (see Figure 6.2).

Related to the tilt concept is the ability to distinguish between mandatory constraints and desired preferences. For example, an information system designed

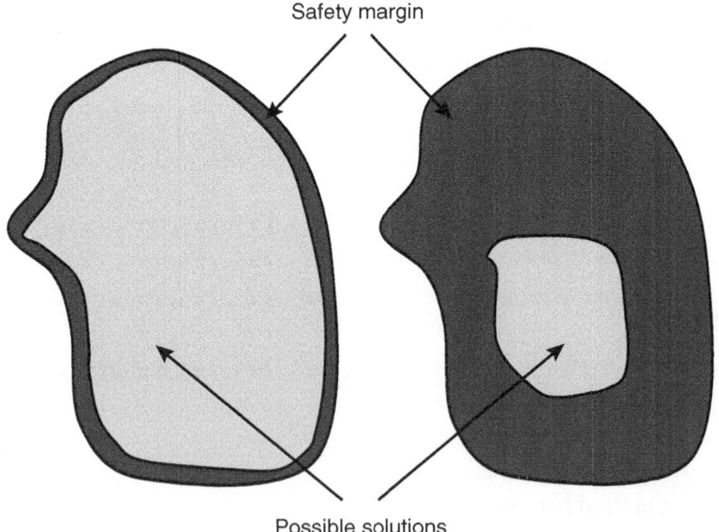

Figure 6.2 Psychology of constraints

to tabulate and report U.S. presidential elections must be ready to operate by the first Tuesday after the first Monday in November of the next leap year. If the product is not ready by that day, it has no value for the next four years. This is definitely a constraint. A requirement to upload a photo of the new executive team member onto the company website by the end of the day on Friday is typically a preference.

Summary

A large share of project troubles is rooted in the inability to capture the initial high-level scope of ventures. There are several techniques that a project manager should use in order to elicit the right business requirements early in the project.

First, in order to overcome this issue, project managers must understand the definition of business requirements and record them properly, either in a separate stand-alone document or in the project charter.

Second, project managers must ask the right questions, including uncomfortable ones such as: "Why are we doing this? What problem are you trying to solve? What happens if we don't do this project?"

Third, a disciplined prioritization approach should be used on every scope definition exercise, and ambiguity time bombs should be eliminated from the project management documentation.

Fourth, concentration on the essence (i.e., the original problem) rather than on the implied or suggested solutions should always reign supreme in a project manager's mind.

And finally, understanding the oh-so-subtle differences between the real, hard constraints and desired preferences is another important ingredient in defining the scope.

References

1. Boehm, Barry. *Software Engineering Economics* (Upper Saddle River, NJ: Prentice-Hall, 1981).
2. Standish Group, *CHAOS Report* (Standish Group International, 1995).

This book has free material available for download from the Web Added Value™ resource center at *www.jrosspub.com*

7

Defining the Detailed Scope: How and Where Do You Find Requirements?

Historical Perspective

Roses, Stars, and the Sun

On April 13, 1471, during the War of the Roses, Yorkist troops under the command of King Edward IV (see Illustration 7.1), and Lancastrian forces led by Richard Neville, the 16th Earl of Warwick, and John de Vere, the 13th Earl of Oxford, met near the town of Barnet some 12 miles north of London. Both commanders arranged their armies east to west on either side of the Great North Road running through Barnet. At four o'clock in the morning on April 14, the soldiers of both armies were awakened and started preparing for the decisive battle. Warwick's army heavily outnumbered Edward's, although sources differ on exact numbers. According to some historians, however, Lancastrian strength ranged from 10,000 to 30,000 men, with 7000 to 15,000 on the Yorkist side. The major problem that both armies had to deal with was heavy fog that covered the entire battlefield, thus making any kind of monitoring or communications with their units somewhat problematic.

Shortly after the fighting ensued, it became clear to any observer that Yorkist forces were headed for a disastrous defeat. Some of the Yorkist soldiers deserted the battlefield and were chased by the Lancastrians; some Yorkists even reached London where they spread tales of the fall of York and a Lancastrian victory.

Illustration 7.1 Edward IV of England

Medieval battles have never been known for their orderliness and organization. Because of the heavy fog, however, the confusion in the field dwarfed anything that had been experienced in military campaigns before or since that memorable day. In the mayhem, John de Vere's forces ended up behind their allies who were part of Lancastrian forces led by Warwick's younger brother John Neville. Neville's regiments, for reasons to be explained later, mistook their comrades-in-arms for enemies and unleashed a volley of arrows on them. De Vere, in his turn, quite logically assumed treachery and attacked Neville's troops. The cries of treason quickly spread throughout the entire battlefield, and as the fog started to dissipate, Edward saw the Lancastrian center in disarray and sent in his reserves, hastening its collapse. One by one, first John Neville, then de Vere, and finally Warwick were killed by Yorkists.

Some historians claim that as many as 6500 Lancastrians perished in that engagement—a mind-boggling number of casualties by fifteenth-century standards. As for Edward, he retained his crown and ruled England for the next twelve years.

Here is one of the most curious parts of this story: how was it possible for Neville's forces to mistake their allies for their enemies? The answer lies in the fact that fifteenth-century armies did not have uniforms; the only way to tell enemy from ally was by the heraldic banners each troop carried into battle. And here is the kicker: Edward's coat of arms contained a depiction of the sun with several wavy rays—sun in splendor (see Illustration 7.2)—while John de Vere had an *estoile*—a star with six wavy rays on its crest (see Illustration 7.3). Unfortunately, the bulk of John Neville's regiment consisted of illiterate peasants who had no training in heraldry (at the time this discipline was typically reserved for someone belonging to the higher echelons of British society). It is not surprising, therefore, that they confused these heraldic signs and reported back to Neville, "The enemy is behind us!"

The project management lesson of this story is that when running projects, especially large and complicated ones, no little detail of the project scope can be overlooked. Ignoring these little and seemingly insignificant details can lead to disastrous results like the ones mentioned in this story. Accordingly, this chapter is dedicated to the problems and issues of the detailed scope definition that has been somewhat overlooked in current project management science.

Illustration 7.2 Sun in splendor

Illustration 7.3 Estoile

Eliciting Detailed Scope

In Chapter 6, the elicitation of high-level scope requirements that would probably appear in the project charter or some other auxiliary scope document was discussed. The next step is the iteration of scope definition that happens some time after the sign off of the project charter but before the technical team members start working on the final designs, blueprints, and bills of materials.

Who Should You Talk To?

A question that gets asked frequently, especially on large and complicated projects is, "Who should I include in scope discussions?" This is a complex matter. Setbacks in the form of cost overruns and missed deadlines are pretty common because the right group of people (or even a single person) were not consulted properly at the scope definition stage.

An example of this scope definition problem is as follows: the project in question was fairly small by this organization's standards, less than $1 million. It involved installing a new high-tech gate on one of the terminals. The project was initiated by the security and engineering departments who managed to get through all the phases of the project and were in the final stages of the execution. About a week before the deadline, one of the engineers suddenly remembered that the new gate had to be operated remotely and should be properly hooked up to their computerized terminal operations system. The IT department was contacted and told to connect the gate to the existing software system by the planned deadline. The computer wizards, while collectively scratching their heads, dropped many of the tasks on their current projects and came to a disheartening (at least for the security team) answer—the software that was needed to operate the gate wasn't the same as the system they were presently running; hence, they would need about a month or two to study it and integrate both packages properly.

This story serves as a perfect example of what can happen when the project manager neglects to include all of the relevant stakeholders during the detailed scope definition phase. The first collective group of primary stakeholders are the clients (aka sponsors), customers, and future users of the product or service that is being built. Clients have the final say in the product scope discussions with respect to what the product does, how it does it, and how sophisticated or simple it should be because they are the ones financing the project. Customers are also important because they will pay for the product and walk out of the stores with it under their arms. On the other hand, they may ignore it and decide to buy the competitor's product. Therefore, it is important that one understands the real needs of all stakeholders.

End users could be a different group from customers (i.e., purchasing can be done by one group of people and the actual usage is done by another). Think about the millions of parents who buy video games for their kids during the Christmas season. On a more serious note, it is typically the users of the product or service who possess the deep knowledge and expertise to provide the project manager with real detailed requirements.

Other groups of stakeholders can include company management, subject matter experts and consultants, project team members, inspectors, legal experts, public opinion, government, and last, but definitely not the least, adjacent departments within the organization.

Why Do We Neglect the Stakeholders?

What happens on numerous occasions—a common behavior within the profession—is that project managers and their team of technical experts decide either independently or after being pressured by their management to ignore one or more stakeholder groups in their detailed scope definition efforts. Some of the common excuses for this behavior follow:

- We are more afraid that the stakeholder will find out too much about the problems we are having and the mistakes that we made than in seeking their help in overcoming the difficulties.
- We are too busy to take time out to communicate and coordinate with our stakeholders.
- We think (or pretend) that it is harder when we involve the stakeholder.
- We think we can do it without the stakeholder.
- We believe stakeholder involvement costs too much money and time.
- There are personality conflicts with key stakeholders.
- Our own management won't let us.
- We are already late with some of our deliverables. Talking to the stakeholder will waste more valuable project time.

Note that in this particular discussion, stakeholders included clients, customers, end users, company management, subject matter experts, and so on.

Project managers should be aware of these excuses that ignore the voice of the stakeholder and be ready to defend their decisions to invest the necessary time and effort into building proper project scope. The value of investment in requirements can be clearly demonstrated by the study conducted by Barry Boehm, 1981[1] that determined the relative costs of fixing an error at various stages of a project (see Figure 7.1). For a detailed discussion of the cost-of-mistake concept, revisit Chapter 6. The question that project managers should be asking their overly hasty team members, managers, and other project stakeholders is, "Would you like to spend one hour discussing the scope with me now or would you rather spend between 40 to 1000 man-hours fixing our scope omissions and defects as we get closer to the end of the project?"

Types of Requirements

One of the popular ways of grouping requirements is by dividing them into *conscious*, *unconscious*, and *undreamed-of* requirements (see Table 7.1). Conscious requirements are typically the easiest to trawl for. These scope items are usually uppermost in customers' minds, and they are almost always indic-

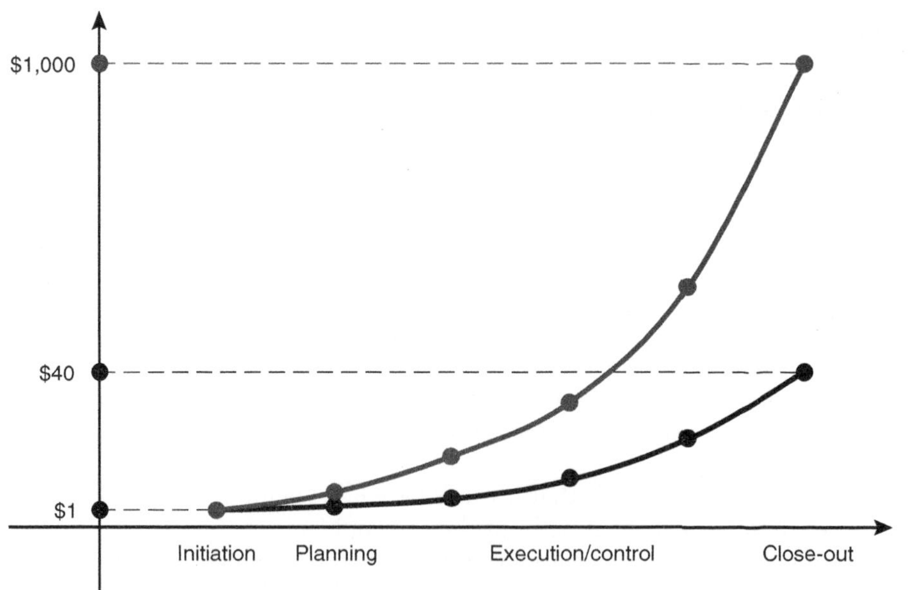

Figure 7.1 Cost of mistake

Table 7.1 Types of requirements

Requirement type	Explanation
Conscious	Most important in customers' minds The essence of something your customers are trying to create or enhance
Unconscious	Items so common and familiar to the stakeholders that they frequently forget to mention them
Undreamed-of	Things that could be very useful to the customer, but for whatever reason—typically lack of technical expertise—they are not aware of their existence

ative of something the customer is trying to create or improve. For example, a small business owner who is trying to increase her revenue stream by selling products on the internet will undoubtedly mention a website with a product catalogue, shopping baskets, and an ability to make payments using most of the popular credit cards. Therefore, it is likely that these requirements would be the first ones mentioned by the stakeholders during one-on-one interviews with the project manager, which makes these requirements fairly easy to catch.

On the other hand, unconscious requirements are a bit more difficult to extract because they are so familiar to the stakeholder that she frequently fails to mention them by assuming that everyone is aware of them. Again, using the small business owner example, including value-added tax into the final price of the product sold via the internet could be considered common knowledge by the business owner, and yet a web developer may not possess sufficient understanding of accounting to add this requirement to the scope of the project. Only inquisitive and thoughtful questioning with follow-up walkthroughs can unearth all of the unconscious scope items.

Undreamed-of scope items are the things that could be very useful to the customer, but for whatever reason (typically a lack of technical expertise) he is not aware of their existence. Once more, returning to the website example, the small business owner may not be aware that all credit card-related information must be encrypted and protected according to industry standards. The burden of informing him about this regulation and thus adding an extra requirement lies on the project manager's shoulders.

Types of Detailed Questions to Ask

Project managers should also be skilled facilitators with a wide array of focus questions at their disposal. These questions can help modulate group dynamics, expand and contract the discussions, and move the group of stakeholders toward closure. Project managers have to be aware that they should be using the questions listed in Table 7.2 to create an environment in which the participants have the freedom to ask difficult questions and provide answers that require making tough decisions.

How to Ask the Right Questions

When developing a detailed scope document, it is very important to ask the right questions to elicit all of the requirements from the customers. The problems of scope definition and documentation could be rooted in unspecified information, unspecified comparison, generalization, or universal qualifier types of statements (see Table 7.3).

Unspecified information: Frequently these statements are somewhat counterintuitive to the average person because she tends to ignore, or just blindly accepts, the underlying assumptions buried in them. For example, the simple statement, "we get the sales reports," should raise the following questions from an experienced project manager (see Table 7.3 for more examples):

- Who is *we*?
- What do you mean by *get*?
- What are these *sales reports*?

Unspecified comparison: A term used when the stakeholder uses words like *better*, *faster*, and so on. For example, "The new container terminal should be better." The questions that should immediately come to mind are:

- Better compared to what?
- Better in what way?
- Who decided that it should be better?

Generalization: This typically occurs when one hears words like *must* or *can't*. For instance, the customer might say, "The new store must be located at the intersection

Table 7.2 Types of questions to ask

Type of question	Explanation	Example
Direct	Seek specific information	What makes this important?
Open-ended	Aimed at stimulating the discussion	What else would be helpful?
Clarifying	Rephrasing the speaker's words	Did I hear you saying this . . . ?
Leading	Propose a new action	And what about . . . ?
Refocusing	Aimed at redirecting the group	This sounds like a great idea which should be parked for now, but what about the original issue?

Table 7.3 Types of statements customers make

Type of statement	Sample statement	Sample questions
Unspecified information	We get the sales reports.	Is it just you or your entire department? Do just specific employees within your team get these? Are other departments privy to these reports? If yes, then who in other departments gets them? What do you mean by *get*? Are the reports printed out and mailed to you or are they faxed? Do you receive them by e-mail? In what format? Do you have a software package that produces them automatically? What is a sales report? What kind of information is contained there? Do you just have one type of report or several?
Unspecified comparison	The new container terminal should be better.	Better compared to what? To the existing terminals at your port or your competitors? Or the best in the world? Better in what way? In terms of square footage, overall container capacity, logistics, usage of computer technologies, security? Who decided that it should be better? What is the reasoning behind this decision to increase capacity, improve logistics or security?
Generalization	The new store must be located at the intersection of two major streets in the Oakmount neighborhood.	Why must you do it specifically that way? Why should the store be located at the intersection? Why major streets? If you are looking for high-traffic areas, have you considered other locations, like malls or shopping plazas? What happens if you can't find a space for rent at the intersection of two major roads? Will you abandon the idea of opening the new store? Will you postpone it? What kind of drop in revenue are you anticipating?
Universal qualifiers	The terminal gate shall always be operated from the main control room.	Is it really always or are there some exceptions? What happens if the main control room is blocked? What should the employees do in case of an emergency (e.g., fire)?

of two major streets in the Oakmount neighborhood." The questions asked by the project manager should be:

- Why must you do it specifically that way? Why should the store be located at the intersection? Why major streets? If you are looking for high-traffic areas, have you considered other locations, like malls or shopping plazas?
- What happens if you can't find a space for rent at the intersection of two major roads? Will you abandon the idea of opening the new store? Will you postpone it? What kind of drop in revenue are you anticipating?

Universal qualifiers: These are found in statements containing words like *never* or *always*. The questions a manager should be asking in this case are:

- Is it really never, or does it happen sometimes?
- Is it really always, or are there some exceptions?

Which Technique Is Best?

There has been some confusion with respect to which scope definition techniques should be used on what types of projects. In IT and software development, managers more or less know that functional and nonfunctional requirements and full-scale use cases typically fall into the category of larger, traditional waterfall projects, while user stories tend to get used on more agile, smaller engagements. We now examine the validity of various requirements trawling techniques on different kinds of projects. To answer these questions, it is useful to divide projects into three broad categories:

- *Rabbit projects* are small and fairly simple engagements with a collocated, tightly knit team and a small number of customers who are willing to invest a lot of their time in the scope definition stage. The techniques that work well on such projects are brainstorming and creativity workshops because of the proximity of the participants and their willingness to participate in the scope definition process.
- *Elephant projects* are, as a rule, large and sophisticated endeavors with budgets of tens or hundreds of millions of dollars such as the launch of a space shuttle, development of a new type of passenger airplane, or construction of a new port terminal. Project teams on such projects are large and likely to be spread out at several locations, sometimes on different continents separated by thousands of miles. There are many stakeholders who most likely do not have much time at their disposal to invest in requirements trawling. As a result, apprenticing (spending time watching the stakeholders perform their daily duties especially in order to understand business processes) can be of great value.
- *Horse projects* are the something-in-between endeavors that retain the characteristics of both Rabbit and Elephant projects. They could be of me-

Table 7.4 Best scope elicitation techniques by type of project

Technique	Description	Rabbit	Horse	Elephant
Apprenticing	Spend time working with an expert	★	★★	★★★
Interviewing	One-on-one discussion with a user or expert	★★★	★★★	★★★
Essence	Find the real problem first	★★★	★★★	★★★
Brainstorming	Facilitate creativity and invention	★★★	★★	★★
Current situation modeling	Examine the legacy system for requirements	★	★★	★★★

Note: three stars = great fit; two stars = adequate fit; one star = bad fit

dium size but have a distributed group of stakeholders. A vast percentage of projects will most likely fall into the Horse category because it is difficult to find a project that possesses all of the characteristics of the Rabbit or the Elephant. As a result of such a blend, most of the techniques mentioned in Table 7.4 rated as great or satisfactory fits for the Horse projects.

The interesting aspect of this table is that apparently techniques such as *interviewing* and *searching for the essence* (i.e., trying to identify the real problem behind every scope item) are absolutely universal no matter what the project is.

What Are the Criteria for Quality Scope Items?

Now that the scope document is complete, what guidelines should be followed to ensure that requirements recorded are of good quality and can be validated by the project stakeholders while at the same time, can be easily understood by all the technical team members (programmers, architects, engineers)? A list of attributes of good project requirements is shown in Table 7.5.

Introducing Measurability

Consider the following example: assume that a client shows up at a custom furniture builder's workshop saying that he needs a dinner table of an adequate size for his family. Without any further discussions and requirements elicitation, how easy would it be to fill this order? Compare this requirement with the following: the table should be 6 feet long, 4 feet wide, and 3 feet high. Is this request easier to implement?

Consider another example. The initial scope item is as follows:

The new container terminal shall be of a sufficient square footage to accommodate load requirements in peak times.

Table 7.5 Attributes of good requirements

Attribute	Explanation
Complete	Have all the details of every scope item been covered (e.g., all possible scenarios, alternatives, and exceptions)?
Consistent	Can the requirement be met without conflicting with other requirements? If not, the requirement should be removed or revised.
Traceable	Is the origin of the detailed scope item known? Can it be traced directly to the high-level product or service feature recorded in the project charter?
Concise	Is the requirement stated simply and clearly? Can it be easily understood by both the customers and technical team members?
Design free	The detailed scope item should be stating what must be done without indicating how. Did we make sure that the technical aspects of the detailed product design are left to the technical experts?
Standard constructs	Requirements are stated as imperative needs using *shall*. Avoid using words *should* or *may*; they create a sense of false priorities.
Unique identifier	Has the detailed scope item been uniquely identified (e.g., R1, R2, R3)?
Prioritized	Has the requirement been assigned a priority relative to other requirements in the document (e.g., must-have, should-have, and nice-to-have)?
Rationale for each requirement	Has the rationale for each scope item been clearly identified and agreed upon by all the relevant stakeholders? In other words, do we really need this?

Compare the old terminal requirement to the following statement:

> *The new container terminal shall have a capacity of at least 600,000 TEUs (twenty-foot equivalent units).*

Which requirement would an architect or an engineer think would be more helpful if he were about to start working on a terminal blueprint?

The initial vague statements similar to those in the aforementioned examples are rather common in the real world process of gathering requirements. Introducing measurability to scope items is one of the key factors in improving the quality of requirements and avoiding future misunderstandings (i.e., rework and budget overruns) as the project progresses from the planning to the execution and close-out stages.

Imposing measurability on scope is, however, one of the most stressful exercises the project manager can go through during the scoping stage. First, one has to discover all of the words and phrases in the scope definition that need to be made measurable. This, by the way, is typically the easier of the two steps. Second, the project manager has to sit down with the stakeholders and compel them to provide real numbers to replace vague wordings in the scope statements. Customers are usually reluctant to do that early in the project because they either don't know the measures required or are unwilling to accept the responsibility for providing them. In other words, their line of thought can go something like this: "What happens if I claim 600,000 TEUs and it turns out that in the peak times the demand reaches 850,000 TEUs?" Providing answers to such questions typically requires a lot of additional work and research, which sometimes is discouraged by senior management because it is seen as wasting time or delaying the start of an important project.

How does one impose measurability on scope items? One of the easiest ways of doing that is by asking the following question:

> *What is considered to be a failure to meet this requirement?*

Examine this method in the following example, which is based on a conversation that took place with a project manager working for a very large retail chain. He was responsible for one of several new store opening projects, and I was assigned to peer review his project documentation.

> AUTHOR: You need to impose some kind of measurability on your deliverables.
>
> PM: Our deliverables cannot have measurability associated with them. It is an all-or-nothing approach. For example, if the store is supposed to have thirty point-of-sale (POS) stations, it should have all thirty stations installed and working for the opening.
>
> AUTHOR: Okay, but what happens if 29 out of 30 stations are working and one is defective? Do you think the company will say no to hundreds of thousands of dollars in revenue and postpone the opening of the store by even one day?
>
> PM: Well, in that case, obviously we will still go ahead with the opening.
>
> AUTHOR: And if 28 out of 30 stations are working?
>
> PM: We would still go ahead.
>
> AUTHOR: And what happens if only one out of 30 POS stations is working, and the remaining 29 are broken?
>
> PM: Well, of course we would have to postpone the opening of the store then.
>
> AUTHOR: Here is what you need to do. Talk to the customer and try to determine a threshold for the number of nonworking POS stations. That number is your measurability parameter.

Assigning Priorities—Games People Play

The topic of assigning priorities and their importance to any project has already been discussed in Chapter 6. It is necessary now to revisit the same issue to reiterate its importance not only with respect to high-level requirements but also to detailed scope items.

As was mentioned previously, prioritization is a method of dealing with competing demands for limited resources. According to the basic principles of economics, every person's demand for goods and services almost always exceeds her means. As a result, most people in the world have to rank their preferences according to their importance and assess what can be squeezed into the existing budget. Similarly, by ranking requirements according to their priority (with input from the stakeholders), the project manager enables the delivery of the highest value items at the lowest possible cost.

Furthermore, while conducting the eternal balancing game between project scope, time, budget, effort, and quality throughout the length of the project, the work of the project manager is greatly simplified if the scope items are ranked in the order of importance or assigned some relative priorities. This becomes especially important if the project budget or timeline is inflexible, or even fixed, thus necessitating cuts in scope for the successful delivery of the project.

Despite all these facts, overcoming stakeholders' resistance to label some of the scope items as low or medium priority is one of the major issues project managers have to deal with on an almost daily basis during the scoping phase. Some of the excuses mentioned by customers could be:

- I absolutely need all of these features. Just make it happen somehow.
- It is not politically acceptable to say a requirement has a low priority; hence, we will label them high, very high and super high.
- We can do it all.
- I believe our technical people can do it all.
- Low-priority items never get delivered. If I agree to your request, I will never see this requirement built.

Typically project managers have to employ the full arsenal of their communication, negotiation, and other stakeholder management skills to resolve these conflicts. However, one of the strategies a project manager can use is to ask the following questions:

- What happens if we drop this requirement? Will the entire project have to be cancelled?
- What is the impact on the original business objectives of dropping this scope item?

Asking these questions allows a shifting of the burden of business-related decision making onto the shoulders of the stakeholder and permits a refocusing of the attention on the big picture—the project goals.

How Do You Know When to Stop?

The caveats of not spending enough time defining the detailed scope of the project have been discussed to a great extent in project management literature. This concept also has been confirmed in numerous studies by various researchers including the Standish Group CHAOS Report[2], Project Management Institute[3] (PMI®), and others. However, a question diametrically opposed to the issue above is: how does one know when he is done with building the scope definition? The following are some of the indicators that can advise a manager it is time to wrap up the requirements stage of the project and move on to the final stages of the planning phase:

- The stakeholders can't think of any other requirements or scope items no matter how many different types of questions are being asked.
- The stakeholders repeat issues that have already been covered. The conversation starts going in circles as the same requirements get mentioned again and again.
- The stakeholders request requirements that are all out of scope. The project charter should have listed all of the high-level features. If the scope were limited to just a three-bedroom home, the requests for a pool and landscaped yard should be out of scope.
- Newly proposed requirements are all low priority. The stakeholders keep mentioning scope items to be included in the project but agree that these are low-priority items.
- The users are proposing features that should be included in one of the next phases. The conversations with the stakeholders start drifting toward the future phases rather than the current release of the project.

Walkthroughs and Peer Reviews

Walkthroughs and peer reviews are one of the most powerful techniques at the disposal of project managers. However, survey results seem to indicate that few companies use walkthroughs in order to validate the scope of the project before moving on to the execution stage. And yet those who tried this technique reported extremely positive results in terms of improved quality, lower-than-before budgets, reduced amount of rework, and most importantly, high levels of satisfaction from the project team and the stakeholders alike.

The issue of walkthroughs and peer reviews is so vast and important that it requires a full chapter of its own (see Chapter 12). A suggestion to project management professionals is to have their project documentation—scope especially—reviewed by all of the project stakeholders including customers, end users, project team members, and other departments in the organization impacted by the project in question.

Summary

When selecting the sources of project scope, make sure to consider all relevant people, especially clients, customers, and future users of the product. It is also imperative to inquire if other stakeholder groups such as company management, subject matter experts, project team members, company lawyers, and the adjacent departments within the organization have anything to say about the project scope.

There could be some pressure from clients, project team members, or even from managers to speed things up and avoid wasting time by forgoing conversations with some of the stakeholders. Avoid such shortcuts at all costs. Always remember that a one-dollar mistake made during the requirements stage can become a thousand dollar defect at the end of the project.

Keep in mind the types of requirements that exist and make an extra effort to capture the unconscious requirements, since they frequently go unmentioned by the customer.

Employ the entire array of various kinds of questions at one's disposal. It will take some time to know which question should be asked at what time, but eventually it will become second nature. Also, don't be too intimidated to ask politically incorrect questions such as, "Why do you think this way is better than the others?" or "When you say 'never' do you really mean *never*, or are there some exceptions?"

Know what requirements trawling techniques are appropriate for the type of project being worked on. Also, keep in mind that one can never go wrong with one-on-one interviews. Try to find the problem first rather than blindly accepting the solution imposed by the customer—the search for the essence technique.

When documenting and especially when reviewing scope documents, remember the quality attributes of good requirements and the concept of measurability.

References

1. Boehm, Barry. 1981.
2. Project Management Institute, *The PMI® Project Management Fact Book, 2nd ed.* (Project Management Institute: 2001).
3. Standish Group, *CHAOS Report* (Standish Group International: 2006).

8

Who Needs Creativity in Projects and How Do You Cultivate It?

Historical Perspective

British Redcoats and American Rebels

Some historians tend to spread stories about the dumb British who dressed up their troops in bright red uniforms and lined them up in rigid formations so that the brave (and smart) American revolutionaries hiding in bushes could shoot at them at their pleasure.

However, other scholars contend that there was, after all, a certain logic behind this idiocy. They argue that brightly colored coats and rigid formations were used to enforce the discipline and to improve the soldiers' morale. First, they claim, if the troops were dressed up in red uniforms and lined up in a square or rectangular formation, it would be very easy for the commanding officer (positioned on some nearby hill) to see the soldiers deserting from the battle and to take proper actions after the battle was won.

If, on the other hand, the battle was lost, it would be very easy for the enemy troops to find British deserters, again, thanks to their crimson overcoats. Of course, the fugitive could always take off his uniform, assuming he had enough time (perhaps that was why they had so many buttons), but young men running around the countryside in their underwear would be almost as conspicuous as soldiers in red jackets.

Try to analyze this solution from the project manager's point of view. At some point in time, probably around the seventeenth century, the British War Office had identified a key problem:

> When the unprotected soldiers of two armies are lined up against each other and [are] supposed to continuously shoot and reload their weapons at very close distances, fear becomes a very important factor. This factor leads to panic and desertion from the battlefield, thus causing us to lose some of the engagements that could otherwise [be] won.

Once the real issue had been identified, the War Office came up with a novel and ingenious solution to a difficult problem—the rigid rectangular formations and bright red uniforms with a lot of buttons (see Table 8.1).

Could this method devised by the British War Office be categorized as creative thinking? What is creativity and innovation? How does one simultaneously encourage and channel creative thinking on challenging projects? This chapter, which is dedicated to harnessing creativity and innovation on projects, will attempt to answer these questions.

Introducing Creativity

How Important Is Creativity?

Words like *innovation* and *creativity* seem to appear in almost every speech or in interviews of prominent CEOs or business leaders. If one thinks back to the last general company meeting or town hall, he can probably remember these terms

Table 8.1 British uniform attributes and their purposes

Solution attributes	Explanation
Rigid rectangular formations	It is fairly difficult for a soldier to desert from the battlefield if he is surrounded by dozens of his peers while marching at a fairly fast pace. It is very easy for the commanding officer to spot someone breaking away from the squad if the squad forms a rectangular shape.
Bright red uniforms	If a soldier deserts from the battlefield and the British win the battle, it would be fairly easy for them to find him after the combat. If a soldier deserts from the battlefield and the British lose the fight, it would be really easy for the enemy to locate him after the skirmish. Thus, the cost of desertion has been maximized for both scenarios.
Multitude of buttons	Having a lot of buttons on the uniform maximizes the difficulty of taking it off.

appearing at least once or twice in the sermon given by the organization's president or vice president. Here is a compilation of some recent quotes[1] of world-famous company leaders:

> We have to continuously create new innovation that lets people do something they didn't think they could do the day before. (Steve Ballmer, Microsoft)
>
> A business has to be involving, it has to be fun, and it has to exercise your creative instincts. (Richard Branson, Virgin)
>
> Obviously everyone wants to be successful, but I want to be looked back on as being very innovative, very trusted and ethical, and ultimately making a big difference in the world. (Sergey Brin, Google)

A survey of management priorities confirms that innovation is almost always in the top two or three strategic priorities mentioned by executives. While almost everyone agrees, however, that creativity is extremely important in the modern business environment, there remains a certain element of frustration associated with it. This issue is about how to turn the flowery rhetoric and gung-ho speeches into pragmatic, down-to-earth, and profitable reality.

What Is Creativity?

Before going into the detailed descriptions of creativity-enhancing methodologies, it's important to determine what innovation really is. After all, the definition of creativity seems to be one of the more elusive enigmas in the corporate world. This elusiveness looks a bit odd in today's age that is filled with practicality and well-defined business processes. While it is perfectly acceptable for a senior manager of any given company to claim that:

> Our team suddenly had an epiphany, and the vision of this great cutting-edge product just appeared in front of us, partly because of the individual brilliance of our technical gurus and partly because of some yet unknown factors.

Does this sound like an acceptable declaration? Compare that statement to the following statement:

> Our team suddenly had an epiphany, and the vision of the process for preparing patients' prescription medicines just appeared in front of us, partly because of the individual brilliance of our technical gurus and partly because of some yet unknown factors.

This obviously is not something customers would like to hear from the manager of their neighborhood pharmacy. Therefore, it would be beneficial to determine what creativity is and what it isn't before attempting to come up with innovation management techniques.

There are generally two kinds of problems: easy and difficult. The approach to easy problems obviously is very straightforward; easy problem implies an easy solution. For example, in order to calculate the average velocity of a vehicle, the distance it has travelled should be divided by the time it took the vehicle to cover the distance. Difficult problems, on the other hand, can fall into two categories:

- Problem is known, but the solution is unknown
- Problem itself is unknown, and the solution is unknown

Human desire to fly, until the end of the nineteenth century, would fall into the first category. So does the aspiration to design an electric car battery that would allow a vehicle to travel, say, 2500 miles between charges. With these challenges the original problems are well defined:

- We cannot fly
- We do not have a car battery that would allow the car to travel at least 2500 miles between charges

In contrast, a detective who is looking for evidence at a crime scene or a painter who is contemplating her next masterpiece falls into the second category. If one asks them, "What are you doing?" the answer will most likely be, "I am not sure, but I will know once I find it." Creative solutions, therefore, can be described as a resolution of a difficult problem.

Creativity should not be confused, however, with novelty. By definition, novelty is necessary but not a sufficient condition for creativity. For example, a new version of word processing software cannot be considered creative unless it manages to address some of the challenging problems the customers had with the previous versions.

In other words, a combination of novel approach and the solution to a difficult problem must exist for the product or service to be, indeed, considered creative.

What Are the Tactical Methods at the Project Manager's Disposal?

Define the Problem

From the definition of difficult problems that was previously mentioned, it is fairly easy to see that a situation where both the problem and the solution are unknown is more challenging than the cases where the problem, albeit very difficult, is well defined, but the solution is still unknown.

Hence comes the first axiom of creativity—try to recognize the underlying problem first, and make sure it is well understood by all stakeholders.

Imagine, for example, that a software engineer has been hired to design a brand new software system for elevators in a luxurious seven-star hotel in an exotic location. The team has been told that innovation, creativity, and the wow factor are strongly encouraged and expected by their clients.

One of the many requirements for the elevator software system may state:

> *The current floor number shall be shown on a digital display in the elevator cabin.*

Since this statement is not a problem but rather a solution, how many degrees of freedom are now at the designer's disposal? Not too many, really; he would be limited to various ways of displaying the floor number on the digital screen. However, if a problem is stated (instead of a solution), the statement may look like:

> *How would the people on the elevator know which floor they are on?*

What options are available?

- Display floor number
- Display animation
- Voice announcement
- Play tones
- Play melodies
- Vibration
- Airflow
- Odors (the chocolate floor!)
- Any combination of several signals

The previous exercise demonstrates that investing time and effort in understanding the actual problem can be the first step in finding a creative solution to a difficult problem (as opposed to considering a solution that is so frequently imposed on project teams by the customers and other stakeholders). See The Problem Versus Solution Discussion in Chapter 6 for a more detailed discussion of this topic.

Maximize Diversity

It would probably be worthwhile to start this section with several shocking revelations made by creativity and innovation researchers over the course of the last century.[2]

- A study of 58 major inventions made in Europe and the United States including photography, fluorescent lighting, ballpoint pens, and computers concluded that at least 46 of these innovations originated outside of their industry.

- Probably the most famous examples of outsiders making a serious impact on an entire industry is the story of Frank Whittle (UK) and Hans von Ohain (Germany) in the 1930s. Working independently, each developed the first prototypes of jet engines. At the time of their discoveries, Whittle was a student at the Royal Air Force College whereas von Ohain was working as a junior research assistant at the Physical Institute at the University of Göttingen.
- Another study of the origins of scientific instruments discovered that 77 percent of innovations in this area originated with users and only 23 percent could be traced back to the manufacturers.
- Try to think of the most progressive, hip, and culturally rich cities in the world. There would be some variation in the answers, but metropolises such as London, New York, Los Angeles, Paris, Toronto, and Vancouver would likely appear frequently on these lists. What is the one unifying factor of these cities? The amazing cultural and ethnic diversities. One can probably find a representative or even a community of residents from each corner of the world living in these urban centers.
- According to the experiments conducted at the California Institute of Technology, diverse project teams have consistently beaten groups consisting of the most talented individuals available.
- Commenting on innovation, Luke Visconti was quoted in *DiversityInc* magazine, "If you want to compete globally, you have to understand that 80 percent of the globe isn't white, and 50 percent of it isn't male."

Once absorbed and analyzed, these facts can lead to several important conclusions. First, if managing a project where innovativeness and creativity are expected to play a big role, project managers should ensure that their team includes, if possible, representatives from the following areas:

- People who are known for generating a lot of crazy ideas and people who can calmly weed out any ideas that are not feasible
- People who work at the company's headquarters and team members who are working on the periphery
- Representatives of both younger and older generations
- Team members who are technology experts and people who are good at understanding business realities
- People from within the company and people from outside the company, including customers and users
- People of different ethnic and cultural backgrounds

Regarding customer involvement, there are several techniques that can be used by the project team instead of, or in addition to, direct customer participation. The first technique is called *direct observation*, which is where customer experiences with the product or service are watched directly, photographed, or videotaped.

For example, a successful Chinese appliance manufacturer, *Haier*, sent their design people to college and university campuses in the United States. One of the problems identified by the researchers was that, because of the cramped dormitory rooms, some students were building makeshift desks by placing boards on coolers. Haier considered this problem to be serious enough to come up with a refrigerator that had a fold out work top. The product proved to be extremely successful.

In addition, customer experience mapping, a process similar to creating a business process diagram, attempts to map the entire customer experience surrounding a specific product or service.

Here is another case: a European-based CIO of a large international bank was transferred to a key North American hub of the company. On his arrival in North America, he visited the local branch of the same bank and attempted to open an account there. To his great surprise, he learned that opening a bank account at the new location involved several dozen fairly cumbersome operations on a computer. In addition, he was told by the clerk that if he wanted his privileges (i.e., overdraft protection, credit rating, etc.) transferred from his European account to the new one, he would have to wait another three weeks so that the proper files could be moved by fax and by mail.

It's easy to guess what the first project initiated by the new CIO was. He ordered the complete overhaul of the outdated account management system during his first month in the office.

Communications

Jeff Bezos, Ted Turner, Steve Jobs—these people are firmly associated with creativity and innovation in the modern corporate world. Unfortunately it is assumed that the success of these individuals is solely dependent on their creative genius and the as-yet-unexplained innovative epiphanies they have been prone to from time to time.

What frequently gets ignored is the fact that these business leaders created proper conditions in order for their creativity to flourish by communicating, observing, and sharing their ideas with like-minded people around them. After all, innovation is frequently about absorbing a wide variety of half-baked designs, notions, principles, and skills and finding the right synergies among them in order to create novel solutions to difficult problems.

For example, Henry Ford, who is credited with the creation of the revolutionary assembly line idea, actually borrowed this idea while watching the butchers perform their duties at Philip Armour's Chicago meat packing company. Ford simply assumed that the same principles used by the workers at this hog disassembly line could be used when building cars.

Star Wars movies are yet another example of combinational chemistry at work. Despite the fact that the original films are considered to be among the most innovative movie concepts of all time, George Lucas once admitted that the plot for the movies was actually a combination of pirate, western, war, and science fiction movies coupled with several Biblical legends.

Thus, the main lesson that should be learned from these stories is that project managers should strive to answer the following questions with respect to creating collaborative environments for their projects:

- How do we create a high level of association and conversation on our projects?
- How do we increase the frequency and quality of communications between different stakeholder groups on our projects?

Some of the possible answers to these challenging questions can be quite simple. To begin with, take the first step and talk to the users, customers, and project sponsors. It is amazing how many project managers and technical experts prefer to receive their project requirements via e-mail or from conversations with their direct managers rather than by just walking a couple of hundred feet to have a face-to-face conversation with the real customer or a frontline worker.

Also, team collocation—placing the distributed team at one geographic location—is yet another way of encouraging conversations among project team members. If collocation is not a feasible option, there should be several (both formal and informal) organized gatherings of internal and external project stakeholders during the initiation and planning phases of the project. These gatherings can range from formal joint brainstorming sessions to company-sponsored barbeques in order to facilitate and encourage interactions among people.

Identify and Challenge Orthodoxies

This book has already mentioned that the question *why* is probably one of the best friends of any project manager. It also has been discussed how this question allows differentiation between the proposed solution and the underlying problem; between the imposed design and a more general requirement. However, this question can be elevated to an even greater strategic level. It can be used to challenge the most sacred cows of the organizational rules, assumptions, business processes, and product features. One can argue that the key to IKEA's success was buried in one very simple question:

> Why does the furniture have to be delivered already preassembled?

Jeff Bezos of Amazon.com asked:

> Why should a bookstore carry only 200,000 titles at a time? Can we expand that number to 2 or 3 million?

Thus, project managers and their teams are encouraged to find and question the orthodoxies that exist in practically any organization. These orthodoxies can take different shapes. Some of them take the form of dogmas deeply ingrained into the corporate mind-set. For example, consider this conversation between a consultant and a president of a small marketing company that for years believed one of their customers, a local telecom giant, was their most important strategic client.

> CONSULTANT: I keep hearing from almost everyone here that Company A is our most important strategic client. Why do you believe that?
>
> PRESIDENT: Well, they are our largest client by far, and we hope that we can get more business from them as time goes by.
>
> CONSULTANT: I have looked at some of the projects you have done for them over the course of several years and compared them to similar projects done for other companies. It looks like you have consistently undercharged them, accepting fairly significant losses on each project.
>
> PRESIDENT: But I have just told you that they are a key strategic client. Because of this policy, we have been very flexible with our pricing in order to win them over and generate more business for us.
>
> CONSULTANT: But it looks like you have lost close to $1,800,000 over the course of the last five years on the projects you have done for them because of this policy. I realize that this organization has been identified as a key client, but don't you think it is time to carefully examine the historical data and make a strategic decision?

Another great tactic is to try to break the *or* approach and replace it with the *and* attitude. The *or* approach implies that a customer can either get one attribute of the product or another, but not both. For example, until recently, there was a firm belief in the telecommunications industry that if a customer wanted cheap phone service, she was limited to landline phones at home. If, on the other hand, a customer wanted a mobile phone, he should, by default, be prepared to pay three or four times more for the same service. This trend continued until some of more progressive telecom companies asked, "Can we provide our customers with cheap and reliable mobile phones?"

In another case, for many years customers were expected to first lather their hair with shampoo, rinse it, apply conditioner, wait for several minutes, then wash it out of their hair. The approach was: if the customers want to take care of their hair, they'd better be prepared to spend a lot of time in the shower. Many people accepted this dogma until Procter & Gamble challenged that tenet by introducing the first two-in-one product Pert Plus® to the market in 1987.

Use Milestones

Another technique is to use milestones in order to aid the project team in finding the most creative solutions to the problems mentioned by the customers. Just like in the simplified elevator example, once all of the possible solutions have been tabled, the team needs to analyze each one to assess them from the point of feasibility, probability of technical delivery, and compatibility with other parts of the system.

Rather than suggesting to the project team to disperse, assess the different combinations of solutions in groups and meet several days or weeks later to discuss the findings. The project manager could arrange for a series of meetings (milestones) separated by several days to iteratively appraise and analyze intermediate findings. Using these milestones as stepping stones, the project team can quickly filter out bad solutions or designs and discern a promising direction for the most fitting and innovative result.

Closely related to this scheme is the *breadth-first principle*. This method implies generating and analyzing a wide array of possible solutions to a problem one layer at a time. Compare this approach to the *depth-first principle* where only a few, or even one, possible solution is generated, and the entire team focuses on the detailed assessment of that particular design. If the solution chosen in the depth-first principle turns out to be bad, the team will have lost a lot of time and effort. Needless to say, choosing only one or two possible solutions instead of several will not benefit the creativity aspect of the designs.

Therefore, it is advisable for project teams to start their search for the optimal solution by employing the breadth-first principle in order to quickly sift through a lot of information at a fairly high level and to dispose of all the inferior solutions as soon as possible.

Once the few promising solutions are left, the team may consider switching to an in-depth analysis of each one of the candidates.

When Should the Creativity Happen?

Another important question that is frequently overlooked in project management literature is: when should innovation happen during the course of a project? After all, shouldn't creativity be equally welcome and therefore encouraged throughout the entire project life cycle, or is there a specific time span when it is most productive?

This is an important question since losing control of the creative processes could lead to serious performance, quality, timing, and budget issues. Imagine that in the process of building a custom luxury home, the construction team has already finished all the major tasks such as erecting the walls and building the roof and is now concentrating on the interior design components. At some point, the architect of the original plan shows up on the construction site and proclaims, "Hey, guys, wouldn't it be really cool to build an underground swimming pool right underneath the house?"

Is this a creative concept? It probably is. Would it be the right time to infuse creativity into the project? Assuming the project has deadlines and a constrained bud-

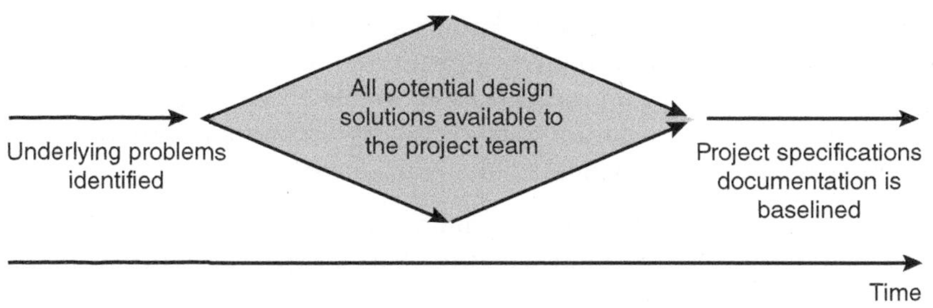

Figure 8.1 Harnessing creativity

get, then probably not. The best approach to harnessing creativity is to start with defining a problem or a set of problems that the team is trying to address. Once the list of problems has been defined, the team should be encouraged to exercise their creative talents and use whatever techniques are necessary—brainstorming, communicating, prototyping—to generate as many solutions as possible. One might say that the team is operating in a divergent mode as shown in Figure 8.1.

At a certain time, probably halfway between *problems defined* and *specifications completed*, the team will exhaust all potential solutions to the problems outlined earlier. Then, the second half of the creative process should be dedicated to weeding out the proposed designs that are not feasible, not doable, or conflicting. The domain of the solution search remains in the convergent mode until the overall design is narrowed down to a single point.

What Are the Strategic Methods at the Executive's Disposal?

Sow Enough Seeds

The senior management of any given company should realize that innovation is a numbers game: the more ideas generated within the organization, the higher the chances are that some of them may become successful products or services.

In this discussion, it is worthwhile to consider the extreme case of the idea generation and analysis business model such as that of a typical venture capital company. Venture capital firms receive thousands of business plans (aka project ideas) from entrepreneurs. A hundred or so of these authors are usually invited to present their case for the senior venture capital partners. After a careful analysis, about 10 proposals receive venture capital funding. The management of the venture capital does not really expect that all 10 carefully screened proposals will become winners. About two or three will fail fairly soon; six or seven may become reasonable income earners; only one or two, however, will turn out to be portfolio stars.

Thus, if the company strives to be known as a cutting-edge innovator in its industry, it should be prepared to invest time and money into the creation of idea-generating mechanisms at the organization. While these mechanisms may take different shapes due to the nature of the business or company structure, there are several universal attributes typical to all organizations:

- Providing creativity training for all employees
- Providing technology infrastructure that enables the employees to share their ideas
- Hiring people who have experience in both innovation coaching and mentoring
- Having a rewards and recognition system for the innovative employees
- Having some kind of portfolio management system in place that is capable of receiving, analyzing, and selecting the best product ideas

Drowning the Puppies

In his speech at the Project Management Institute (PMI®) Research 2006 conference in Montreal, famous product and portfolio management expert Robert Cooper claimed that, according to his own research, there is a strong correlation between innovativeness and portfolio management methodology known as *drowning the puppies*.

According to Cooper, companies that are recognized in the world as innovation leaders—Procter & Gamble, Johnson & Johnson, Kraft—have all used this project portfolio management technique to select the best product ideas and to dispose of the less promising projects. Figure 8.2 demonstrates this approach in a very simplified manner, purely for illustrational purposes. For more information on how to select projects and manage the portfolio pipeline, please see Chapters 15-19.

The idea behind this methodology is that the senior management of a company reviews a multitude of new project proposals and, according to whatever criteria is applicable, selects the top 10 most promising ideas. The scope, timing, budgets, risks, and probabilities of success are known at a high level at that time of the process.

These 10 ideas are then moved to the concept or project-charter stage where more detailed scoping, estimation, and risk management activities take place. With much more detailed information available, the management committee again reviews all 10 projects in order to assess their feasibility and success potential. It is quite possible that, by this stage, several of the project ideas may be considered not feasible as new information becomes available or because of a change in market conditions. Hence, the executives might make a decision to drop or postpone several ventures (projects J, H, and I in the example).

The process repeats iteratively at the end of each predefined stage. The ventures that still appear to be promising are given a green light while the projects that are found to have low probabilities of technical or commercial success are dropped.

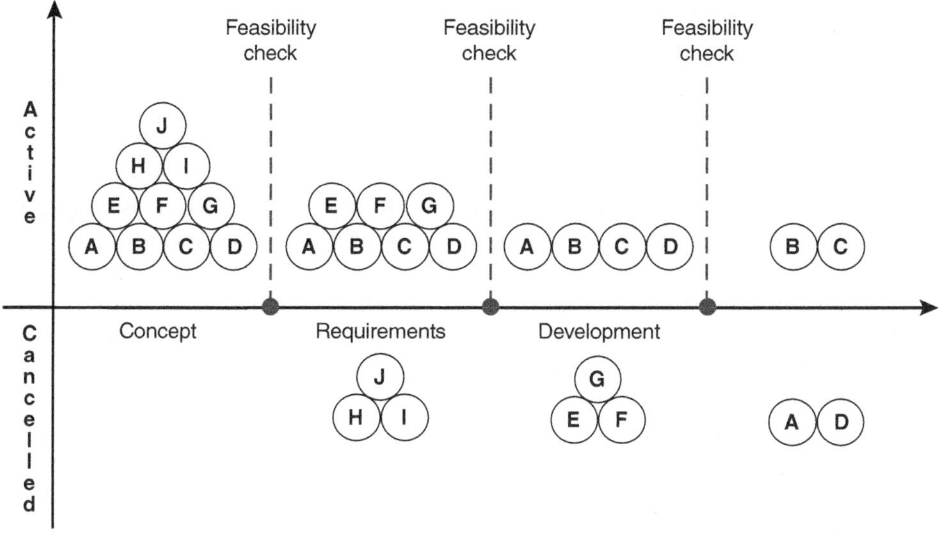

Figure 8.2 Drowning the puppies

At the end of the process, only a few (two in the example) out of the large number of original proposals are implemented and introduced to the marketplace. The name of the methodology suggests that despite whatever sentimental attachment the project sponsors—sometimes senior people in the company—have to their proposals, it should be overcome for the purpose of selecting the best, the strongest, and the most innovative products that will benefit the organization.

Summary

The definition of creativity states that it is a novel solution to a difficult problem. There are two types of difficult problems: the ones in which the problem is properly defined, but the solution is missing and the ones in which the problem itself has not been properly formulated.

Thus, it is much easier to tackle challenging issues when the problem statement has been properly articulated. As a result, a project team that is dealing with a challenging project should take the first step of properly defining the underlying problems behind customer business requirements and try to use brainstorming or other techniques to generate as many solutions as possible.

Project managers should always try to maximize the diversity of their teams. Groups consisting of the representatives of various age, sex, ethnic background, skills, experiences, and technical knowledge domains have been proven to consistently outperform the teams comprised of crème de la crème technical experts.

Furthermore, team leaders must increase both the quality and quantity of the communication and interaction opportunities among team members, customers, users, and other key project stakeholders. Innovation typically thrives in an environment where collaboration and free exchange of ideas is encouraged and nourished.

The entire team should be trained and encouraged to think in a challenge-the-orthodoxies mode. Identifying stale and frequently mistaken assumptions and constraints has been the source of many great discoveries and revolutionary business ideas.

A proper mix of milestones and the breadth-first principle will allow project teams to quickly uncover the maximum number of potential solutions and to weed out the features that are not feasible, technologically impossible, or have little chance of commercial success.

Controlling creativity is also an important ingredient for project success. Allowing innovation to run rampant can have a number of negative effects on project timing, budget, and quality. Therefore, the best place for creativity to emerge is between the point when all of the challenging problems have been defined, and the point where detailed specs for the project have been finalized.

On a strategic level, company executives must realize that innovation is essentially a numbers game; the more ideas generated within the organization, the higher the chances that some of them will transform themselves into revolutionary products or services.

Finally, having a project portfolio management system in place that would gather the creative ideas, analyze them, select promising project candidates, and guide them through the project pipeline is an important creativity-boosting tool at management's disposal.

References

1. http://www.woopidoo.com/business_quotes/creativity-quotes.htm
2. Kim, S. *Essence of Creativity: A Guide to Tackling Difficult Problems* (New York: Oxford University Press, 1990).

9

How Do You Incorporate Scope Definition into Project Management?

Historical Perspective

Raise the City or Lower the Highway?

The Central Artery/Tunnel Project (CA/T), better known by the public as the Boston Big Dig project, was initiated with noble objectives in mind (see Illustration 9.1). The state government of Massachusetts decided to undertake this venture in order to address serious traffic congestion on many of Boston's historically twisted streets, which had been built long before the beginning of the twentieth century. The finished project included:

- Rerouting Interstate 93 into a 3.5 mile (5.6 km) tunnel under the city
- Construction of the Ted Williams Tunnel to connect Interstate 90 to Logan International Airport
- Construction of the Leonard P. Zakim Bunker Hill Memorial Bridge over the Charles River
- Building Rose Kennedy Greenway in the space vacated by Interstate 93

The CA/T endeavor turned out to be the most expensive highway project in the history of the United States. While the original estimate for the project in 1985 was $6 billion (in 2006 dollars), over $14.6 billion of taxpayers' money has been spent. Once the interest charges—to be paid by 2038—are factored in, the total bill balloons to a whopping $22 billion.

Illustration 9.1 Boston Big Dig

What caused this 267 percent cost overrun on this megaproject? While there were many issues within the traditional project management areas such as budgeting, scheduling, overly optimistic estimates, and poor risk management, the most glaring errors were made during the scoping stages of the venture. Consider the following analysis of both high-level and detailed-level scoping omissions and mistakes made by the project team and the politicians.

Earlier in the life of the project, several disastrous decisions were made. In order to appease all the stakeholders and to ensure that the project proposal received a green light, proponents of the Big Dig included the following features—in addition to the ones mentioned earlier—to the scope of the project:

- The project shall enhance the urban environment rather than degrade it
- The project shall not take away any housing
- The project shall not shut down any of the Central Artery's six lanes during construction
- The project shall outfit North End apartments with air conditioning, soundproof windows, and firm mattresses as residents settle in for a decade of construction
- Companies such as Fidelity Investments shall not lack electricity or telephones for even a few hours as contractors dig up miles of utilities to make room for underground highways

- The project shall build temporary roads to the post office distribution station
- The project shall ensure that cars from the airport tunnel won't exit onto residential land
- The project shall preserve, as open space, three-quarters of the land that the Central Artery's demolition would create
- The project shall pay to catalog artifacts dating back to colonial days
- The project scope shall include an aggressive rodent-control program

Guess what? The mitigation part of the scope eventually accounted for about one-third of the Big Dig's cost—more than $7 billion—$1 billion more than the entire original estimate for the project. Added to this plight was the final design of the costly Zakim Bridge. Initially expected to be a much cheaper tunnel, the design was not finalized until much later in the execution stage of the project.

Another issue that arose later in the project could be directly linked to the original promise not to shut down any of the Central Artery's six lanes. As a result, the construction team had to implement a very costly solution—jacking up the Central Artery, which meant replacing the highway's half-million-ton support columns with temporary supports so that the columns could be removed to make way for the tunnels. On hearing about the potential cost of such a feat, Congressman Barney Frank quipped, "Rather than lower the expressway, wouldn't it be cheaper to raise the city?"

In general, beginning the work on pieces of the project before the final designs were completed was one of the trademarks of the Big Dig, and this meant expensive changes to the scope of work. These and other mistakes led not only to a 267 percent cost overrun but also to numerous quality issues once the project was completed. These included a major leak in the Interstate 93 north tunnel that forced the closure of the tunnel while repairs were conducted. A fatal collapse of a 3-ton concrete ceiling panel onto a car killed the only passenger and injured the driver.

Any experienced project manager, upon reviewing this story, will point out right away the poor scope elicitation and management practices on the Big Dig project, especially the failure to consider scope impact on other project parameters including schedule, risks, and especially budget.

This chapter is dedicated to one of the murkiest areas in project management—incorporation of scope definition into the overall project management process.

A Word about Methodologies

As was mentioned earlier, it is not the purpose of this book to create a universal methodology with rigid documentation flow and templates but rather to show the interaction of various concepts such as project charter, project plan, high-level scope document, detailed-level scope document, and detailed-design document.

While project management documentation is fairly universalized across industries, scope documents still have different names, structures, and flows. The objective for this chapter is to portray an amalgamated view of the documentation flow on a given project while considering the realities and differences of modern project management methodologies in various industries.

It is worthwhile to begin the discussion with regard to IT and software development industries since they already have a fairly well developed methodology for the integration of project management and scope definition (business analysis) processes.

Initiation

The project initiation phase is the most crucial phase in the project life cycle because it is the phase in which the following tasks are typically accomplished:

- Identification of the project manager
- Confirmation of project objectives and rationale
- Development of the project charter and high-level scope document

Once a project manager has been appointed by senior management, he is responsible for defining the scope and assembling his team.

During the initiation stage, the project manager will have to meet with the project sponsor and other key stakeholders, collect all the necessary information, and create a draft of the project charter.

Among other parameters, a rough order of magnitude budget and schedule must be generated by the project manager based on the high-level scope definition. According to accepted standards, as discussed in Chapter 3, these estimates should be in the +75 to −25 percent range.

In IT and software development industries, the scope of the project (the document that the project manager sometimes relies upon to generate the project charter) is defined in a separate high-level scope document called vision and scope (see Figure 9.1). The key part of Vision consists of a listing of all the significant features that will compose the scope of the project. For example, if one describes the features of a custom family home, the list of high-level features might look like:

- Feature 1: Three levels
- Feature 2: Between 5000 and 5500 square feet
- Feature 3: Five bedrooms
- Feature 4: Four bathrooms
- Feature 5: Separate three-car garage
- Feature 6: Outdoor swimming pool

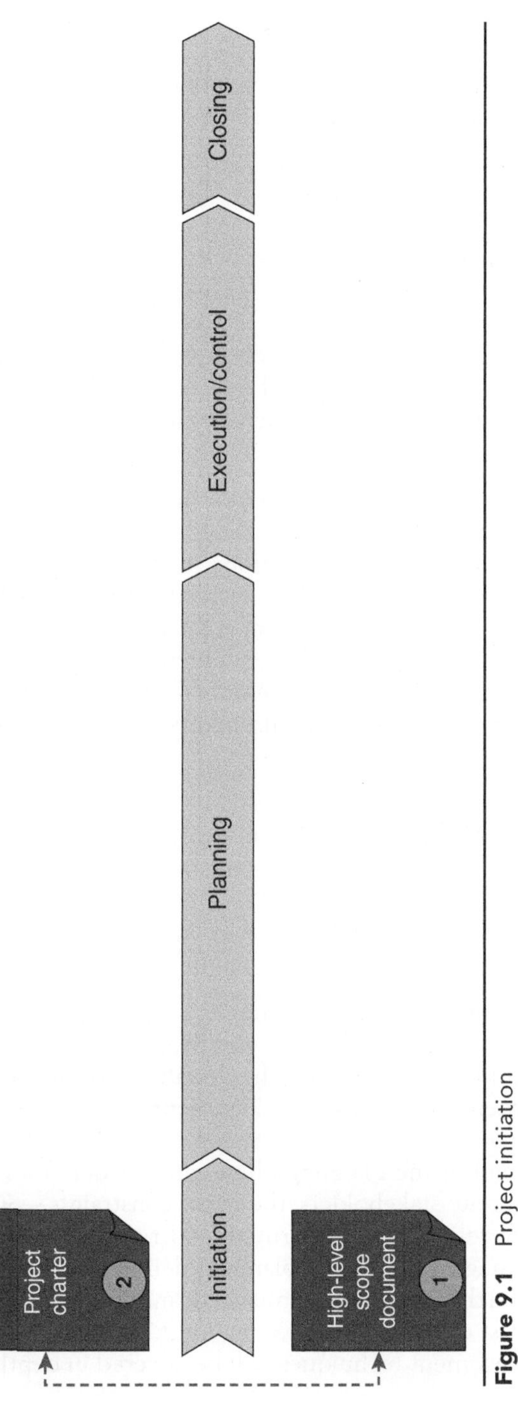

Figure 9.1 Project initiation

Planning

The key step in the planning stage is delivery of the project plan document. This will be discussed in detail in Chapter 10. For purposes of discussion in this section, the basic scope of the project plan is:

- Refine scope
- Confirm requirements
- Determine deliverables
- Prepare schedule by decomposing project tasks, sequencing them, and assigning resources
- Determine budget and plan purchases, acquisitions, and contracting
- Define communication protocol
- Confirm assumptions, risks, dependencies
- Develop project plan

Since scope is the most influential variable in all projects, the project manager typically relies on the information outlined in the detailed-level scope document—system requirements specifications in the software development industry—to generate schedule and budget estimates as well as human resource requirements and a list of potential project risks. This technical design scope should not be confused with elicitation of the detailed business scope covered in Chapter 7 (see Figure 9.2). For example, Feature 6 (pool) from the previous section can be broken into the following requirements (components):

- Requirement 1: Dimensions—pool dimensions shall be 30 feet long by 20 feet wide
- Requirement 2: Shape—pool shall be of rectangular shape
- Requirement 3: Depth—pool depth shall gradually increase from 3 feet to 5 feet
- Requirement 4: Fountain—pool shall have a built-in fountain
- Requirement 5: A diving board shall be installed

Usually the target for the project manager is to refine these estimates with a +30 to −15 percent accuracy by the time the project plan is finalized. It is worthwhile to note that in other industries the detailed-level scope document has various names: statement of work, scope document, specifications document, specs, among others.

Finally, at the end of the planning phase, project definition and scope are validated with appropriate stakeholders, the triple constraints—project scope, budget, and schedule—are refined and confirmed, and risk assessment activities advance to the mitigation stage. The project planning deliverables (the components of the project plan) are further developed, enhanced, and refined until they form a definitive plan for the rest of the project (see Figure 9.3). Scope validation methods and proper scope management techniques will be covered in depth in Chapter 12.

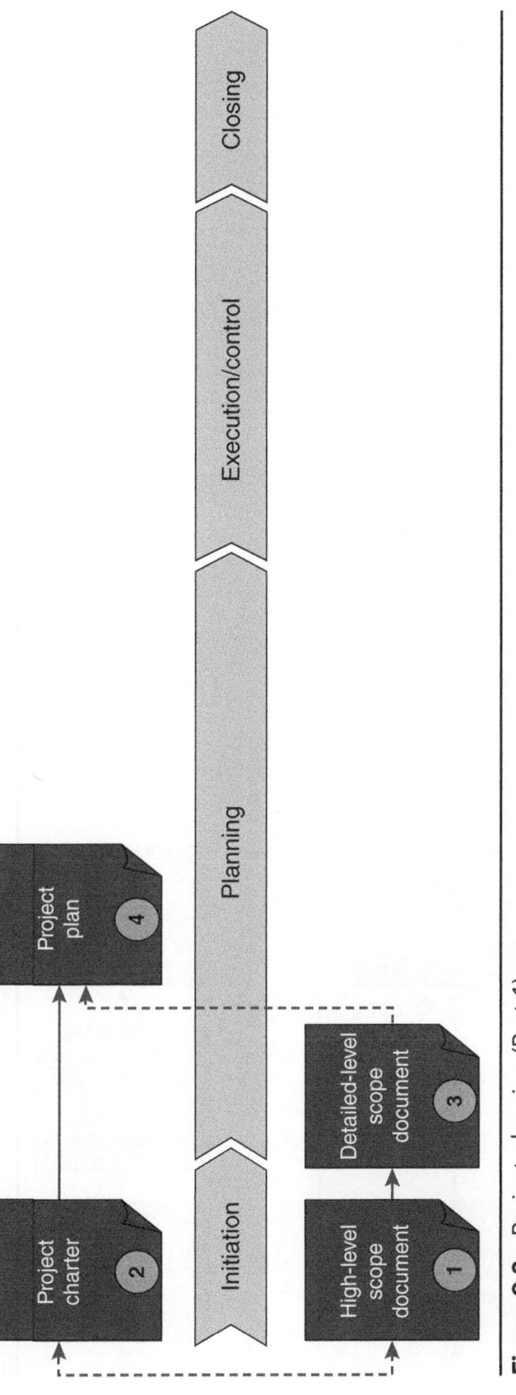

Figure 9.2 Project planning (Part 1)

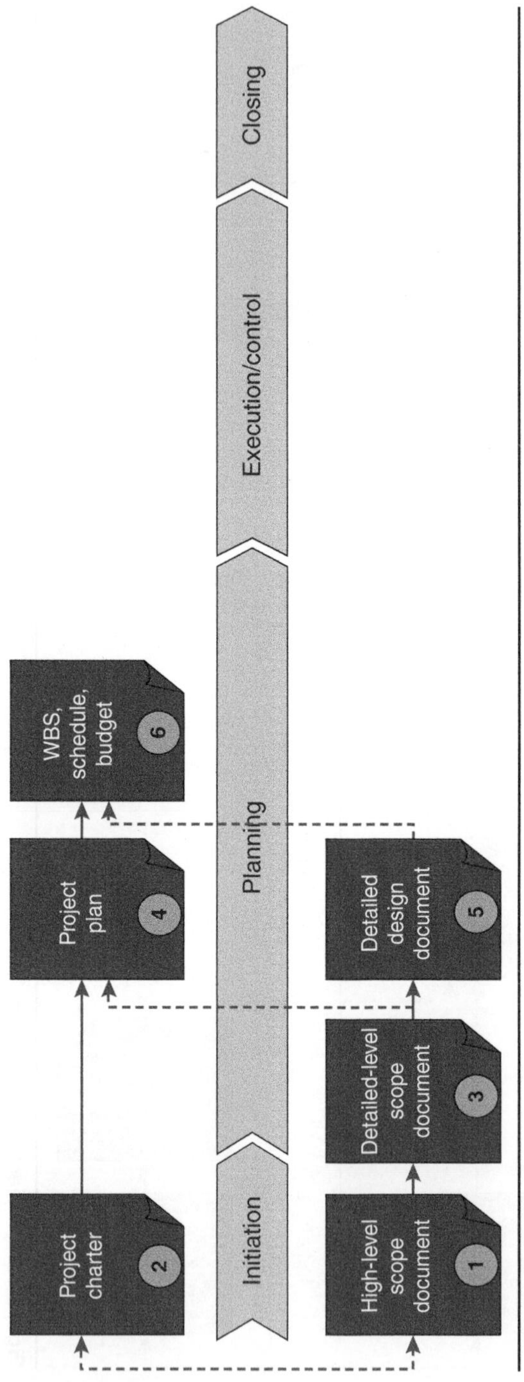

Figure 9.3 Project planning (Part 2)

Other Approaches to Initiation and Planning

Project Charter Can Include High-level Scope

In some cases, both in and outside of software development industries, the project manager may decide not to develop a separate high-level scope document and instead include all the high-level features in the scope section of the project charter (see Figure 9.4). The rest of the project flow is no different than the processes described in the previous section; the detailed-level scope document is developed followed by a project plan.

No Stand-alone Scope Documents

The second option frequently employed by managers who are overseeing smaller and less complex ventures is not to develop a separate scope document at all. Here, both high-level and detailed-level scope are included as sections in the project charter and project plan respectively (see Figure 9.5).

Execution and Control

The development of the detailed design documentation, referred to as blueprints, bills of materials, or technical design specifications, can be handled either in planning or at the beginning of the execution stage of the project. The detailed design provides input into the final iteration of estimates and other project parameters refinement before the actual hands-on work can start.

Another one of the key purposes of the planning phase is to define the exact parameters of a project and ensure that all the prerequisites for the execution and control stages are in place. These include:

- Follow plan and monitor status
- Control cost, schedule and scope
- Select and manage contractors
- Purchase equipment and services
- Manage communication and team
- Monitor risks and issues
- Publish status reports and meeting minutes
- Conduct reviews and acceptance

Change requests are also one of the key influences that can alter the balance of project constraints. In general, once the potential impacts on the project have been identified, confirmed, and analyzed by the project team, they should be communicated back to the change requester, key project stakeholders, and (if necessary) the executive team/steering committee. If the change is approved, the project plan must be updated, and this should be communicated to all key parties involved

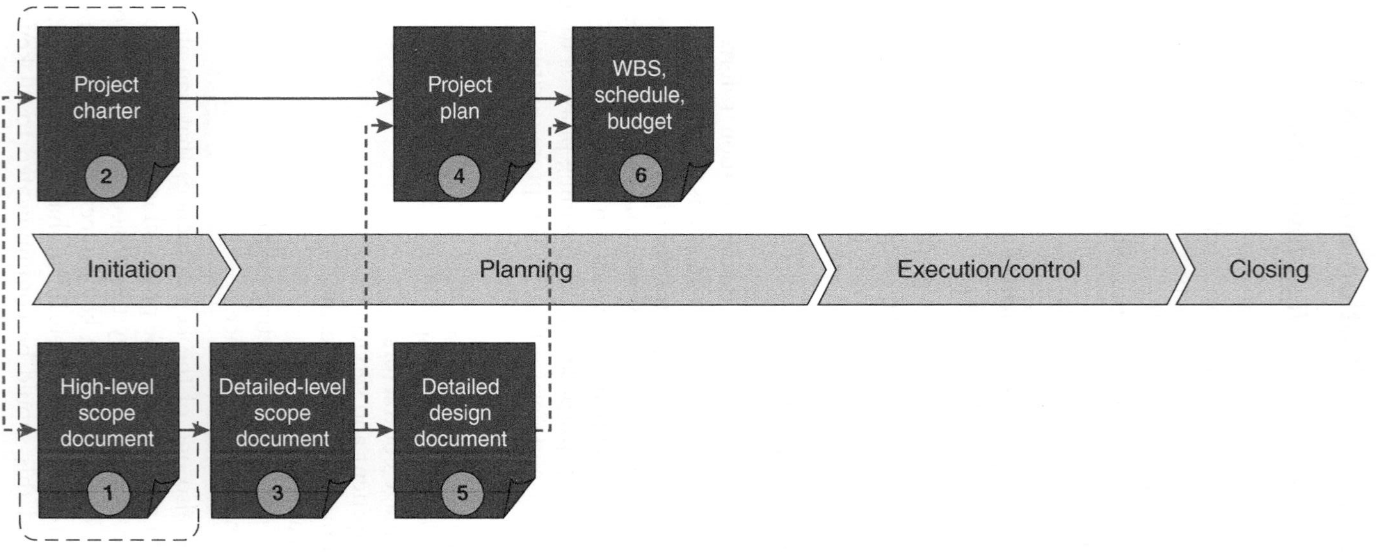

Figure 9.4 Variation A—unified project charter and high-level scope document

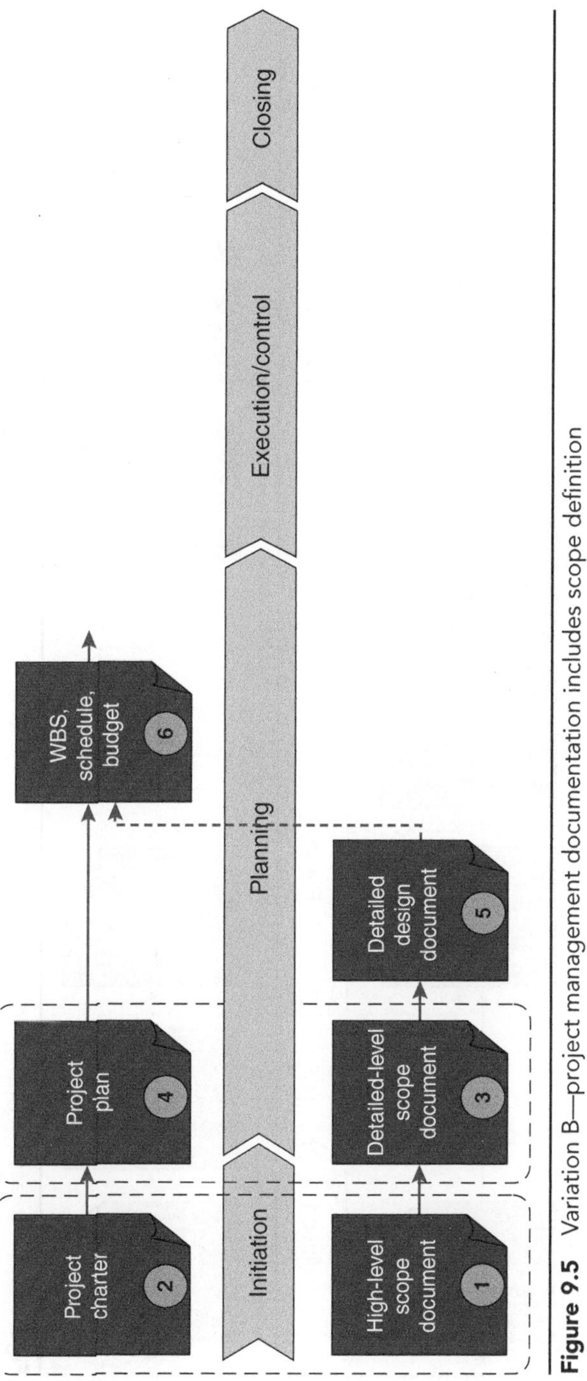

Figure 9.5 Variation B—project management documentation includes scope definition

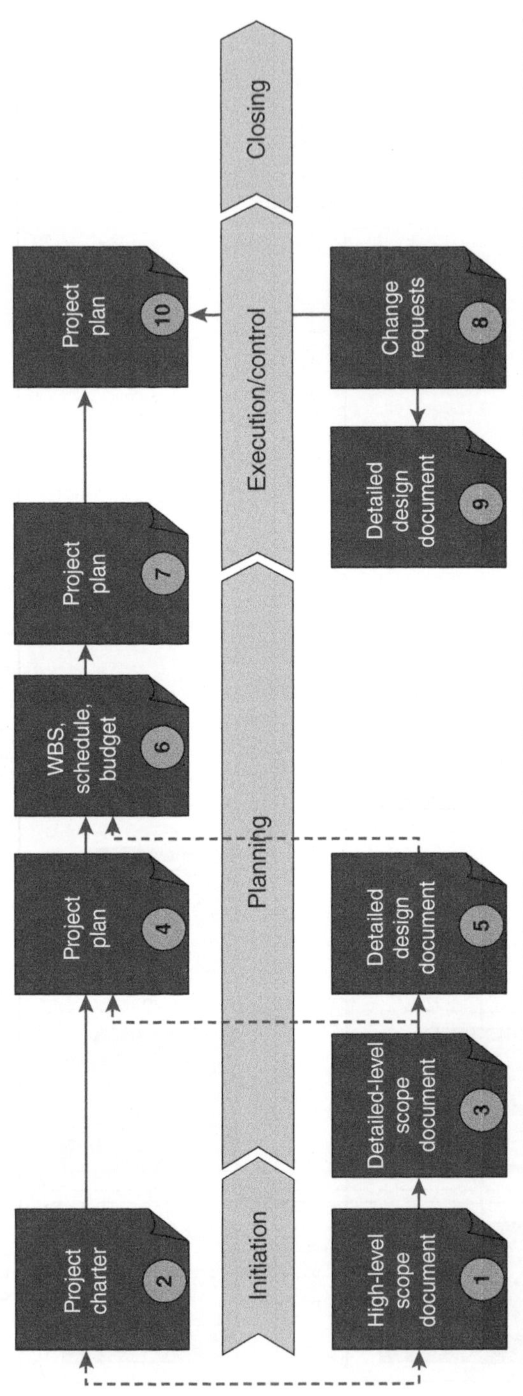

Figure 9.6 Project execution and control

via a status report (see Figure 9.6). More detailed information on handling scope changes and managing stakeholder expectations will be covered in Chapter 13.

Meetings and Meeting Minutes

Once the project moves into the execution and control stages (or even earlier if necessary), the project manager should book ongoing regular (typically weekly) project team meetings to collect and disseminate project information, discuss new issues, assign tasks, and obtain updates on project status.

In addition to running and facilitating the weekly meetings, project managers should be responsible for the creation and distribution of meeting minutes typically no later than 24 hours after the meeting.

Project Status Reports

Status reports are created and used on projects to increase project transparency and to improve project team accountability. Project managers should obtain project status information and distribute it via status reports to all project stakeholders. The frequency of project status reports should be predetermined during the project plan creation but typically should be on a weekly or biweekly basis. The list of project status report recipients should also be determined in the planning stage.

Close Out

Lessons learned is an important project document that serves the following purposes:

- Ensures that mistakes are not repeated at the cost of project delay, budget overruns, and customer dissatisfaction
- Improves the understanding of potential risks
- Improves communication

No later than two weeks after the completion of a project, the project manager should use the last project meeting to discuss project results with team members and other project stakeholders in order to determine the positive and the negative events on the project.

The lessons-learned document should be filled out and submitted for stakeholder feedback. Once all the feedback has been incorporated, the document should be published (preferably a PDF version) to allow for easy access (see Figure 9.7). The why-invest-time-and-effort-in-the-lessons-learned document will be discussed in depth in Chapter 14.

Documents produced to describe the product or service of the project (e.g., plans, specifications, technical documentation, drawings, electronic files) must also be validated and prepared for the transfer to the appropriate parties.

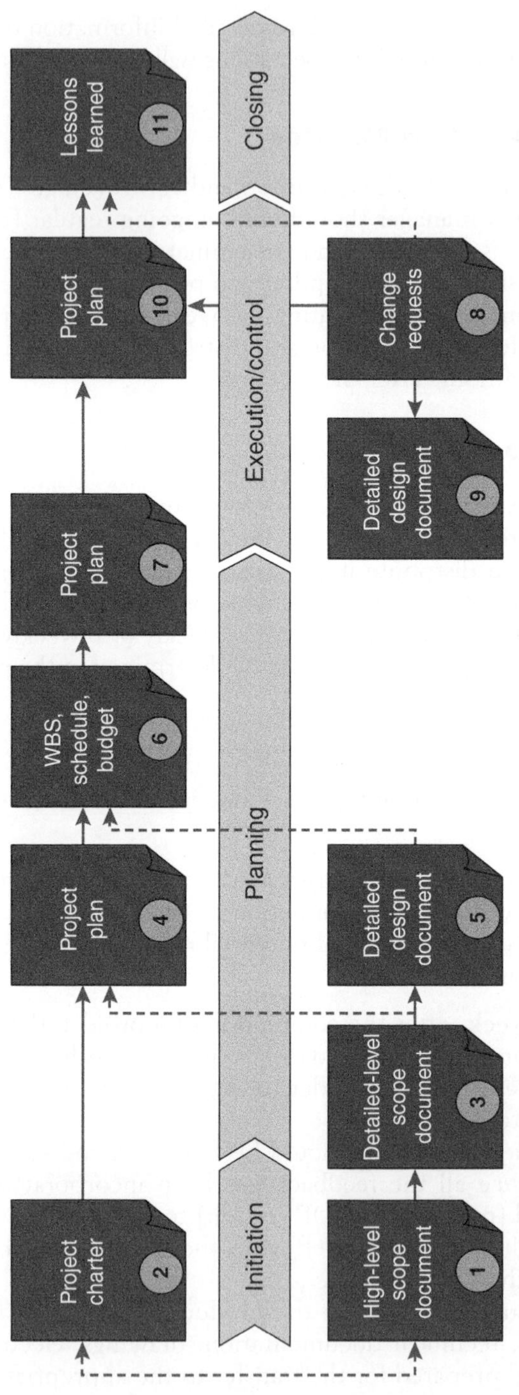

Figure 9.7 Project close out

Summary

Proper integration of scope definition into the overall project management process is one of the keys to success in managing projects.

The high-level scope document (called a vision and scope document, high-level scope document, or high-level specifications) is created before or concurrently with the project charter in order to capture the high-level features of the final product. The collection of these features aids the project manager in assessing the preliminary project budget, schedule, risks, and other important project parameters.

Once the project moves into the planning stage, the detailed-level scope document is produced. This document captures granular business requirements without going into the design mode. There are several names for the detailed-level scope document—statement of work, scope document, specifications document, specs, among others—depending on the industry and even the company. This detailed scope acts as input into the project plan and provides the project manager with all the information necessary to generate more accurate budget, schedule, and resource requirements for the project.

The detailed design document (referred to as blueprints, bills of materials, or technical design specifications) represents the final stage in the scope elicitation process and allows for the final iteration of project plan refinement to be conducted.

After the project has moved into the execution and control stages, special attention should be paid to scope management to prevent scope creep and to the elimination of all unnecessary additions to the scope of the project at the expense of time, budget, or extra risk.

Furthermore, the project manager is expected to communicate all potential changes to the project scope as well as to other key parameters through meeting minutes and status reports.

Once the project is completed, a lessons-learned document should be generated by the project team and other key stakeholders in order to compare actual versus budgeted costs, schedules and scope items, and to pass on important and relevant advice to the next generation of project managers who could be involved in similar ventures in the future.

This book has free material available for download from the Web Added Value™ resource center at *www.jrosspub.com*

10

How Do You Write a Great Project Plan?

Historical Perspective

Operation Overlord: Planning for Private Ryan

There are some serious misconceptions about warfare during the twentieth century, and the blame should be placed on the movie industry. Think about war films: armies are lined up in two wide rows facing each other on the field (if one is watching a movie about battles that took place before the twentieth century), or troops are in trenches or other fortifications being attacked by the other side. Explosions, guns firing, soldiers falling down, dead or wounded lying around, acts of personal heroism—this is typically how battles are depicted in the movies and on TV.

Unfortunately, what is not shown in these films are the weeks, months, and sometimes years of preparation that it took to ensure the victory in these battles. Consider Operation Overlord (the name given to the Allied landing at Normandy), which was made famous by the film *Saving Private Ryan* (see Illustration 10.1). Imagine the task of transporting 1.5 million people—forty-seven divisions including nineteen British, five Canadian, one Polish, and twenty-one American—across the English Channel. Incidentally, the fleet had to be drawn from eight different navies and was comprised of 6,939 vessels including warships, transport boats, and merchant ships. Consider, too, the fact that the whole exercise could take place only during the night with both a full moon and a spring tide. A full moon was needed to illuminate the waters of the channel, and high tide was required to avoid German defensive obstacles.

Illustration 10.1 Omaha Beach

Add to this the fact that the terrain for the landing was relatively unknown. The BBC went so far as to request that its listeners send them their holiday pictures of France for a fake exhibition because the Allies obviously did not want their intentions known by the Germans. Further, special planes had to be used to determine whether the famous beaches—Utah, Omaha, Gold, Juno, and Sword—could support the weight of tanks.

In addition, the Allied scientists had to develop several technological marvels for the purpose of that operation alone. These included:

- Mulberry—a mobile, prefabricated concrete harbor that could offload cargo on the beaches in order to supply the troops during the invasion thus eliminating the need to capture one of the heavily defended Channel ports
- PLUTO—the pipe-line-under-the-ocean that enabled planners to supply their forces with gasoline and diesel
- Hobart's Funnies—a fleet of modified Sherman and Churchill tanks assembled by General Percy Hobart that included flamethrowers, mortars, amphibious vehicles, and bulldozers (see Illustration 10.2)

Illustration 10.2 Duplex Drive (aka Donald Duck) Sherman Tank with Flotation Screen

Furthermore, several deception operations were undertaken by the Allied intelligence agencies to cover up their real plans. Operation Bodyguard was initiated to convince the Germans that the invasion would be taking place in other parts of France and even as far away as the Balkans. Operation Fortitude North, on the other hand, was designed to convince the Axis that an attack on Norway was imminent. Another deception campaign was initiated closer to D-Day, which involved flooding German embassies in neutral countries with misleading information in order to cause them to ignore actual news emanating from northern France.

Finally, the landings had to be coordinated and preceded by naval and aerial bombardment in order to soften up the considerable German defenses on the coast.

This is only a partial list of all the key preparations undertaken by Allies for the successful invasion of Normandy. But, as mentioned previously, one gets to see only after-the-landing scenes in the movies. The thorough and scrupulous planning that took place before the operations usually gets ignored by the media.

Therefore, as one could have guessed by now, this chapter is dedicated to the art and science of writing a project plan. It is also one of the crossroads chapters of the book since it relies on the topics discussed in Chapters 3–9, including estimation, negotiations, creativity, and detailed requirements.

Several Important Disclaimers

Writing a how-to chapter on creating project plans is a challenge because literally hundreds of different versions of this document are available in the marketplace. Their sizes range from two- or three-page documents to 30-page templates developed specifically for the megaproject-type ventures. The subsections included in this document also vary wildly from only high-level scope, time, and budget to detailed four-level hierarchies. Herein lies the difficulty of coming up with a project plan that would universally fit the needs of all project management professionals.

The goals set forth in this chapter were guided by the question: what is the minimal and mandatory information one should have in the project plan for a medium-size project? Hence, if the reader is engaged on ventures dedicated to building space shuttles or other megaprojects, she may find this template somewhat inadequate. The assumption is that the template can be expanded to include other necessary sections and subsections to the document as needed.

By the same token, it is not recommended that the author reduce the outline of the template by deleting some of the sections. It is much more productive to include a simple *n/a* (not applicable) under any unnecessary subsection followed by a brief comment explaining why this part of the document had not been filled in. This way the author of the project plan can demonstrate to readers that this particular aspect of the project had been given some thought but was deemed to be unnecessary. If the author simply deletes an entire section, future concerns might arise from stakeholders asking, for example, why an MS Project version of the Gantt chart wasn't included.

The project plan document that will be discussed is a widely accepted style that includes eight project management areas: scope management, time management, cost management, quality management, human resource management, communications management, risk management, and procurement management. Note that there is actually a ninth area known as integration management. As it actually involves writing the project plan, it was purposely omitted in this section.

The Project Plan Contents

Revision History Table

Like any important and constantly changing document, the project plan should contain a revision history table (see Table 10.1). The purpose of the table is to record version number, version date, name of the person making the change, and a short revision description. Document versioning will be covered in Chapter 13 in more detail.

Why is it necessary to keep a record of all the changes made to the document? First, one can expect to make up to several dozen revisions to a project plan during the planning and execution stages. Stakeholder feedback, customer-initiated

Table 10.1 Revision history table

Version number	Version date	Added by	Revision description
0.1	01-Sep-2009	John Smith	First draft of the document
0.2	15-Sep-2009	John Smith	Changes in scope and time made after the review with the project team
0.3	20-Sep-2009	John Smith	Changes and additions in scope, risks, and budget sections made after the stakeholder review
1.0	10-Oct-2009	John Smith	Document sign-off

updates, and technical project team inspections act as sources of updates and modifications to the document. By the same token, during the execution stage, change requests, various risks and other events may have an impact on other aspects of the project. Committing all of this information to memory is probably not the most efficient use of a project manager's brainpower.

Second, people have a tendency to save e-mail files on their hard drives. As a result, they continue referring to the older versions of the document while the newer, fresher versions have already been posted in the project documentation repositories. Therefore, "what version of the document are you looking at?" becomes one of the most frequently asked questions in conversations between the project manager and project stakeholders.

Overview

Document Purpose

It is worthwhile to start the document with an explanation of its purpose since some readers might not be very familiar with project management and would not fully understand the objective of the project plan.

A sample text for the project plan overview follows:

> This document is the project plan for the <Project Name>. It addresses scope, deliverables, risks, assumptions, milestones, schedule, budget, and teamworking practices required to achieve a successful outcome. The project will be placed under the change control process after sign-off. Updates to the project plan must be reviewed and approved by the project manager and by any relevant stakeholders for the section that is changed.

List of Relevant Project Sponsors and Stakeholders

A list of all the relevant project sponsors and external stakeholders should be included in the overview section (see Table 10.2). Among other things, this table

Table 10.2 Sample list of key project stakeholders

Project role	Name	Organizational role
Project champion	Robert Smith	COO
Project sponsor	John Black	CFO
Customer	Leslie Brown	VP, sales
Stakeholder	Cassandra Jones	Director, marketing department
Stakeholder	Alexandra Smalls	Director, legal department
Stakeholder	Joseph Chan	Director, IT department

serves as a quick reference to who should approve the project plan, scope documentation, and all subsequent change requests.

Project Scope Management

Project Goals

Under project goals, one should provide a high-level description of the project scope. Identify why the project was initiated and what opportunities it is supposed to seize or what problems it is intended to solve. Note that the original project goals would have been outlined in the project charter, so it would be a good idea to revisit the original document.

Project Feasibility

The next element is project feasibility. It is important to mention which model was used to assess the project's feasibility (e.g., net present value, internal rate of return, payback, weighted-scoring model, strategic importance, strategic risk management). Keep in mind that the first feasibility estimate was done in the project charter, so revisit the original calculation and assess whether the inputs into the formula (project cost estimates, increase in revenue, change in costs, discount rates) have changed. Another important factor to remember is that the measures of feasibility mentioned in the project plan template should be synchronized with the factors used by the senior executives of the organization to assess the value of the ventures at the portfolio process checkpoints. This is described in detail in Chapter 16.

Scope Inclusions and Exclusions

Next, one should mention several key features that will be included in the scope of the project. Provide a list of the high-level scope items that should be excluded from the scope of the project. For example, the scope inclusions section of the document might state:

- Feature 1: Three-bedroom, two-bathroom Victorian style family home
- Feature 2: Separate two-car garage
- Feature 3: Swimming pool

The scope exclusions part might list:

- Fence around the property
- Property landscaping
- House furnishings
- Household appliances

The following sections allow the project manager to establish the scope boundary and to list the high-level items that will be specifically excluded from the list of deliverables in order to avoid possible unpleasant surprises in the future.

Scope Definition Documentation

There are several possibilities available for this section of the document. If the project is very small and does not require any additional scope documentation (a fairly rare occasion), this section can be used for a detailed description of the project scope. If the project is of medium or large size, separate scope documentation definitely should exist in the form of a separate stand-alone document. These documents tend to have a variety of names and titles as one moves from industry to industry, from company to company, and even from one department of the same organization to another. In software and IT industries, they are called system requirements specifications, software requirements specifications, and detailed design; in the engineering field and several other fields, they are called requirements specs, statement of work, bill of materials, and blueprints.

The point of this chapter, as was the case with Chapter 7 and Chapter 9, is not to dwell on a specific document name but rather to highlight the importance of the detailed scope documentation in general and provide a reference to it in the project plan in particular. Thus, it is very important to provide a link or a location of the scope definition documents in this section of the project plan.

Project Time Management—Schedule and Milestones

Estimation Methodology

Under time management, one should mention what methodology was used to obtain the estimates (e.g., top-down, bottom-up, historical, or expert judgment). Note that the project charter required a +75 to −25 percent degree of precision;

at the completion of the project plan, the estimates should be at +30 to −15 percent.

Project Duration

One should indicate project duration in days, weeks, months, years, or whatever is applicable to the size and the complexity of the project. Keep in mind the presentation techniques mentioned in Chapter 3:

- +/− qualifiers (e.g., 6 months ± 2 months)
- Ranges (e.g., 4 months to 8 months)
- Cases (e.g., best case—4 months, most likely—6 months, worst case—8 months)
- Course dates and time periods (e.g., 3 quarters instead of 270 days)
- Confidence factors (e.g., We are 95 percent sure the project will be done within 90 to 118 days.)

Project Milestones

Furthermore, one should include key project milestones as shown in Table 10.3. Provide +/− qualifiers for each date. The idea behind this table is that senior managers and customers are probably unlikely to examine complicated Gantt charts that were created in *MS Project* or some other project management software. Thus, a list of key high-level milestones could be of great assistance to explain in a user-friendly, easy-to-understand fashion the general schedule for a project.

Table 10.3 Sample key project milestones

Project phase/activity	Completed by
Initiation	
Project charter	12-Sep-2009
Kick-off meeting	20-Sep-2009
Planning	
Project plan	30-Oct-2009
Requirements document(s)	20-Oct-2009
Execution	
Activity 1	15-Nov-2009
Activity 2, and others	20-Nov-2009
Note: All dates provided are +/– 2 weeks	

Gantt Chart

If the project required the creation of a Gantt chart using *MS Project* or some other project management software, include a link to the *.mpp* file. These files are unlikely to be reviewed by business and nontechnical stakeholders, but project management professionals and technical team members might need to see a more detailed view of the schedule and specific tasks.

Project Cost Management—Budget

This section of the document should contain a project budget table. The level of detail appropriate for the project plan varies from company to company and from industry to industry, but it should at least include variable costs, fixed costs (overhead), and other expenses including bonds, forward contracts, foreign contracts, contingency, and escalation costs (see Figure 10.1 for a sample project budget). Furthermore, the total cost figures should also include +/− qualifiers as was the case in the duration estimates.

Project Quality Management

Subsequently, one should describe which quality management tools and techniques will be used in the project to ensure proper quality management and control:

- Document control
- Training
- Customer complaints
- Design and development
- Peer reviews
- Inspections
- Customer feedback
- Document management
- Testing
- Change control

Preferably, the project plan should also specify the timing of these activities or indicate if they are ongoing tasks. For example:

- Appropriate safety and security training will take place in the first week of the execution stage of the project
- All key documents including project plan, scope and design documentation, and change requests shall undergo peer reviews and inspections before the sign-offs
- Testing will take place at the end of the execution phase between Jan 15 and Jan 25

Total project cost estimate								
Item	**Unit**	**Quantity**	**Labor cost**	**Equipment cost**	**Material cost**	**Outsourcing cost**	**Sub-total**	**TOTAL**
Variable costs								
Excavation	m^3	2,000	$ 2,500	$ 1,500	$ –	$ –	$ 4,000	
Backfill	m^3	400	$ 2,700	$ 1,300	$ –	$ –	$ 4,000	
Steel	m	700	$ 20,000	$ 10,000	$ –	$ –	$ 30,000	
Concrete–footings	m^3	103	$ 3,000	$ 1,000	$ 1,000	$ –	$ 5,000	
Concrete–abutments	m^3	247	$ 30,000	$ 8,000	$ 25,000	$ –	$ 63,000	
Concrete–deck slab	m^3	170	$ 10,500	$ 5,000	$ 7,500	$ –	$ 23,000	
Steel–reinforcing	kg	50,000	$ –	$ –	$ –	$ 75,000	$ 75,000	
Bearing plates	kg	1,700	$ 2,000	$ 1,000	$ 3,000	$ –	$ 6,000	
Guardrail	m	50	$ 2,000	$ 1,500	$ 5,900	$ –	$ 9,400	
Paint	N/A	N/A	$ –	$ –	$ –	$ 40,000	$ 40,000	
Sub-total variable costs							**$259,400**	
Fixed costs								
Project management							$ 15,000	
Utilities							$ 2,500	
Facilities							$ 3,500	
Travel							$ 3,000	
Site clean-up							$ 5,000	
Other							$ 2,000	
Sub-total fixed costs							**$ 31,000**	
Other costs								
State tax (5%)							$ 14,520	
Bonds							$ 3,000	
Contingency (@10%)							$ 3,100	
Sub-total other costs							**$ 20,620**	
Total project cost								**$ 311,020**

Figure 10.1 Sample project budget

Project Human Resources Management

Project Team

Under the human resources section, one should list all of the project team members and their roles. For the project roles, try to use each person's role on the specific project rather than his title in the organization (see Table 10.4).

Responsibility Assignment Matrix (RAM)

It would also be a good idea to assign responsibilities for each key task to specific personnel on the project. This will help the project manager avoid potential future surprises and miscommunications, especially in a traditional, functional organization where the resources are assigned by the departmental managers and directors. RAM depicts the responsibilities of various project resources in completing tasks or deliverables for a project (see Table 10.5 for a partial RAM).

Table 10.4 Sample project team

Project role	Name
Project manager	Brenda Yang
Scope specialist	Cathy Nadeau
Public relations expert	Daryl Leung
Legal expert	Justin Robinson
Engineer	Michael Moniz
Architect	Paul Sutherland
Foreman	Rob Teves
IT specialist	Sara Whyte

Table 10.5 Sample RAM

	Project team members				
Deliverables	**Project manager**	**Scope specialist**	**PR expert**	**Engineer**	**Architect**
Project plan	X				
Scope definition	X	X			
PR campaign			X		
Design documents				X	X
Blueprints and bill of materials				X	X

Project Communications Management

Communications Planning and Distribution

Under the communications management section, it is a good idea to decide who should and who wants to receive what documentation at the beginning of the planning stage. This will help to avoid complaints from people who needed to receive the documentation but were not notified. By the same token, senior managers might request to be excluded from the meeting minutes mailing list and be sent status reports instead. Table 10.6 contains a partial list of key project documents that have to be distributed during the project.

Project Meetings and Meeting Minutes

At this point, one should describe how often project status meetings will be conducted and when (e.g., project status team meetings will be held weekly on Wednesdays at 2:30 pm). Also, specify how the meeting minutes will be created, who will be responsible for writing them, and how they will be distributed and stored. For example:

> Project status team meetings will be held weekly. The project manager will be responsible for keeping proper meeting minutes and publishing them within 24 hours after the project meeting. Also, meeting minutes shall be e-mailed to all project stakeholders upon their requests.

Table 10.6 Sample information distribution matrix

Document	Distributed to	Frequency
Project charter	All project stakeholders	• Once before the sign-off • Posted on the intranet afterwards
Project plan	All project stakeholders	• Once before the sign-off • Every time a significant change is made to it • Posted on the intranet afterwards
Meeting minutes	Project team and other stakeholders based on individual requests	• Weekly • Posted on the intranet afterwards
Status reports	Customers, senior management	• Biweekly • Posted on the intranet afterwards
Lessons learned	All project stakeholders	• Once • Posted on the intranet afterwards
Change requests	Change control committee, project team	• As needed • Posted on the intranet afterwards

Project Documentation

One should include a reference to the project documentation locations. For instance:

> All project documentation related to this project will be kept in the following folder: F: /Projects/Project ABC

Project Risk Management

The project risk management section should not differ too much from the risk management section of the project charter discussed in Chapter 5. The only distinction is that by the time the project reaches the planning stage, some of the assumptions, risks, and constraints have either materialized or become obsolete. On the other hand, new risks might be identified and will need to be recorded as the project progresses from the initiation to the planning stages.

There are two schools of thought on whether old but still valid assumptions, constraints, and risks should be transferred from the project charter to the project plan. Some organizations think that if these items have already been mentioned in the project charter, they shouldn't have to be copied into the project plan. The document, according to this particular philosophy, must contain only new assumptions, constraints and risks.

The other school insists that in reality once the project plan is written, people rarely return to review the project charter. Hence, they argue, all relevant risk management factors must be restated in the project plan.

Either of these schools of thought is fine, but the second alternative is usually chosen due to the simple fact that people typically prefer to keep track of one document rather than two.

Assumptions

It is good to articulate some of the assumptions one might have made related to the project, but write no more than five or six (see Table 10.7). Assumptions are typically good things that are supposed to happen on the project, but one is not entirely sure they will happen.

Table 10.7 Sample list of assumptions

ID	Description
A1	We assume that all the resources required for the successful delivery of this project will be available.
A2	We assume that the subcontractor involved on the project shall be able to complete the bridge painting by the deadline indicated in the project schedule.

Constraints

One should record some of the constraints that might exist, but again, record no more than five or six (see Table 10.8). Constraints are certain things that limit options with respect to the successful delivery of project products or services. They typically, but not exclusively, include deadlines, budgets, and availability of resources.

Risks

The next step is to record some identified risks and, here again, try to limit it to five or six. It is also desirable to add the planned responses for each one of the risks outlined (see Table 10.9). Risks are the uncertain things that can jeopardize a project's success.

Project Procurement Management

In this section, one should indicate the selection process (e.g., preferred supplier, request for information, request for proposal or quote). Describe which parts of the project will be outsourced to external contractors, who these contractors are, and how they will be managed. In general, larger companies have fairly well defined guidelines on outsourcing and subcontractor selection. If these guidelines exist, be sure to reference these policies in the project plan.

Summary

This chapter explained the process for writing a project plan. It described the absolute minimum of information required in this document for planning a me-

Table 10.8 Sample list of constraints

ID	Description
C1	Project budget was capped at $300,000.
C2	Only one senior architect shall be available to perform work on design documentation.

Table 10.9 Sample list of risks

ID	Description
R1	There is a possibility of a major contractor's employees going on strike.
R2	The municipality might require additional environmental cleanup leading to an increase in project budget and timeline.

dium-sized project. If the project is larger, more sophisticated, or has additional requirements specific to a given industry or a company, one should expand and tailor the plan according to the project's specific needs. If the venture is smaller and simpler, adding *n/a* with a brief explanation in each applicable section is recommended rather than deleting the section altogether. It will demonstrate for others viewing the plan that the irrelevant sections were at least considered, and keeping all sections in the plan serves as a good checklist.

The project plan should include a revision-history table to keep track of all the changes, updates, and modifications made to the document.

An overview statement describing the overall purpose of the document, especially for the stakeholders who are not very proficient in the area of project management, is highly recommended.

The average project plan should cover at least eight project management areas. The sections to be included are:

- Scope management section—contains project scope description and reference to the detailed scope documentation
- Time management section—includes the project schedule and key milestones
- Cost management section—contains the project budget broken down into variable, fixed, and other costs
- Quality management section—describes quality tools and techniques that will be used on the project
- Human resource management section—outlines the project team and the tasks they will be responsible for
- Communications management section—explains the distribution of project documentation
- Risk management section—lists all relevant assumptions, constraints, and risks
- Procurement management section—clarifies all the relevant procurement and outsourcing guidelines for the project

11

How Do You Troubleshoot Scope Problems?

Historical Perspective

General Hadik and the Glove Fiasco

In 1757, during the Seven Years War, an interesting episode took place in Berlin. Austrian general of Hungarian descent András Hadik de Futak (see Illustration 11.1) was in charge of a light cavalry brigade consisting of 4000 to 5000 hussars. On October 17, for some unexplained reason, instead of attacking the forces of Prussian King Frederick, Hadik redirected his troops and attacked the Prussian capital of Berlin. Five hundred soldiers defended the city, of which 200 were raw recruits and several hundred were local city guards. As a result, it was not very surprising that the attack on Berlin was a very short one and resulted in Hadik's army gaining control of the city.

After taking care of the remaining city guards, the general marched to the city magistrate and without much ado started demanding a hefty contribution from the city officials. The haste in his actions was very well justified; Prussian General Friedrich von Seydlitz was rumored to be somewhere in the vicinity of Berlin with a formidable force of his own.

Unfortunately for the Austrian general, the members of the city magistrate were also aware of von Seydlitz's whereabouts, and this knowledge gave them some negotiating power. According to some historians, it is believed that the following dialogue took place between Hadik and the Berliners:

HADIK: I demand a contribution of 600,000 thalers!

MAGISTRATE MEMBERS: Sorry, we are a bit short on finances.

Illustration 11.1 General Andras Hadik

HADIK: Damn it! OK, five hundred!

MAGISTRATE MEMBERS: Really, we don't have that kind of money.

HADIK: I am a reasonable man, but . . . well, how about four hundred?

Finally, the negotiations ended up with Hadik receiving only 200,000 thalers instead of the originally requested sum of 600,000. Incidentally, the general himself pocketed a hefty part of that contribution to the Austrian government—about 12,000 thalers. He also decided that his adjutant deserved to receive a bonus of another 3000 thalers, again withdrawn from the original German contribution.

The German magistrate members were about to bid farewell to the Austrian marauder when Hadik suddenly remembered that Berlin was very famous for the leather gloves produced by local artisans. He demanded that the city pack for him two dozen pairs of ladies' gloves stamped with the city's coat of arms so that he could present them as a gift to the Austrian Empress Maria Theresa. The magistrate employees obliged this strange wish and delivered a package of gloves to Hadik. Remembering the proximity of Friedrich Seydlitz, the Austrian neglected to check the contents of the package either on the spot or at a later time.

The legend claims that he arrived at the royal palace in Vienna and proceeded to tell the story of the heroic siege of Berlin to the Empress and the rest of the court. As a final gesture (and with anticipation of great honors and promotions), he handed over the package of German gloves to Maria Theresa. The Empress opened the parcel, examined its contents, and then proceeded to slap the general several times across the face with the gloves.

As it happened, the sinister Berliners gained a little revenge on the greedy general by making sure all of the Empress's gloves were for the left hand.

What lessons can be learned from this story? First, the general should have been very clear when defining his requirements; the requested package should have contained equal numbers of left- and right-handed gloves. Second, Hadik should have conducted a scope validation exercise upon the delivery of the package to ensure that the final product was indeed delivered according to his specifications.

The two mistakes discussed here are just a small portion of the warning signs of serious problems that could erode the scope definition efforts on projects. Therefore, this chapter is dedicated to potential issues one might encounter during the scope definition process, their symptoms, and the ways to address them.

Skills Issues

Poorly Trained Professionals

One of the key problem areas of project scope definition is the lack of properly trained professionals who have knowledge and ability to elicit the right requirements from the project stakeholders. Some people might argue that this situation is slightly better in the IT and software development industries where scope definition responsibilities have been removed from project management and assigned to a group of professionals called business analysts.

Unfortunately, this problem isn't limited to the lack of properly trained professionals. Scope definition in many industries implies the creation of blueprints and bills of materials, thus ignoring the preliminary work that has to be done in collecting and analyzing the business requirements for projects.

Technical Experts versus Scope Experts

In many organizations, management frequently assume that a technical expert (e.g., architect, engineer, designer) automatically qualifies to collect, build, and analyze project scope. While this approach sometimes works on smaller ventures, assigning untrained technical people to build scope on larger, sophisticated projects can prove to be a very challenging task indeed.

This issue is, unfortunately, quite common. It brings to mind a conversation with a group of executives at a government agency involved, among other things, in several construction megaprojects. The debate involved project scope definition and its place in the science of project management. The problem this organization faced was fairly similar to the issues encountered by many firms. The pure construction element of the project represented only a fraction of the overall scope. Other elements that needed to be considered included public relations, environmental cleanup, legal, real estate, IT, security, engineering, and logistics, to name a few. This organization typically assigned such projects to one of the functional team members in the construction department, such as a senior architect, and time after time the scoping issues would arise as soon as the execution phase began. The conversation with this group of executives went as follows:

> CONSULTANT: So, how does the scoping process work on such multi-departmental projects?
>
> EXECUTIVES: Well, the representative of the construction department is responsible for creating the construction scope.
>
> CONSULTANT: And what about other areas—PR, environment, legal, etc.?
>
> EXECUTIVES: They are supposed to produce the scope of their areas.
>
> CONSULTANT: OK, but who unites all of these scopes into one document? How do you know everything has been covered? How can one identify inconsistencies between scope items originating from different departments? How can you prioritize them? Who is responsible for arranging peer reviews and document walkthroughs?
>
> EXECUTIVES: This is where our main problem lies. It is impossible to find one person who is an expert in public relations, law, construction, engineering, IT, etc.
>
> CONSULTANT: Have you considered assigning a department-independent project manager and providing him with proper training in the scope definition area? He can be responsible for business-level requirements, while technical experts will take care of the detailed technical design.
>
> EXECUTIVES: Interesting idea. By the way, what the heck is a *walkthrough?*

What Can Be Done?

First, come to grips with the fact that it is absolutely essential for any organization involved with larger, more sophisticated projects to properly train their project managers in the areas of scope definition and management. Second, do not make the mistake of assuming that a great technical expert in a specific area can easily become a scope definition guru. Remember, scope definition does not imply technical design involving detailed blueprints and bills of materials but rather high-level and detailed-level business requirements. If a technical expert expresses interest in the requirements elicitation area, one need not discourage his interest. Simply make sure that that person receives proper training before assigning him to elicit scope from the stakeholders (see Table 11.1 for a summary of methods described in the skills issues section of this chapter).

Product or Service Issues

Product or service issues are sometimes discovered when a product or service is delivered, and the client voices her dissatisfaction with it or even rejects it outright. In other cases, the products are delivered to the market and receive poor reviews or do not sell as well as expected. A partial root cause of these problems can lie in insufficient interaction between the real customers and the project team members who are responsible for scope definition. In other words, customers or users were unavailable during the planning stage, or they were too high in the company hierarchy to be bothered with inquisitive scope elicitation questions, or the organization decided to save some money on focus groups. This lack of interaction and, more importantly, insufficient education of the stakeholder can lead to the development of unrealistic customer expectations.

What Can Be Done?

Recognize that the involvement of customers at all stages of a project is absolutely essential to a product's success. They need to be involved at the initiation and planning stages in order to help define the high-level and detailed-level scope of the project, respectively. Their presence is required at the end of the planning and at the beginning of the execution phases in order to validate scope and detailed design documentation. Scope validation tools and techniques will be covered in detail in Chapter 12. Furthermore, customer expectations should be continually managed all the way to the close out stage of the project in order to

Table 11.1 Skills problems

Skills problems	How to fix them
Lack of properly trained professionals who have the knowledge and the ability to elicit the right requirements out of the project stakeholders	Train project managers in the areas of scope definition and management
Technical experts cannot automatically become scope definition specialists	Same as above

Table 11.2 Product or service problems

Product or service problems	How to fix them
Insufficient interaction between the real customers and project team members	Communicate and interact with the key customers throughout the initiation, planning, and execution stages of the project.
Lack of stakeholder education about project management and technical solutions that are available	Educate the project stakeholders about the project management processes, current technology capabilities, and technical expertise (including limitations) of the team.
Poor project selection decisions made by the senior management	See Chapters 15–18, which are dedicated to project portfolio management.

avoid the dreaded expectations gap that seems to happen every time the project manager decides to limit his interactions with the customers. A more detailed discussion of stakeholder management procedures is provided in Chapter 13.

There is another possible root cause for poor product performance once it hits the market. Unfortunately, that problem lies well beyond the scope of project team responsibilities. This is, of course, referring to project portfolio management, which will be discussed in detail in Chapters 15–18. In short, this root cause can be described as a bad project idea generated by the executives—an idea that can't always be fixed by applying technical or other abilities of the project team. For example, when the Ibaraki prefectural government in Japan decided to build a $268 million airport that no major airline was planning to use, whose failure was it that the product was not successful: the project teams that delivered the airport on time and on budget or the politicians who initiated this project without any regard to the economic and demographic realities of their region? See Table 11.2 for a summary of methods described in the product or service issues section of this chapter.

Project Management Issues

External Pressure

Too often project managers are pressured to start the execution stage when the scope definition effort is far from being completed. Sometimes it happens because management thinks that investing more time and effort in gathering project requirements is a waste of valuable project resources. Sometimes (and this happens more often), the firm deadline for the project is set before the scope definition or even initiation phase is completed.

In these scenarios, the unpredictability factor in the project-related estimates is completely ignored, and the release date is imposed while all of the estimates are, at best, in the +75 to −25 percent range. What typically happens is that management realizes that the project cannot be completed on time if the scope elicitation efforts continue. This forces a shift into the execution phase, which is often guided by the foolhardy motto: we shall start building and figure out our scope as we go. This decision leads to omissions that reappear later when it costs a lot more to fix a problem than if the issue had been addressed at the scope definition stage.

Too Much Scope

In some cases, the project team agrees to deliver too much scope for a given budget or timeline. At a certain point in time, the stakeholders realize that the project cannot be completed on time or within the specified budget. The resulting responses vary from company to company. In some cases, the project team is ordered to roll up their sleeves and work harder. And what happens when a group of individuals gets overworked? They get tired. What happens when people get tired? They make mistakes. What happens to the cost of making a mistake as one progresses through the project timeline? It grows exponentially. What is management's response? Work harder. What happens when people work 16-hour days? It's easy to see that it becomes a self-feeding cycle of doom that destroys project results and employee morale.

Quick De-scoping

In other cases, management finally gives in and orders a quick and frequently unorganized de-scoping of the project. The interdependence of various scope items, and the fact that dropping a scope item requires extensive fact gathering followed by analysis, often gets ignored.

Another variation of the agreeing-to-deliver-too-much-scope problem is a change in project constraints (e.g., slashed budgets, shortened timelines) while the scope remains the same.

What Can Be Done?

First, project teams should not sacrifice scope elicitation efforts for the sake of speeding up the project. These shortcuts are almost never successful. Second, project managers should avoid firm commitments to deadlines and fixed budgets, whenever possible, before project scoping is completed. Also, using various negotiating techniques to obtain additional degrees of freedom, as discussed in Chapter 4, is a powerful tool at the project manager's disposal to alleviate these problems. Furthermore, stakeholder education about the risks of rushed shifts from planning to execution phases of the projects is absolutely essential. See Table 11.3 for a summary of techniques described in the project management issues section of this chapter.

Table 11.3 Project management problems

Project management problems	How to fix them
Pressure to start the execution stage before the scope definition effort is complete	Do not sacrifice scope elicitation efforts for the sake of speeding up the project. Educate your stakeholders about the risks of rushed shifts from planning to execution.
Project team accepts the responsibility for too much scope for a given budget or timeline	Avoid firm commitments to deadlines and fixed budgets whenever possible before the project scoping is complete. Use various negotiating techniques to obtain additional degrees of freedom.
Quick and frequently unorganized de-scoping of the project	Define feature priorities as soon as possible in the scope definition stage.

Scope Elicitation Issues

Frequently, the project team and other stakeholders discover that important project requirements have been missed when the project is well into the execution stage.

Lack of Communication

Sometimes these missed requirements are caused by customers and users who do not have a very clear idea of what they really need. In other cases, poorly trained project managers are responsible. Another cause is the lack of communication between different departments that leads to the omission of important details.

One project manager described an extreme case of this type of miscommunication. The case involved two departments in a government organization: the logistics department, which was responsible for building and maintaining roads, and the engineering department. At one point in time, the engineering department decided that it would be a great idea to implant special devices into the surfaces of roads leading to a local port in order to monitor and forecast the truck flow to the terminals. It was indeed a great idea because the employees at the terminal frequently complained about unpredictability of incoming traffic. The engineers acquired these fairly expensive sensors and the software required to analyze the data then proceeded to embed them into the road surface. Closer to the end of the year, at a department heads' meeting, the director of engineering reported on his team's accomplishments and proudly mentioned the sensor project as one of the highlighted achievements of the year. To his great surprise, the director of logistics started laughing uncontrollably, and it took a couple of angry stares from other executives to calm him down. Still struggling to control himself, the head of the logistics department was finally able to explain his reaction.

His team was scheduled to resurface these same roads in the coming year. Thus, the engineers' efforts along with a hefty sum of taxpayers' money were basically wasted because of the lack of coordination between the two departments.

Scope Imposed by a Higher Authority

Another frequent problem with scope definition is that the requirements are imposed by a higher authority without any regard to whether they truly represent the needs and aspirations of real users. A variation of this problem occurs when functional managers prevent project managers from communicating directly with the customers.

Absence of Prioritization

Yet another issue that can jeopardize the scope definition process takes place when the scope items are not prioritized, or all of them have high priority. What happens in this scenario is that a team's flexibility in cutting scope is severely limited if it turns out that the initial time and budget estimates were overly optimistic.

What Can Be Done?

Missed or overlooked requirements can be avoided by the customers' active involvement in the scope definition process, proper training of project managers in scope elicitation techniques, and thorough document walkthroughs and inspections. In addition, the project manager should ensure that people responsible for scope definition get access to the real customers and users.

Finally, all of the scope items must be prioritized and assigned to must-have, should-have, and nice-to-have categories. Education of the stakeholders about the importance of prioritization is another important factor when battling scope elicitation issues. See Table 11.4 for a summary of procedures described in the scope elicitation issues section of this chapter.

Documentation Issues

Undocumented Scope

In some scenarios, different and sometimes competing groups of stakeholders cannot arrive at a consensus of what the final product should look like. Consequently, the decision is made to start working with what is currently available and to hope differences can be reconciled in the future. In some extreme cases, the decision is made to forego the documentation effort altogether. As mentioned previously, sometimes the eagerness to begin the construction of the product

Table 11.4 Scope elicitation problems

Scope elicitation problems	How to fix them
Requirements are omitted because the customers do not have a very clear idea of what they really need, project managers are poorly trained, or there is a lack of communication.	Involve the customers in the scope definition process. Ensure that the project managers receive proper training in scope elicitation techniques. Conduct thorough document walkthroughs and inspections.
Scope is imposed by a higher authority.	Make sure that the project manager or anyone else responsible for scope definition gets access to the real customers and users.
Scope items are not prioritized at all or all of the features are assigned a top priority.	Prioritize all of the scope items. Educate the stakeholders about the importance of prioritization.

can compel the project manager, voluntarily or unwillingly, to transition to the execution stage of the product while there are still open issues remaining with respect to the project scope. And a poorly defined scope can be a byproduct of a lack of appreciation among the stakeholders for the importance of well-defined requirements.

Vague Scope

A common complaint expressed by technical team members responsible for building products is the ambiguity and vagueness of the scope documentation. Left uncorrected, this can lead to other serious issues including project failure. These technical people might take it upon themselves to independently follow up with various stakeholders in order to gain some understanding of the vaguely stated scope items. In some cases, they might end up talking to the wrong stakeholder (e.g., an internal functional manager) rather than a real customer. Even if they do end up talking to the right person they might, and probably will, forget to update the project documentation. And if they do remember to update scope documents, they could fail to consider the impact of their particular interpretation of a vague statement on other requirements and project constraints. In an even scarier scenario, the technical experts might decide to forego consultations with stakeholders regarding the stated requirements and rely on their own interpretation or, God forbid, imagination.

In the best-case scenario, technical team members will continue harassing the project manager by complaining, and justifiably so, that they are unable to work with documentation of such poor quality. This will, in turn, lead to repeating the scope definition process with one unpleasant twist—it will be taking place in the middle of the execution stage.

Lack of Measurability

Lack of measurability easily could lead to the same kind of behavior described in the last section. Statements such as *the new container terminal shall be of a sufficient square footage to accommodate load requirements in peak times* might again compel the engineers or architects to either independently contact the stakeholders or decide what *sufficient square footage* means according to their own perceptions and imaginations. Needless to say, customer expectations very frequently turn out to be somewhat different than the opinions of the technical team members.

What Can Be Done?

Once the first drafts of the documents have been completed, they should undergo several rigorous examination processes including peer reviews by experienced project managers who are preferably unrelated to the project in question, inspections with technical teams, and walkthroughs with customers. Only several iterations of these processes will enable the project team to remove all the discrepancies from the scope description and provide the technical team with quality documents that will become the foundation of the detailed designs including blueprints and bills of materials. And as mentioned previously, proper training in the scope definition area is absolutely essential. See Table 11.5 for a summary of techniques described in the documentation issues section of this chapter.

Table 11.5 Documentation problems

Documentation problems	How to fix them
Undocumented or poorly documented scope	Educate managers about the consequences of moving into the execution phase without properly understanding the project scope. Do not begin a project with a poorly documented scope.
Ambiguity and vagueness of the scope documentation	Develop scope definition templates either as standalone documents or as sections of the project charter and project plan. Provide project team members responsible for scope documentation with proper training. Conduct peer reviews, team inspections, and customer walkthroughs of all the important documents.
Lack of measurability	Same as above

Scope Management Issues

Finally, the last group of problems typically starts after the scope of the project has been finalized, and the team has moved into the execution stage by starting to build the final product. In almost any venture, there are several problems associated with this particular stage.

Customers Communicate Directly With the Technical People

The first problem is that the customers, either due to the lack of understanding of scope control procedures or because of some more sinister reasons, start talking directly to the technical team members responsible for building the final artifact. This occurs through informal one-on-one conversations, phone calls, or e-mail messages while circumventing the project manager and other key project stakeholders. The technical team members might then be pressured into making changes and adjustments to the scope, bypassing detailed impact analysis of the requested modifications and their benefits. As a result of such manipulations, several issues most likely will surface:

- Uncontrolled modifications and additions can have a negative impact on other project features
- The quality of the final product might suffer as such changes are rarely assessed and documented
- Project scope will increase while time and budget constraints remain the same
- New risks can surface because of ad hoc improvements to the project scope
- Technical team members will be distracted from their assigned duties, thus jeopardizing the overall project schedule

More information on uncontrolled project changes and how to deal with them is provided in Chapter 13.

Scope Changes Frequently

Another problem is that the customers change their opinion about what the final product should look like after the specifications documents have been baselined. This can happen for the following variety of reasons: stakeholder lack of understanding of technical difficulties of changing scope, especially on larger, more sophisticated ventures; poor scope definition efforts during the planning stage; internal strife among different stakeholder groups; and even political, economic, or technological shifts in the marketplace. If left unattended, these frequent changes will have exactly the same effect on the project as the ones described in the previous section.

Table 11.6 Scope management problems

Scope management problems	How to fix them
Customers communicating directly with the technical project team members	Educate the stakeholders about the dangers of ad hoc, uncontrolled scope changes. Implement proper change control policies. Conduct a thorough analysis of every change request, it's potential impacts, necessity, additional effort, and time needed to implement it.
Frequent scope changes	Conduct a thorough analysis of the necessity of each change request. Ask the stakeholders to determine whether the value of implementing the proposed change minus all of its negative impacts is greater or less than the cost of not carrying it out.

What Can Be Done?

One of the techniques available to project managers who are determined to gain control of the project scope is the education of project stakeholders on the inherent dangers of making unplanned modifications to the project scope. The project manager should find a way to explain to all parties involved that uncontrolled changes can lead to increased exposure to risks, low product quality, and can have detrimental effects on budgets and time lines.

Implementation of proper change control policies is an essential step in harnessing the scope management process. It should, among other things, incorporate a very thorough examination of the necessity of a proposed change, the technical impacts, and the effects on timeline, budget, and risk exposure. All stakeholders should be making their decisions regarding the validity of the change based on the following formula:

> *Is the value of implementing the proposed change minus all of its negative impacts higher or lower than the cost of not carrying it out?*

For more information regarding assessment of the changes and modifications of the project scope, please see the section in Chapter 13, What Is the Impact of the Change? Table 11.6 contains an overview of techniques described in the scope management issues section of this chapter.

Summary

One might have noticed a definitive repeating pattern while reading this chapter. Certain suggestions kept reappearing in the *how to fix them* columns of the tables. It probably would be more efficient to highlight all the key methodologies for battling scope problems according to their importance rather than to group them by the problems they address.

The most important ingredient in preventing scope issues is the training of scope definition experts, either project managers or people holding other titles (e.g., business analysts in IT or software development industries).

Ongoing involvement and communication with all stakeholders in general and customers and users in particular is another cornerstone of the scope elicitation, definition, and management process.

Educating the stakeholders about project management, scope definition, and the overall impact of their decisions on the budget, duration, resource requirements, quality of the final product, and potential risks is also very important in avoiding serious scope issues.

Project managers should resist any attempts to sacrifice scope elicitation and definition efforts in order to speed up the project's progress. Invariably, such endeavors result in serious problems with quality, missed deadlines, and overblown budgets.

Making any firm commitments with respect to project budget, timeline, or resource requirements before the entire scope has been finalized is also not recommended for project managers and other project team members. Project managers are also strongly encouraged to extensively use the negotiation techniques described in Chapter 4 when discussing various project estimates and commitments with other stakeholders and key customers.

Finally, scope management is another key methodology in preventing scope creep and unapproved change in the scope that can affect the success of the project.

12

Who Needs Walkthroughs, Inspections, and Peer Reviews?

Historical Perspective

Mutiny on the High Seas

In 1707, a British fleet under the command of Sir Clowdisley Shovell was returning home after a long mission (see Illustration 12.1). The convoy encountered heavy fog upon entering the English Channel. The admiral gathered his officers and navigators to get a definite fix on their location. After a short consultation, the officers reported to Shovell that the fleet was safely off the coast of France. The admiral was about to issue an order to sail north to England when a sailor approached and asked him for permission to speak.

The sailor told Sir Shovell that he was keeping track of their position by using his own navigational equipment. He also informed the admiral that the officers were badly mistaken and that the fleet was much closer to English shores than they had anticipated. Therefore, according to the sailor, it was very dangerous to proceed to England at full speed since they were in danger of wrecking on the Scilly Isles. Sir Shovell ordered the man hanged as a mutineer.

Hours later, the flagship and three other boats smashed into the rocks. Sir Shovell was swept ashore where, according to one of the legends, he was murdered by a woman who wanted his emerald ring.

Incidentally, the sailor indeed, according to British naval law, deserved to be hanged. The danger of mutiny was a real problem on English ships due to bad

Illustration 12.1 Admiral Clowdisley Shovell

living conditions, diseases, and corporal punishment. Therefore, only the officers were allowed to keep and use navigational equipment. Admiralty's logic was that if the sailors didn't know where they were, they would be less inclined to rebel against the officers.

This story has been used frequently by historians to demonstrate the incompetence, stubbornness, and even pompousness of some military leaders. Nonetheless, the first mistake the admiral made was that of wasting his project resources. After all, what project manager in his right mind disposes of his precious project team members in the middle of a project?

On a more serious note, this story serves as a great example of how a project can go terribly wrong if the project manager chooses to ignore the critique and feedback from stakeholders in general and from technical team members in particular.

The Overlooked Techniques

In Chapter 7, the concept of walkthroughs, inspections, and peer reviews was discussed as being among the most powerful techniques at the disposal of project managers. An interesting paradox was also briefly discussed: research showed that few organizations used these techniques, yet those that did use them reported extremely positive results.

Personally, I found these research results rather surprising. I learned these techniques fairly early in my career, liked the concepts and started applying them on all of my projects fairly consistently and, at times covertly, because of the pressure from some of my superiors to quit wasting technical people's time on silly meetings. My personal results from using these techniques have been rather positive as well.

Disturbed by this paradox, I decided to review the issue further over an extended period of time with the experienced project managers and executives attending my courses at British Columbia Institute of Technology. My students came from almost every industry such as construction, engineering, pharmaceutical, government, utilities, oil and gas, software, and IT, to name a few. By surveying and evaluating the use of these techniques across all these industries, I fully expected a different result, at least in sectors with deeper roots in the fields of project management, engineering, construction, and government. The results from this study were again pretty surprising. Surprisingly enough, few of them (excluding some of the IT and software people) ever confirmed that they were indeed using or even aware of this powerful technique.

To complete this study, my next step was to try to convince my students to try these techniques in real-world practice. The majority of my project manager students readily agreed to give them a try. My executive students, on the other hand, took a lot more convincing but finally agreed to give them a try as well. Their assignment was to try using walkthroughs, inspections, and peer reviews to validate the scope of the projects, to identify otherwise unexpected risks, and to decrease the amount of mistakes and rework required. The results from this study were, to say the least, staggering. All of those who tried the techniques reported great results including, but not limited to, projects that finished before deadlines, high quality final products or services, and, most importantly, highly satisfied customers.

Based on this study and other research, walkthroughs, inspections, and peer reviews are among the most overlooked techniques of value in the field of project management, particularly outside the high tech and software industries. For those who are still not convinced and those who might have to convince others, this discussion will continue and will describe how to go about using these techniques.

Peer Reviews, Inspections, and Walkthroughs

Why Conduct Peer Reviews and Walkthroughs?

Unfortunately, due to the lack of reliable information from other sectors, readers will have to rely on data collected in the high-tech field and then construct generalized extrapolations to the rest of the world. An expanded discussion on the reviews will begin with a very interesting statistic originating from the IT and software industry:

> Forty-five percent of project costs industry wide is rework.

Ponder this number for a while. If one chooses to believe in the power of extrapolation to one degree or another, it appears that by eliminating the amount of rework completely, all project budgets can be cut in half. Durations would probably fall by a significant number as well.

At first glance, this assumption seems significantly overstated. However, upon further analysis, this number does not look excessively abnormal if one remembers the cost-of-mistake study conducted by leading thinker Barry Boehm, which claimed that a mistake that costs one dollar to fix at the initiation stage of a project will typically balloon to a \$40–\$1000 deficiency by project closure. If one uses financial modeling to recreate a possible scenario on a given project and tries to assess the return on investment by catching the mistakes early in the project process:

Given: Initial project budget = \$100,000

Number of mistakes, omissions, unidentified risks, hidden constraints = 50 (a fairly plausible, if not conservative, number)

Cost to fix, per mistake (early) = \$5 (Actually, it is \$1 per mistake, but, once again, one should err on the conservative side.)

Cost to fix, per mistake (late) = \$1000

Scenario 1—catch the mistakes early

Cost of fixing = \$5/mistake × 50 mistakes = \$250

Actual project budget = initial project budget + cost of fixing = \$100,250

Scenario 2—catch the mistakes late

Cost of fixing = \$1000/mistake × 50 mistakes = \$50,000

Actual project budget = initial project budget + cost of fixing = \$150,000

By comparing these scenarios, it is not very difficult to accept that approximately 40 to 50 percent of project expenditures could be spent on rework.

It would also be worthwhile to calculate an ROI on the catch-the-mistakes-early investments:

$$ROI = \frac{(\$50,000 - \$250)}{\$250} - 1 = 1800\%$$

To paraphrase Karl Wiegers[1], an 1800 percent return on investment is not something to be sneezed at.

So, what can happen without the walkthroughs, inspections, and peer reviews? Here is a very typical scenario (a bit exaggerated for illustrational purposes):

> Step 1: The project manager, sometimes with the help of other resources (e.g., business analysts in IT field, architects in the construction industry, mechanical engineers in product development), develops a project plan and a scope document (statement of work).
>
> Step 2: The technical project team members are still working on other very important projects, and their functional managers frown upon distractions that might keep the team from their urgent tasks.
>
> Step 3: Customers or end users are not consulted about the final designs because these documents are fairly technical. Also, annoying questions, corrections, and other disruptions need to be avoided.
>
> Step 4: The project manager presents the project plan and statement of work documents to the technical people and possibly does a quick walkthrough during the project kickoff meeting.
>
> Step 5: The project team members discover a great many deficiencies, mistakes, and risks in the documentation, but unfortunately, major commitments with respect to time, budget, and scope have already been made.
>
> Step 6: The project team pulls together and, based on sheer will and long hours, delivers a product that somewhat resembles the scope described in the documentation. In addition, despite all of these heroic efforts, the project is late and over budget.
>
> Step 7: Finally, customers walk in the doors and, after a cursory inspection of the product, find dozens and dozens of defects, omissions and mistakes.

The subsequent sections of this chapter will attempt to explain what should be done with respect to walkthroughs, inspections, and peer reviews in order to avoid this depressing situation. Figure 12.1 provides the reader with a high-level overview of the documentation review process.

How to Conduct Walkthroughs, Inspections, and Peer Reviews

What Documents Should Be Reviewed?

Typically, it is a good idea to review all of the major project documents including scope. The more documents reviewed fairly early in the process, the less chance of missing scope items, unforeseen risks, and hidden constraints. Having said that, in real life, assembling the entire group of project stakeholders or even stakeholder subgroups is a difficult and time-consuming task that might not be encouraged at some organizations. Therefore, it seems quite logical to concentrate on the most important of the project documents.

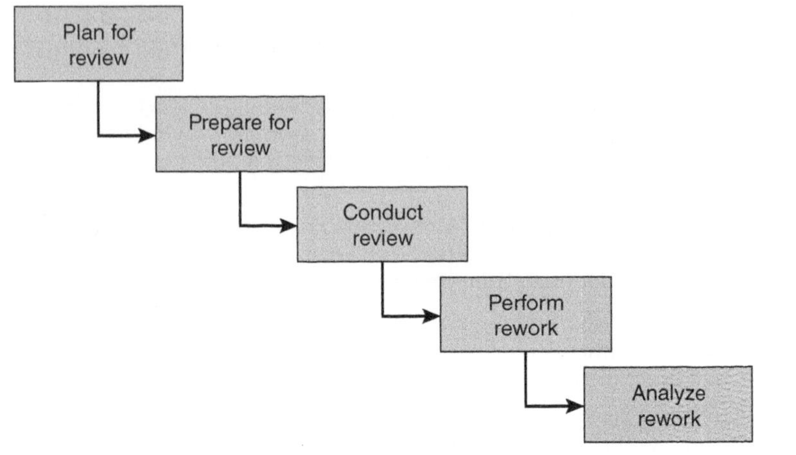

Figure 12.1 How to conduct peer reviews and inspections

The primary documents for project team members and customers would definitely be project plan and statement of work (scope document and requirements document) because they contain crucial information for the project's success. It is also very useful to briefly familiarize the project team with the project charter in order to inform the technical team members about the project itself, the key scope items, and constraints. It is absolutely essential, however, for a project manager to conduct a full-scale walkthrough of the project charter with the customers and key stakeholders.

How Do You Organize Peer Review and Walkthrough Meetings?

The best way to conduct peer reviews and walkthroughs (especially on larger, more complicated projects) is to have them at regular intervals during the document development stage. At least two or three meetings should be scheduled closer to the end of the project charter, project plan, and scope document development stages.

Note that there is a serious chance that the functional managers might say that the technical people are too busy to attend such meetings. Some other stakeholders might occasionally claim they are too busy as well and refuse or ignore one's invitations to the walkthrough meetings. Experience suggests that the best way to convince these people is to share the cost-of-mistake chart with them and ask them whether they would consider it a worthwhile investment to spend a couple of hours now in order to avoid spending several hundred to a thousand hours later solving issues that could have been prevented.

It is a good idea to reserve a two-hour block of time in a medium- to large-sized well-ventilated conference room several days in advance. At least two hours might be needed because the documents (especially on larger projects) tend to be fairly long. Thus, even walking a group of, say, 20 or 30 people through a 50-page document will probably take the entire two-hour meeting.

On the other hand, keep in mind that walkthroughs and reviews of project documents, especially the ones taking place earlier in the process, are very vigorous and spirited affairs that could drain all of the project manager's energy and even sometimes hope. Thus, allocating more than two hours for the meeting could have some inherent dangers; people will get tired, they will start losing their collective focus, and they might even become a bit cranky.

Speaking of vigorous meetings, I still remember my first reviews when I walked into the room all bushy tailed and cocky, convinced of my own infallibility, and left the meeting a couple of hours later with the document completely covered in red ink with required follow-ups, clarifications, corrections, and even complete rewrites marked everywhere. Walkthroughs and peer reviews can sometimes be a very humbling experience indeed. Always remember that a humbling experience that lasts a couple of hours early in the project is a very small price to pay for discovering the aforementioned one-dollar mistakes, errors, and omissions.

Preparing for the meeting also involves sending a first draft of the document to all meeting participants with a request that everyone is expected to review the document with a critical eye and come prepared to voice her concerns, suggestions, and improvements. Mentioning that a document is a first draft that could change dramatically after a series of reviews and walkthroughs is especially important because sometimes organizational and country-specific factors mean some people could otherwise be reluctant to voice their criticism of another person's work. A byproduct of a conservative hierarchical organization might create a situation where any word uttered by one's superior is considered to be a commandment. In other cases, especially with the advances of globalization, people working on a project might be reluctant to voice their concerns because of their cultural backgrounds. For example, in many parts of south and east Asia, telling a person, "I think you made a mistake here" or "you overlooked a couple of important risks" could be considered an insult and, more often than not, will never be mentioned to the project manager who is perceived to be an authority figure on a project. Therefore, it is very important to consider the company culture and the traditions of the people involved in the project and adjust one's message accordingly.

The next step is to conduct a quick document walkthrough either using the document itself or some kind of presentation software. It is good idea to plug a laptop into the overhead projector so that everyone can see what is being discussed and recorded. Using a Word document is a good option so that all of the comments, critique, feedback, and follow-up items can be recorded right there. It also is helpful to let people word their comments themselves rather than to rephrase them. This way one can avoid future misunderstandings about the content of the feedback.

Whatever form is chosen—comments in a Word document or remarks in a notebook—it is worthwhile to re-record all of the action items from these meetings into some kind of issues list, then disseminate it to all of the meeting participants and other project stakeholders. Incorporating this issues list into the meeting minutes and sending it out to all the stakeholders is an effective and time-saving technique.

Conducting Peer Reviews and Inspections

There are two very distinct types of peer reviews. One is called the proper format review and the other is called the correct technical context review.

The proper format review is typically done by an experienced project manager external to the project. Accordingly, this person is usually not familiar with the detailed technical scope of the project; in fact, it is better if that person hasn't even heard about the project before. The problem is that someone who has been involved extensively in the project and has participated in many of the project discussions is less likely to be as alert and vigilant when reviewing project documentation. In addition, he might subconsciously be subject to the group's assumptions. A colleague came up with a very accurate description of these phenomena; he referred to them as *soaping of the eyes*. For instance, the technical people on the project team might think that they have a very good idea of what *seamless integration* means. An experienced peer reviewer who hasn't been burdened by team influence will flag this phrase as inappropriate right away.

Therefore, the proper format reviewer's mission is not to validate the technical scope of the project, its schedule, budget estimates, or to ask the question: "what problem are you trying to solve?" Her job is to make sure that the document follows the best practices of project management. The documentation guru's primary responsibility is to capture deficiencies and mistakes such as ambiguous language, missing measurability, completeness, consistency, prioritization, and proper constructs.

Unfortunately, these kinds of reviews cannot answer questions like:

- Can this scope item be delivered at all?
- Can this scope item be delivered with the budget and timeline provided?
- Are there any technical inconsistencies in the scope?

This is where correct technical context reviews or inspections come in handy. The technical team members are more likely to focus on the correctness of technical information, unidentified risks, and overlooked resource requirements in the documents rather than the way in which documentation is written. For example, statements like:

> Build a large four-bedroom three-bathroom Tuscan-style home on a budget of $100,000 by the end of next month.

would generate different feedback from the guru than from the technical project team members. The documentation guru would almost certainly notice an inappropriate use of the word *large* and would ask the project manager to associate a measurable attribute with that particular term. As a result, the word *large* could be replaced with statements like *5000 square feet* or *three-level, 6000 square feet.*

On the other hand, technical team members might have an idea (not necessarily a good one) of what *large* means or they might just miss it because of the lack of training in documentation reviews. They would, however, likely make a comment such as "buildings of this size cannot be built on a budget of $100,000 and be completed in a month and a half."

Who should be invited to peer reviews and inspections? With proper format reviews, it is fairly straightforward: the project manager, the documentation guru, and one of the most experienced project leaders in the company who has been properly trained in the fine art of critical reading. The technical document inspections will require the presence of the project manager, team leaders of each functional group involved in the project, all technical team members, quality assurance people, subject matter experts in each of the functional areas, and several key representatives from the customer side.

Conducting Customer Walkthroughs

For a stakeholder walkthrough, one should consider inviting clients or customers (whichever is applicable) and, if possible, the end users of the product. Note that each one of these groups could be, in turn, subdivided into several clusters; some of these clusters could be primary and some of them could be secondary, but both are important. It also would be a good idea to invite key representatives from the technical team since some of the questions posed by the customers and users might be ones that only they could answer. Technical team representatives are needed in order to explain and justify the estimates. If one is working on a multidepartmental project at a fairly functional organization, inviting other department heads also could be valuable because they could end up providing resources for the project.

Peer Review and Walkthrough Challenges

Some of the issues encountered by project teams during the peer reviews, walkthroughs, and inspections include large requirements documents, large inspection teams, and geographical separation. Probably one of the most dangerous things that can happen at these meetings is having reviewers lose focus and sometimes even interest due to exhaustion. Tired or disinterested people pay less attention to the document in question and hence miss the errors and deficiencies hidden in the document. Sitting in a stuffy room for hours and hours staring at a screen as page after page of a 200 page document slips by can be very tiring.

What are the tools, then, at one's disposal for battling walkthrough fatigue? If dealing with larger documents, try scheduling several reviews in stages. This way the duration of reviews is reduced and the focus of the participants is maintained. Try not to exceed a two-hour time limit on meetings. Also, when booking a conference room, pick the largest and the best ventilated room possible. Nothing kills the thought process like the lack of oxygen.

Sometimes review teams can get very large, especially on key project documents like project plan or project scope definition. Having fifty or more people commenting and providing critiques of one's documentation can turn into chaos very quickly. Therefore, it could be useful to break the inspection teams into groups for initial inspections. Once the major issues discovered in these separate meetings have been analyzed and addressed properly, the final joint technical team and customer walkthrough involving all the project stakeholders can take place.

Geographical separation can also present certain challenges. Try using tools like video conferencing, teleconferencing, or tracking and comments functions in word processing software.

What Kinds of Questions Should You Expect (and Ask)?

So what kinds of questions can one expect from the walkthroughs with the customers and the technical team members? Table 12.1 lists some of the questions the project manager should expect when engaging in the walkthroughs, inspections, and peer reviews.

While the walkthroughs are mainly the arena for customers, clients, and users to ask questions and provide feedback, this is also an opportunity for the project manager to pose inquiries of his own. Make the effort to document *why* each requirement is needed, as one might often find that as many as half of the requirements can be eliminated. In other words, one can often cut the scope of a project by approximately 50 percent just by asking:

- Why did you include this requirement?
- How is it related to your original problem?
- Is this a requirement or more of a design decision?

What to Watch Out For: Defect Checklists

So what are the things all reviewers should watch out for during walkthroughs, peer reviews, and inspections? When reviewing scope and other project man-

Table 12.1 Questions asked during inspections and walkthroughs

Question	Document	What should the project manager do?
Why are your estimate ranges so wide?	Project charter and project plan	Explain that the appropriate ranges for the initiation stage estimates are +75 to −25 percent for regular projects and +300 to −75 percent for software development and R&D ventures.
Why will it take so long?	Project charter and project plan	Go over the project schedule and explain how the estimates were obtained.
Why will it cost so much?	Project charter and project plan	Go over the project budget and explain how the estimates were obtained.
Can you finish the project faster?	Project charter and project plan	Explain the concept of project management triangle (scope, time, budget) or pentagon (scope, time, budget, effort, and quality) and find out which areas can be manipulated to deliver the project more quickly.
Can you find some ways to do it more cheaply?	Project charter and project plan	Explain the concept of project management triangle or pentagon and find out which areas can be manipulated to deliver the project more cheaply.
We have to add another high-level feature.	Project charter	Try to assess which problem the requested feature will solve and, if necessary, add to the issues list. If required, schedule an offline meeting.
We have to add another detailed scope item.	Scope document	Try to assess which problem the requested requirement will solve and, if necessary, add to the issues list. If required, schedule an offline meeting.
With respect to project feasibility, who came up with revenue projections?	Project charter	Explain the underlying logic in arriving at future revenue forecasts.
You should also mention regulatory projects, competitive advantage, etc., in the project feasibility section.	Project charter	Have a discussion with the participants, and add to the document if necessary.
Have you considered this risk?	Project charter and project plan	Quickly assess the risk and flag for incorporation into the documentation. Arrange for an offline meeting or follow-up, if necessary. Add to the issues list.
You need to communicate to person X from department Y; he should be involved in this discussion.	All documents	Add to the issues list. Schedule a follow-up meeting with that person.

Question	Document	What should the project manager do?
Director of department Z will have to assign resources to this project.	All documents	Add to the issues list. Schedule a follow-up meeting with that person.
Hey, that is not what I needed!	Scope document	Briefly discuss the problem with the stakeholder. Add to the issues list. Arrange for an offline meeting or follow-up, if necessary.
Oh, I have just realized that we will also be needing this feature	Scope document	Briefly discuss the new scope item with the stakeholder. Add to the issues list. Arrange for an offline meeting or follow-up, if necessary.
You forgot to include this	Scope document	Briefly discuss the new scope item with the stakeholder. Add to the issues list. Arrange for an offline meeting or follow-up, if necessary.
There is a conflict between these two (or more) scope items.	Scope document	Add to the issues list. Arrange for an offline meeting or follow-up, if necessary.
We do not have the capability to make that happen.	Scope document	Discuss why this can't be done and what are the alternative ways of reaching project objectives. Add to the issues list. Arrange for an offline meeting or follow-up, if necessary.
I can interpret this statement in several ways.	All documents	Rephrase the statement in a proper format to remove any ambiguity.

agement documents, the stakeholders should be asking themselves the following questions:

Organization and completeness of the documentation:

- Are all parts of the documents written at a consistent and appropriate level of detail?
- Does the scope definition document provide an adequate basis for design?
- Are priorities assigned to each scope item?
- Is there any information missing in the document? Are there any TBDs in the documents?
- Are all possible alternatives, exceptions, risks, and constraints covered?

Technical feasibility:

- Is every requirement in scope?
- Can all the scope items be implemented with all the known constraints?

Table 12.2 Words to beware of

Words	What to do about them?
Acceptable, adequate	Define acceptability and how the product and stakeholders can decide what is acceptable and what is not.
Efficient	Explain how efficiently the product performs operations or how easy it is to use.
Fast, rapid	Specify minimum, maximum, and desired speed.
Flexible	What specifically should the product do in response to specific changes in the environment or business objectives?
Improved, better, faster, superior	Quantify how much faster constitutes adequate improvement.
Maximize, minimize, optimize	Provide maximum and minimum acceptable parameters for each value. You can also provide desired range, too.
Seamless, transparent, graceful	Translate into observable product characteristics.
Several	How many? Provide a specific number or maximum and minimum acceptable parameters for each value.
State-of-the-art	Define what this means.
Sufficient	How much is sufficient?
Support, enable	Define exactly what functions would constitute support or enabling.
User-friendly, simple, easy	Translate into observable product characteristics.

Measurability:

- Do all of the scope items have appropriate measurability attributes associated with them?

Ambiguity:

- Do all the key statements in the document have only one possible meaning?
- Can the statements be misinterpreted by any of the stakeholders?

Dangerous words:

- Table 12.2 provides a list of potentially troublesome words and phrases that frequently appear in project management documentation in all industries and types of organizations

Summary

Document walkthroughs, inspections, and peer reviews are surprisingly underutilized in many industries despite strong evidence that these practices have a great positive effect on the quality of project results.

Considering the fact that close to 45 percent of project costs are rework and that costs of fixing a mistake grows a thousand-fold as one progresses from the project initiation to the close out, using these techniques is a very worthwhile and rewarding investment.

In a perfect world, most of the project management documentation should be reviewed by the proper audiences. In the worst-case scenario, however, the stakeholders, including the team and the customers should at least review the project charter, project plan, and the scope documents.

When conducting reviews and inspections, one should reserve a large, well-ventilated room for an ample amount of time but for no longer than two hours. E-mail the document in question ahead of time, and inform the reviewers that a first draft is being sent. Tell them that the document might change drastically as feedback is received, analyzed, and incorporated. Be aware of the cultural and organizational obstacles when conducting candid and open reviews.

Understand the difference between customer walkthroughs, proper format reviews done by the experts in the organization, and correct context technical team inspections. Use them all at proper times in the project.

Be aware of the types of questions that might be asked and know how to act in each scenario. Maintain an issues list during each meeting so that all problems and questions are recorded for future follow-up. Also, use a defect checklist as a guide in assessing the quality of documentation.

Finally, when one is walking into the review conference room, he should leave his ego at the door.

Endnote

1. Wiegers, Karl. *Software Requirements,* 2nd ed. (Microsoft Press, 2003).

13

Why Should you Manage Scope and Customer Expectations?

Historical Perspective

The Camel Is a Horse Designed by Committee

French shipbuilders produced a curious quartet of battleships over the course of 12 years in the late nineteenth century: the *Hoche* and her sisters *Marceau, Magenta,* and *Neptune*. It has been argued by some naval historians that because of the accumulation of demands by multiple departments for various features, these vessels eventually lost any resemblance to battleships. A foreign critic described one of the ships as "a half-submerged whale with a number of laborers' cottages built on its back." A domestic columnist, while being understandably more sympathetic, referred to the *Hoche* as *Le Grand Hotel*.

During the 1880s, French shipbuilders, for some inexplicable reasons, decided to design their ships by uniting the scoping, designing, and building phases into one very confusing process. As a result, it took a staggering 12 years to build *Hoche* and her sisters as every new and cool naval development was added to the ship design irrespective of the compatibility with the original blueprint. As a result of such rampant scope creep, the *Magenta* (see Illustration 13.1) underwent several transformations (see Table 13.1).

Consequently, when *Magenta* was completed in 1893, she was 300 tons overweight and had lost 30 percent of planned stability. The *Conseils de Travaux* charged with overseeing the construction were accused of behaving like medieval

Illustration 13.1 Battleship *Magenta*

Table 13.1 Scope changes on the Battleship *Magenta* project

Sequence of changes	Description of changes
Initial design	Armament—three 13.4-inch guns Top speed—14.5 knots Displacement—9800 tons
First change	Change armament from three 13.4-inch guns to two 13.4-inch guns and two 10.8-inch guns
Second change	Change armament from two 13.4-inch guns and two 10.8-inch guns to four 13.4-inch guns and no 10.8-inch guns
Third change	Lengthen and broaden the ship to increase its speed to 16 knots
Fourth change	Add massive military masts and armored conning tower
Fifth change	Add torpedo nets and searchlights
Sixth change	Add a battery of quick-firing guns

bishops building a Gothic cathedral, and the ship itself was being compared to a three-storied chateau rising 40 feet above the armored belt with 60 guns of different calibers. It was calculated that if the *Magenta* had trained all of her guns to one side, she would have capsized and sunk.

The final straw was unpretentiously provided by the ship's captain who claimed, "A ship may go into battle only once in its life, and then be inactive

Illustration 13.2 Battleship *Hoche*

for thirty years. The superstructure [while] annoying in battle, notably improves habitability for ordinary life." No wonder the ship was dubbed *Le Grand Hotel*!

These unfortunate vessels were arguably the worst battleships in the French navy. Their service lives were not long. The *Magenta* was broken up in 1911 and the *Hoche* (see Illustration 13.2) was sunk as a practice target on December 2, 1913.

The lessons of this case study are fairly obvious: good project results cannot be achieved if the project manager loses control over the scope and fails to curb the expectations of the stakeholders.

How Formal Should Scope Management Be?

Although scope management becomes one of the key activities once a project has entered the execution stage, there has been some lack of consensus regarding the appropriateness of the scope management process on various projects. The question of appropriateness stems in part from customer reaction to the process, especially if expectations are not properly managed. The real question is: how extensive and formal should the change request procedures be for projects of varying size and complexity?

While it is practically impossible to provide everyone with a universal framework that would fit the needs of any project, the principles that are discussed in this chapter are applicable to all ventures, large and small, simple and sophisticated. The only difference would be the degree of formality associated with this methodology. For example, on a very complicated megaproject, there would likely be a need for a lot of documentation, formal meetings, and, at times, sophisticated negotiations accompanying every change request. On a small simple endeavor, all of the principles that are discussed could remain at the verbal level with perhaps one summary e-mail exchanged between the parties. Consequently, this chapter targets projects somewhere in between these examples with the assumption that an experienced project manager should be able to fine-tune the degree of formality according to the complexity of her project.

Managing Scope and Stakeholder Expectations

Why Manage Expectations?

Customer satisfaction is not a matter of delivery but of how well delivery matches the client's expectations. Therefore, controlling customer's expectations is one of the key success factors especially once the project has left the planning stage behind and entered the execution phase.

There are several reasons behind the necessity to limit stakeholders' expectations. First of all, no matter how good one is at capturing and documenting project scope, no matter how many times the team has inspected and peer-reviewed the project documents, there will always be omissions, mistakes, and errors. Since nobody on a project team is perfect, customers should be psychologically ready to accept certain imperfections as they progress through the execution stage. A straightforward communication of this simple fact would limit stakeholders' expectations in a healthy way.

Second, people in general and project customers in particular are not always logical. To illustrate this point, consider a situation where a person who has a coupon from a chain restaurant for a significant discount learns upon arrival that the coupon is not valid. All his protests are put to rest by a polite service person who points to a line printed at the very bottom of the document in an almost invisible font that reads: Valid only at participating businesses. On one hand, especially from a legal standpoint, this situation is completely the customer's fault. After all, he was expected to read the entire document and arrive at the proper conclusion. On the other hand, did the restaurant chain do a particularly great job of managing the customer's expectations? Probably not since the vast majority of people have a short attention span when it comes to marketing media, and they tend to ignore the small font at the bottom of coupons. So remember, being logically or even legally correct is not the same as making the customer happy.

Another reason to limit stakeholders' expectations is that people tend to perceive things differently, especially if they are from different cultural backgrounds, different industries, or even different departments at the same company. As a result, a manager might think that she and her counterpart are discussing a scope item using fairly similar language only to discover much later that they had been talking about two completely different things.

One way of controlling customer or stakeholder expectations is to include a scope exclusions section to the project management documents to explicitly state the features that will be excluded from the project scope. This section of the document should be highly visible and created using the same font as the rest of the document.

One example of differing perceptions is the story about Lady Astor's (one of the first British female politicians) election campaign sometime around 1918–1919. According to the legend, Viscountess Astor (see Illustration 13.3) was canvassing for her first parliamentary seat in the port city of Plymouth. Because of her status and because she was new in town, she was allotted a senior naval officer as her escort. At one point during their improvised campaign, they ap-

Illustration 13.3 Lady Astor

proached one of the houses near the port and knocked on the door. A little girl appeared and the following exchange took place:

> LADY ASTOR: Is your mother home?
>
> LITTLE GIRL: No, but she said if a lady comes with a sailor they are to use the upstairs room and leave ten bob.

On a more serious note, consider the following situation: a project involves the development of a customer relationship management (CRM) website for a resort-booking call center. The final details of the system are being discussed with the director of customer management, a young lady who is not very well versed in the intricacies of software development. At one point, she is asked about the desired system availability, or uptime. The following exchange takes place:

> DIRECTOR: Oh, this is a very important system, so I expect the highest availability possible. It should be available 100 percent of the time.
>
> CONSULTANT: Well, 100 percent availability is basically impossible; even the most complicated systems have to be maintained and upgraded once in a while.
>
> DIRECTOR: So, what is possible?
>
> CONSULTANT: Theoretically, you can have 87 percent, 95 percent, or 99.9 percent uptime . . . ."
>
> DIRECTOR: We only want the best! I shall choose 99.9 percent.
>
> CONSULTANT: OK, but you do realize we will need $20 million to $25 million for that? By the way, why would you need that level of uptime? To put it in perspective, 99.9 percent implies that the system will be off for less than nine hours a year.
>
> DIRECTOR: Oh, I get it now. You misunderstood me. What I wanted is for the system to be up between 9:00 a.m. and 5:00 p.m. on weekdays. We don't care what happens to it outside of these times.

What happened in this conversation? For the consultant, the best possible availability of the system meant 99.9 percent of uptime and multimillion-dollar expenses associated with it. Whereas her best possible availability implied that the system be available only during working hours Monday through Friday. Obviously, the perceptions were quite different and had the consultant not pushed for clarification, they could have encountered some serious issues later in the project.

It is also important to keep in mind that technical team members often have their own expectations. Sometimes these expectations tend to leave the realm of reality and practicality and venture into the world of uninhibited fantasy and imagination. A manager's brain should go into high alert mode as soon as a sentence starting with the words, "I know this is crazy, but wouldn't it be cool if we did this . . . ." is uttered any time during the execution stage of a project. While absolutely desirable and sought after during the scoping and design stages of a project (during brainstorming exercises, for example), the same attitude during an execution stage could be a sign of the dreaded phenomenon known as *gold plating*. This happens when a technical team member independently decides to further enhance the product, thinking that it would please the user although the user has never asked for such improvements and probably has no use for it.

What happens if a project manager decides at some point in time that since the scope has been documented, reviewed, and baselined, the need for active stakeholder management is diminished? Figure 13.1 illustrates a possible scenario. At some point in the project, call it point X, the line of communications between the project team and the customers is broken or severely weakened. The customers might think that they have provided all of the relevant information, and the project team might decide that they would be distracted needlessly from their active duties if they spent more time talking to the customers. What happens from that moment on is that an expectations gap starts to appear on the project, a gap between what the customers want and what the project team will deliver. This divergence can occur for a number of reasons, including change in customer preferences, technical abilities of the project team, or imperfections in the original scope documentation, to name a few.

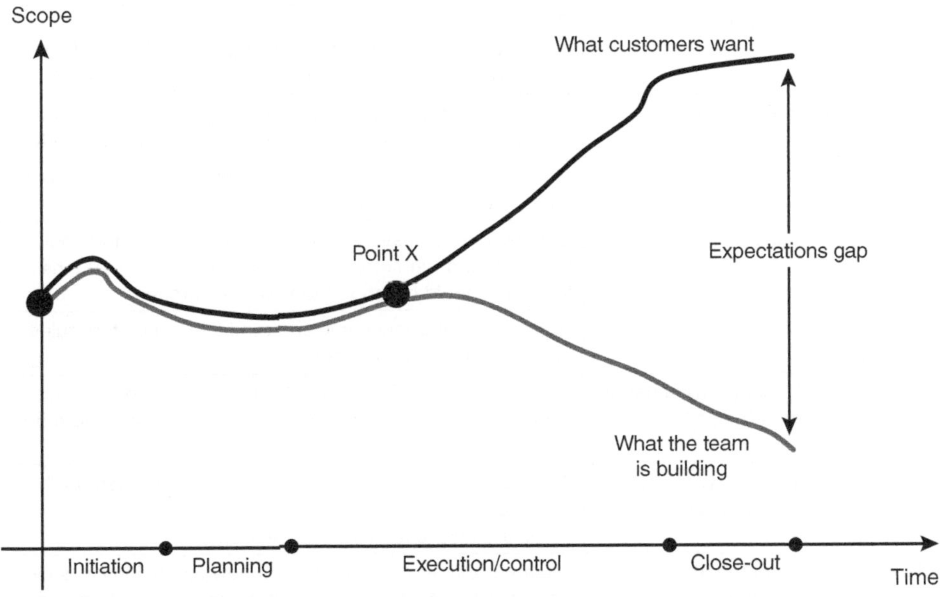

Figure 13.1 The expectations gap

The end result of this process is almost always very sad and disheartening—customers show up at the end of the project, inspect the results and find a lot of mistakes, deficiencies and discrepancies between the final product and their own expectations, either real or illusory.

How Much Do Things Change and Why?

Why do scope changes happen on projects? Despite the project manager's dislike of unexpected alterations, in many cases they do have a rightful basis. Table 13.2 lists some of the reasons why changes can happen on projects along with some relevant examples.

The primary focus of this section is the compounded effect of scope creep on the overall scope of a project. Uncontrolled changes can lead to a scope explosion on the project, much like a miniscule interest rate compounded with necessary frequency can drastically impact the size of one's debt.

Research studies indicate that an average rate of scope change on projects is around two percent per month. This doesn't sound like much but a simple calculation will yield a staggering 27 percent growth in the project scope over the

Table 13.2 Why changes happen

Type of change	Explanation/example
Large scope and complexity of the product	Chances that some scope items could be overlooked increase drastically when one compares building a family house with the construction of a modern port terminal.
Poorly or loosely defined requirements	Not enough time was allotted for proper scope definition, or the requirements specialists were not trained properly.
Changes in business objectives and plans	R&D budgets were cut, or the weight of the company portfolio shifted to other priorities.
Technology changes	Competitors released a new product with new and cool features, and the company management feels that these features should be added to their own product.
Changes in laws, policies, directives	A government agency implemented new regulatory rules in the middle of the project.
Customers and users who change their minds about things	The customer realizes that a house with a pool, a tennis court, and a four-car garage will look more imposing than a house without all these features.
Customers and users who learn neat ways of doing things	A customer reads a trade magazine and discovers that engineered stone countertops are more attractive and durable than the laminate countertops.
Technical team members independently decide to improve the product	A team member learned about a new technology or saw an interesting feature in the competitor's product and unilaterally decided to tinker with the scope.

course of one year. To put this number in perspective, if the initial project budget was $1 million with a scope change rate of two percent, the budget would balloon to at least $1,270,000 by the end of the year. The words *at least* are added because late changes in the project cost proportionally more than if the same scope items were to be implemented at the beginning of the venture.

A simple implementation of a change control process will decrease the monthly growth rate to 0.5 percent, which in turn leads to approximately six percent annual increase in scope, instead of 27 percent growth. Table 13.3 demonstrates various scenarios of monthly scope change rates and annual increases in the scope of the project.

Interestingly enough, some project managers incorporate average scope growth rates into their estimates. For example, if the expected project duration is two years, the average expected scope creep is 2 percent per month, and the initial project budget is $500,000, the the project manager will add 61 percent to the original project scope in order to come up with the overall budget, resources, and duration estimates.

On a more strategic level, it could be a valuable exercise for many organizations to actually capture certain statistics with respect to the scope changes. This data might include:

- Total number of change requests received per project
- Number of change requests broken down by category (approved, rejected, deferred) per project
- Number of change requests by source per project
- Costs of assessment for each change request (including time, effort, and budget)
- Costs of implementation for each change request (including time, effort, and budget)

Analysis of such data could provide project managers with an invaluable source of information when planning and estimating future organizational projects.

Are All Changes Necessarily Bad?

As was mentioned earlier, it is a natural instinct of any project manager to dislike last-minute scope changes. Once a manager has spent copious amounts of

Table 13.3 Impact of scope creep

Scenario	1	2	3	4	5	6	7	8
Monthly scope growth rate	1%	2%	5%	7%	1%	2%	5%	7%
Project duration (months)	12	12	12	12	24	24	24	24
Final scope increases by	6%	27%	80%	125%	27%	61%	223%	407%

time on scoping, scheduling, budgeting, and all other related project management tasks, she wants to take a deep breath, lean back in her chair, and relax a bit while the well-oiled project machine chugs along, destined to deliver great results. However, is all change in scope on a project inherently bad?

Managers likely are familiar with examples of when scope creep has devastated projects, causing them to be late and over budget or to be graceless monstrosities that nobody wanted. Having said that, are there any good changes that improve the final outcome? Discovery of a major flaw in the original design, new risks that were foreseen, change in the market conditions—shouldn't managers try to address these changes as soon as possible? The key question for project managers and the rest of the stakeholders including customers and users is purely economical:

> Will the value of implementing the proposed change (minus all of its negative impacts) be greater or less than the cost of not carrying it out?

For example, imagine that you are on a multiday hiking trip. You are not familiar with the area and your friends provided you with a map of the region, warning you that it was fairly outdated. On the second day of your trip you arrive at the bridge across the mountain river. You discover that the bridge is in very poor condition and obviously has not been repaired in the last 20 years. You and your hiking buddies are carrying some heavy equipment, and there is a chance that the bridge will not support your weight. If the bridge failed to support your weight, you would plunge from a height of 200 feet onto a cluster of giant boulders. However, according to the map, there is another bridge 10 miles north of this first one. If your party chooses to change their itinerary and cross the river via the other bridge, the length of your journey will increase by 20 miles (10 miles in each direction). Would you accept the modification in plans and go looking for the other bridge or would you reject the change and proceed across the fragile one? Most people would choose the first option because the value of protecting one's life is definitely higher than the 20-mile hike plus any other inconveniencies associated with it.

Consider an alternate scenario. The first bridge across the river is still in bad condition, but it crosses a very calm shallow creek. The distance between the bridge and the water surface is a couple of feet. Consequently, the worst-case scenario for you and your friends is that you would be forced to take a cold bath. What would an average person do in this case? The majority of people would prefer to cross the first bridge because the value of keeping dry is less than the cost of an additional twenty-mile hike.

How Do You Manage Project Scope?

It should be fairly evident by now that little enhancements, if left unattended, can wreak major chaos on any given project. Having said that, announcing to all the stakeholders after completion of the scope definition phase that the project requirements are henceforth frozen is imprudent and impractical. As was mentioned earlier, not all of the changes are inherently bad. A much better approach would be to:

- Baseline the scope definition documentation when the manager and stakeholders think that the document is good enough
- Communicate to the stakeholders in general and to customers in particular that changes will be subject to the project management pentagon laws (i.e., to add or remove features usually will mean that project budget, duration, number of resources, and quality will change)
- Explain that the cost of implementing scope changes tends to be positively correlated with how late in the project they were submitted—implementation of a technical change right after the end of the planning stage versus implementation of the exact same request one week before project close out will differ drastically in the cost and the effort required
- Begin the execution stage of the project and manage the inevitable changes by trying to minimize their effect on the project

The proper execution of the last point can be facilitated by using a proper change control process. When implementing scope change control, try to avoid complicated procedures. Scope management should be as simple and efficient as possible. Keep in mind that if the process is too complicated and cumbersome, the stakeholders will almost always find some creative ways to circumvent it. Communicating with and applying political pressure to the project technical team, thus removing the project manager from the equation completely, might accomplish this.

Figure 13.2 demonstrates a typical change control methodology. Once the request for a change has been made, it must be reviewed by the project team to assess all of the potential impacts. All the pros and cons of the new modification must then be presented to the stakeholders with respect to budget, timeline, possible risks, impact on quality, among others, so that a go or no go decision can be made. In the case of a go decision, all relevant project documents should be updated.

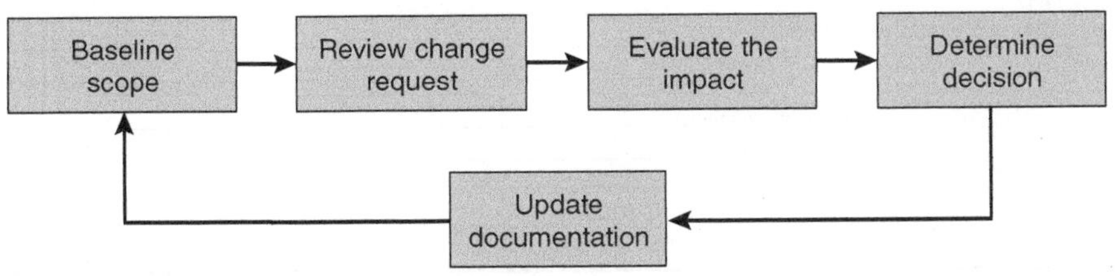

Figure 13.2 The change control process

What Does a Good Change Request Look Like?

A change request template similar to the one shown in Figure 13.3 is recommended. This template can become a great tool because the top part of the document, called section *A*, is the actual request to alter the scope of the project. An interesting aspect is that the customer fills out section A to the best of his abili-

Change Request Number

Section A–To be filled out by the requestor

Requestor: ____________ Phone: ____________ Email: ____________

Date of request: ____________

Type of change? Problem ____________ Enhancement ____________

Recommended priority? High ____________ Medium ____________ Low ____________

Description of the proposed change:

Reason for change:

Section B–To be filled out by the project technical team

Impact on	Budget	Duration	Extra resources	Other impacts
Technical area 1				
Technical area 2				
Technical area 3				
Technical area 4				
Technical area 5				
Technical area 6				
Technical area 7				
Technical area 8				

Section C–To be filled out by the customer and the project manager (or CCB)

Approved? ____________ Explanation: ____________

Rejected? ____________

Deferred? ____________

Additional comments: ____________

Assigned priority (if approved) High ____________ Medium ____________ Low ____________

Figure 13.3 Change request template

ties. This part could be referred to as a first filtration mechanism on the path of scope creep. In using this template, a typical conversation between the project manager (PM) and the change request petitioner (CRP) might go something like this:

> CRP: I have been talking to Bob in marketing, and he told me that it would be really cool to add (insert a low-priority but cumbersome scope item here).
>
> PM: That's great. I will send you a change request template.
>
> CRP: Why?
>
> PM: Well, since you are the requestor, it is logical to assume that you are the one who knows the most about the details of scope and the value this feature will add to the final product.
>
> CRP: And?
>
> PM: Don't worry, you need only provide some basic information, describe the change in as much detail as possible, and provide the reasons for this modification. It shouldn't take more than thirty minutes.
>
> CRP: OK, I will give it a try.
>
> PM: If you encounter any problems with the document, give me a shout. I will gladly help you out.

At least 20 to 30 percent of the time, the change request petitioner was never heard from again. Why? The total utility of not filling out this document was far greater than the utility she was expecting to derive from the implementation of this change. Or, to put this into more colloquial terms, the scope change was not even worth 30 minutes of her time.

What Is the Impact of the Change?

Assuming a change is indeed worth the 30-minute effort, the next step is to assemble either the entire project team or at least all of the technical team leads from different areas. Their job is to assess the combined impact of such a request on key dimensions of any project: scope, time, budget, duration, and quality. The questions that should be asked by the project team are presented in Table 13.4.

In addition, the various risks that could potentially emerge as a result of implementing the change request should be identified and assessed. It is also recommended that the team assess the value added to the project by the modification requested. In general, the team should employ the same approaches that were used for generating the original scope. These include:

- Why are we doing this?
- What happens if we don't do this change request?
- Who is the client?

Table 13.4 Assessing the impact of change

Type of questions	Specific questions
What is the technical impact?	• Are there any conflicts with other scope items?
	• Is there an impact on blueprints, bills of materials, technical drawings, design documents?
	• What other documents will have to be updated?
What is the impact on timeline and budget?	• What technical work must be done by engineers, construction crews, developers, or architects?
	• What management work must be done (project manager's time)?
	• What documentation must be updated?
	• What meetings need to be conducted (everyone involved)?
	• How will the change affect the sequence, dependencies, effort, and duration of all the tasks in the project plan?
	• What is the impact on budget?
Other impacts	• Is the requested change feasible with all known constraints and staff skills?
	• Will the change affect any indirect areas like marketing, public relations, customer support, or training?
	• What is the impact of the change on all other areas of project management such as quality and communications?

- What problem are we trying to solve?
- If we don't know this, then who does?
- Who else could be impacted by this feature?
- How much money are we ready to spend?
- How much time do we have?

As a result of this exercise, all segments in section B should be filled out, and the merit of the change request should either be discussed between the project manager and the customer or be analyzed by the change control board (CCB). Based on professional experience, out of the remaining 60 to 70 percent of customers who filled the request form, approximately 50 to 60 percent decided not to go ahead with the modification requested because the combination of negative impacts outweighed the value that such a change would have brought to the project.

A very prominent cost of the change request that frequently gets ignored is that the mere evaluation of the proposed modification takes time and costs a lot of money whether or not the customer or the CCB accepts or rejects the request. This implies that by simply asking the project team to analyze the request, there will be a resulting increase in effort and money, and it will probably extend the duration of the project.

Once more simple financial modeling can be used to assess the impact of request analysis:

- Task 1—Project manager's time to process the request: 4½ hours
- If necessary—time to help the customer fill out section *A* of the document: ½ hour
- Task 2—Initial team assessment requiring a meeting to introduce the request to a team of 30 people: 2 hours
- Task 3—Additional meeting of five experts to further analyze the modification: 4 hours
- Task 4—Project management time to arrange and facilitate these meetings: 10 hours
- Task 5—Project management time to document it all: 8 hours
- Task 6—Five-member CCB meeting to approve or reject the change: 1 hour

While it is impossible to calculate the additional time these activities will add to the overall project schedule, it is fairly easy to assess the effort required and extrapolate it to the additional fiscal costs:

- Task 1: 5 hours × 1 person = 5 man-hours
- Task 2: 2 hours × 30 persons = 60 man-hours
- Task 3: 4 hours × 5 persons = 20 man-hours
- Task 4: 10 hours × 1 person = 10 man-hours
- Task 5: 5 hours × 1 person = 5 man-hours
- Task 6: 1 hour × 5 persons = 5 man-hours

Thus, the total effort expended on this not extremely complicated change request is 105 man-hours. If the blended rate is $150 per man-hour, the total cost would be $15,750. Using the language of economists, $15,750 represents a *sunk cost*. The company incurs them regardless of whether the change request is approved or rejected.

Documentation

A number of issues can arise on projects if the document management process is not handled correctly:

- Changes get implemented, but the documentation is not updated
- Several versions of the same document are being used by the project team and the stakeholders
- Several people have access to the same document and can add or delete information without other people's knowledge
- Project stakeholders are not aware of or do not have access to the project document repository

There are several recommendations regarding document management on projects that should be considered. Implement and maintain version control of the documentation. For example, before the document has been signed-off (e.g., baselined, approved), assign version numbers in the following format: 0.N (i.e., 0.1, 0.2, 0.3, and so on). Once the document has been signed-off or approved, switch the numbering system to 1.N, (i.e., 1.0, 1.1, 1.2, and so on). In both cases, the version number increases by 0.1 every time the document owner makes a change. This helps to avoid confusion with various versions of the same document existing in various forms such as attachments to old e-mails, documents saved on peoples' computers, or hard copies lying around on employees' desks. This numbering system should be clearly communicated to all project team members and stakeholders so that each party can verify which version is being used during interactions with one another.

Experience shows that having two or more people with read/write access to the project document is a recipe for a disaster. A one author-one document relationship should be maintained throughout a project. In addition, the project manager shouldn't assume that all stakeholders regularly check the project documentation folder on the shared drive and are aware of all the changes and updates made to documents. Therefore, it would be a good idea to send a broadcast e-mail to all relevant parties every time any key project documents get updated. For example:

> Please note that the project plan document for the Deltaport Terminal project has been updated. Project budget information in Table 3.8 now reads, "the project budget for the Deltaport Terminal project shall be $125 million +/− $20 million." The latest version of the project plan document is now version 1.15.

Summary

Once the project moves into the execution phase, scope and customer expectations management become one of the key responsibilities of the project manager.

Management of customer expectations is needed because people are not always logical and might have differing perceptions. Control over team members should be maintained to avoid potential gold plating.

There are several reasons why changes might arise on projects. These could include a poorly defined scope, shifts in strategic business objectives and technology, and changes in regulatory laws. Furthermore, customers sometimes request modifications because they change their minds about the project scope or because they discover new, previously unknown features.

Uncontrolled changes, even if imperceptible at first, can quickly snowball into serious complications (e.g., project scope can balloon by 50 percent, 100 percent, and even 400 percent).

Project managers working at companies that tend to suffer from chronic scope increases are strongly advised to add future scope creep to their estimates. Capturing historical data regarding scope changes on previous projects is therefore highly recommended.

Not all scope changes are inherently bad. Answering the following question should assess every request for modification or addition to the project scope: will the value of implementing the proposed change (minus all of its negative impacts) be greater or less than the cost of not carrying it out?

Follow a process to deal with changes. Depending on the complexity and size of projects, the formality of the process will vary, but analyzing the change and assessing its impacts on all aspects of the project is essential.

Keep in mind that such analysis could be quite costly especially late in the project. Assessments of change requests almost invariably add time and financial cost to the project regardless of whether the requests are approved or rejected at the end of the day.

Finally, make sure that all the contents and versions of relevant documentation are kept up to date, and communicate those changes to all relevant stakeholders.

14

Why Invest Time and Effort in the Lessons-Learned Document?

Historical Perspective

The Case of Backfiring Reparations

The Franco-Prussian War that took place between the July 19, 1870, and May 10, 1871, was a conflict that involved some 900,000 French and 1.2 million German soldiers. The conflict was the result of a culmination of years of tension between the two nations brought about by Prussian statesman Prince Bismarck's determination to unify Germany under Prussian control, and the French emperor's desire to regain the prestige lost at the hands of Prussia in the Austro-Prussian War of 1866 and to maintain his dominance in Europe. Events culminated soon after the deposition of Isabella II in 1868 when Prince Leopold of Hohenzollern-Sigmaringen, nephew of King Wilhelm I of Prussia, was nominated for the vacant Spanish throne. The government of French Emperor Napoleon III viewed the idea of having German Hohenzollern monarchies on two of its borders as a threat and demanded that Wilhelm order Leopold to withdraw his candidacy. The King agreed to do so and Hohenzollern's nomination was retracted.

Not yet satisfied, French Foreign Minister Gramont instructed Ambassador Count Benedetti to meet with Wilhelm and demand further commitments, especially a guarantee by the Prussian king that no member of any branch of his Hohenzollern family would ever be a candidate for the Spanish throne. The King refused these demands, and the results of this meeting were recorded for release to the media, which became known as the Ems Dispatch. It is believed that Prince Bismarck purposely edited the telegram in a manner designed to give the French the impression that King Wilhelm had insulted Count Benedetti and that the Count had insulted the King; all this was done to inflame public opinion on both sides. Bismarck's plan worked. France mobilized and on July 19, declared war, but only on Prussia. The other German states, however, quickly joined Prussia's side. In short, after a five-month campaign, the Prussian army led by *Generalfeldmarschall* Helmuth von Moltke defeated French armies in a series of battles fought across northern France (see Illustration 14.1). After a lengthy siege, Paris finally fell on January 28, 1871, and the final peace treaty—the Treaty of Frankfurt—was signed on May 10, 1871. The siege also marked the birth of anti-aircraft artillery developed by the Germans to shoot down hot air balloons being used as couriers by the French.

Here is where the things got interesting. Prussians, who were in a state of euphoria at the time over the victory and a proclamation of a unified German empire, imposed a set of absolutely draconian demands on the French in the Treaty of Frankfurt:

- France had to give up the provinces of Alsace, Lorraine, and many parts of Vosges to the Germans
- France was responsible for paying a reparation of $5 billion francs
- Additional parts of France were to be occupied by the Prussians until the full payment had been received

Illustration 14.1 Battle of Mars-La-Tour

Needless to say, such conditions angered the French who remained angry for the next 40 years as they waited patiently to pay back their neighbors for the humiliation endured in 1871. (Before going forward, stop and think about what lessons the French should have learned from the Treaty of Frankfurt.)

The return of the Alsace-Lorraine territory became an obsession with the French according to some historians who insist that this was one of the main catalysts for France's involvement in World War I. This time the French, with the rest of their allies, emerged victorious and began to look forward to retributions on the hated Prussians. Here is a partial list of the penalties imposed on Germany by the Treaty of Versailles signed in 1919:

- Reparations of 226 billion reichsmarks in gold (around £11.3 billion)
- Severely limited army (no more than 100,000 troops) and navy (15,000 men, 6 battleships)
- Complete ban on manufacture, import, and export of weapons including armed aircraft, tanks and armored cars
- And, of course, the return of the Alsace-Lorraine region to France

How did the population of Germany feel around 1919? Now it was their turn to hold a grudge against the despised enemy. Public opinion became so intense and militant that support grew for the German revanchist movement, which demanded the return of not only Alsace-Lorraine, but the Polish Corridor and Bohemia, Moravia and Silesia. Approximately thirteen years after the signing of the Treaty of Versailles, guess who played on these public sentiments and on the wounded pride of the Germans in order to win the parliamentary elections? His name was Adolf Hitler.

As with previous chapters, there is a point to be made in conveying the stories of these two treaties. Arguably, many of the problems described could have been avoided had the French learned a valuable lesson in 1871: no matter how resolute the victory, do not humiliate the losing side to the point where the only thing remaining on their minds is payback.

This chapter is dedicated to analyzing the lessons learned from past projects in order to avoid repeating the same mistakes on new ventures.

What Is *Lessons Learned*?

Lessons learned can be defined as a document that contains a comparison of original estimates-versus-actual figures for key project constraints that include: scope, budget, time, the causes of performance variances, any corrective actions that were undertaken and their reasons, outcomes of the corrective actions, unexpected risks that occurred in the course of the project, and any mistakes that were made.

Why Are They Neglected?

Lessons-learned documents are frequently overlooked in the project management practice. Both executives and project managers, for their own reasons to be discussed later, ignore this step in the project process.

Company Reasons for Neglecting Lessons Learned

Once a project is completed, many senior managers are naturally eager to transfer the project manager and the rest of the project team to other projects in the organizational pipeline, and they don't give much thought to the lessons-learned process or its value. After all, there is always a shortage of good people and more ventures to be undertaken.

A frequent argument given by functional managers is that lessons-learned documents are a questionable investment of time and money. Why waste time on these documents since nobody reads them anyway? The other half of this argument is, "I don't see the tangible benefits of project postmortems."

Try to understand the logic behind such statements by analyzing the economic value involved. The costs of creating project post-mortem documentation are necessary as are the benefits one can expect to derive from them. The cost is fairly straightforward. It is determined by adding up all the man-hours spent on the document then multiplying them by the average hourly rate. If, for example, the project team consists of 20 people including the project manager, then the following effort and cost breakdown is:

- Meeting to obtain feedback—20 people × 1 hour = 20 man-hours
- Preparation of the document by the project manager—1 person × 5 hours = 5 man-hours
- Review of the document with the team—20 people × 0.5 hour = 10 man-hours
- Incorporation of the feedback by the project manager—1 person × 5 hours = 5 man-hours
- Total Effort = 40 man-hours
- Total Cost (@ $100/hour) = $4000

The straightforward economic cost of the post-mortem report is $4000. This figure does not include the postponement of other projects in order to complete the document. Basically, the logic behind the usual arguments is that the costs of preparing the lessons-learned documentation are obvious to functional management while benefits are not.

Project Team's Reasons for Neglecting Lessons Learned

One should consider the costs of writing the post-mortem document from the point of view of an average project manager. A good project manager does not have to be convinced to write a project charter or a project plan because the benefits of doing that are fairly straightforward and obvious. After all, who wants to be responsible for a project where the scope is not defined, budgets and schedules are not set, and the risks are unknown and undocumented?

The attitude towards the post-mortem documentation is somewhat different. When the project is completed (i.e., the product is released and all outstanding issues are fixed), the following events typically take place:

- The project manager and team members experience project fatigue. ("We've just spent two weekends in a row here, and we've worked until 11 p.m. on weekdays. The last thing we want to discuss is the lessons-learned document.")
- The project manager and team members are under pressure from senior management to move on to other projects.
- The project manager is convinced that no one will read the document once it is completed.

With respect to the last point, when a project manager is writing a project plan or project charter, she is primarily making her own life easier. Therefore in her opinion, she is justified in her resistance to the management's pressure to stop wasting time on unnecessary documents.

However when a project manager is writing lessons-learned documents, she realizes that she is actually trying to help other people without seeing any tangible benefits for herself. Logically, this makes her resistance to management's arguments somewhat weaker and less inspired.

Why Do Lessons Learned?

Organizational Benefits

While apparently less obvious to many functional managers, the organizational benefits of project postmortems are fairly straightforward as well. Project managers working on similar projects will typically run into similar obstacles. Once the first project team has identified certain problems and developed the solutions to address the issues, it is really counterproductive and quite costly for the organization to force other project teams to waste time analyzing and assessing the same difficulties time and time again on other projects. If taken seriously and done correctly, project postmortems can save organizations a lot of money.

Sharing lessons learned from past projects improves the risk management activities on all future endeavors. Project managers and their teams are human and sometimes make mistakes that jeopardize the overall success of their projects. Documenting these mistakes and sharing them with the rest of the project managers helps ensure that the same blunders are not repeated at the cost of project delay, budget overruns, and customer dissatisfaction.

Ineffective communication is cited routinely as one of the leading causes of project failure. Preparation and dissemination of the lessons-learned documentation has a positive effect on project communications. For example, if a certain preferred supplier has increased the lead time on orders placed at their organization from five weeks to 10 weeks, is this a valuable piece of information for all other project managers who would have to deal with the same company? Obviously, the answer is yes.

Personal Benefits for Project Managers

There are several hidden benefits for managers who make project postmortems a worthwhile investment of their personal time. But before the discussion can begin, picture a typical year of an average project manager.

A typical project manager handles five to 10 projects in any given year. One could argue that by the end of the year, which is also a time for performance reviews, the typical project manager has probably forgotten most of the specifics pertaining to the projects done in the first two quarters. Unfortunately, this can lead to nasty surprises for project managers during those performance reviews. For example, an actual dialogue between a corporate program manager (PM), who was a big believer in writing and saving all of his lessons-learned documents, and his manager during an annual performance review is as follows:

> MANAGER: I am giving you a below-average rating because two of the projects you were assigned to were late and over budget.
>
> PM: Well, I recently looked at the lessons-learned documents from these projects, and they show that Project ABC budget was revised due to 10 change requests submitted close to the end of the execution stage. These changes inflated the project budget from $200,000 to $275,000.
>
> MANAGER: And what about Project XYZ? It was late, as far as I can remember.
>
> PM: Yes, it was. But I had three developers taken off my team and assigned to higher-priority projects. Again, deadlines were revised and approved by management and stakeholders.

Thus, lessons learned is a great tool that can be used to protect project managers from arbitrary judgments of their bosses. In addition, the lessons learned, or project post-mortem document, can be used in all potential future negotiations on similar projects. For example, if a $100,000 budget and six months duration was once imposed on a project team and the actual cost of the project was $150,000 and a duration was close to 12 months, the project manager can use this historical data as a serious argument in negotiations with customers and management. The line of reasoning might sound something like the following:

> Look, project *A* was completed several months ago, and although there were no major issues or risks encountered, it took 12 months to complete all the

deliverables. Do we really want to repeat the same mistake and impose an unattainable deadline only to revisit this issue at a later time?

How Do You Write Lessons Learned?

What kind of information should be included in the project postmortems? After all, there is a lot of project data that could be mentioned in the document, but one must remember that long documents tend to be ignored by readers. While the information mentioned in lessons learned could vary from industry to industry and from company to company, the guiding principles always remain the same.

When working on the document, imagine a situation where you have been invited for coffee by a best friend and project management colleague who is working for the same organization. He has just been assigned to a project that is very similar in nature to the one you have recently completed, and he wants to gain insights relevant to his next venture. To paraphrase David Letterman, what are the top 10 things your friend should be aware of when working on project *A*? What should he know about the potential risks, typical constraints, and behavior of certain team members, customers and functional managers?

This is precisely the approach project managers should take when working on the project postmortems; what kind of advice can be passed on to the next person in charge of a similar project?

How to Gather Information

There are several ways of gathering materials for the lessons-learned documents. The most straightforward method is to ask team members to think about and record what goes well and what doesn't go so well ahead of time. If possible, have a meeting to gather all the feedback or, alternatively, have people e-mail their lists to the manager. In addition, project customers, sponsors, and other key senior people are excellent sources for gathering this type of information, especially if a project manager wants to capture the external perceptions about the project's successes and shortcomings.

Meeting minutes from the project, assuming they were created and archived by the project manager, are a great source of data for the lessons-learned documents. It can be a fascinating experience to click onto all the files containing sequenced meeting minutes, and see what kind of problems emerged during the project course, their impacts on the scope, schedule, and budget, and how they were addressed. The most important issues and their solutions should also be incorporated into the lessons-learned documentation.

One of the major challenges of gathering information for the lessons-learned documents is the potential resentment of project team members and other stakeholders who might perceive the process as a witch hunt to single out and discipline the people responsible for the project slip-ups. Therefore, it is absolutely essential to ensure that an atmosphere of trust is established from the very beginning of the postmortem process and to verify that the document in question is viewed by all as a compilation of opportunities for improvement rather than reasons for dismissing employees.

It is worthwhile to mention that the protection demonstrated in the project manager performance review example discussed earlier is relevant to other teams as well. In other words, when the detailed memories of a project fade, and when unjustified accusations directed toward team members either from the senior management or from customers emerge, the lessons-learned document can be a handy tool. It is also worthwhile to mention that the forecasted-versus-actual data document can be used as a tool in the negotiations on future projects' constraints especially against imposed deadlines and budgets, as stated previously.

What Information Should Be Included?

The lessons-learned document can be divided roughly into two sections. The first section (see Table 14.1) should contain the historical information regarding project goals, change requests, and estimated-versus-actual information on scope, budget, and time line.

The project scope/goals section should contain a high-level description of the original project scope that can be derived from the project charter and a listing of all change requests. For example, the original scope statement might have read:

> To build a three-bedroom, two-bathroom Victorian-style family home by June 30, 2009.

Table 14.1 Historical project information

Section	Information to include
Project scope/goals	Describe problem/opportunity (see project charter) and outcome achieved. Include the list of all change requests.
Project timeline	Compare the original project time line to the actual one. If there is a significant variance, explain what caused it (e.g., underestimation, change requests, changes in priorities).
Project budget	Compare the original project budget to the actual one. If there is a significant variance, explain what caused it (e.g., underestimation, change requests, changes in priorities).
Documentation and other deliverables	List all of the relevant project documentation, and indicate where the documents are filed.

Table 14.2 Discussion of project results

Section	Information to include
Lessons learned	• What worked well—or didn't work well—either for this project or for the project team? • What needs to be done over again or differently? • What surprises did the team have to deal with? • What project circumstances were not anticipated (e.g., project management processes, technical and design processes, resource management, team approach and focus, escalation)?

The list of change requests might have included the following records:

1. Add a two-car garage to the project scope.
2. Add landscaping to the project scope.
3. Add fence around the property to the project scope.
4. Add a 50 × 20 foot swimming pool to the project scope.

Project time line and project budget sections should mention the original estimates, the actual figures, and if there is a considerable discrepancy between the two numbers, an adequate explanation should be provided. Some of the possible explanations for significant variances could include optimistic estimates, imposed deadlines, scope creep, or change requests. For example, the project time line section might state:

> Estimated Duration—8 months; Actual Duration—11.5 months. An additional 3.5 months was required to assess, design, and implement the four change requests submitted by the client (see the project scope/goals section discussed earlier).

Finally, a list of all the relevant project documentation should be provided along with the location of the files. The second part of the lessons-learned document should be dedicated to a discussion of things that went well and, more especially, to the things that didn't go so well on the project; include advice for future generations of project managers on how to address these issues (see Table 14.2).

Summary

Lessons learned is a document that compares original estimates to actual figures for the key project constraints including scope, budget, and time. This document also discusses the causes of performance variances, describes any corrective actions that were undertaken, provides reasons and outcomes of the corrective actions, lists the unexpected risks that occurred in the course of the project, and outlines any mistakes that were made.

Some senior managers and individual project managers tend to ignore the creation and dissemination of the lessons-learned document. Senior management is often eager to see the resources, including the project manager, transferred to other projects, whereas project managers often do not recognize enough benefits from these documents to justify clashes with their bosses in order to pass their knowledge and wisdom on to other people at the company.

The benefits of lessons learned are very significant, however, albeit not highly visible at first glance. The key idea is that once the first project team had encountered certain problems, issues, risks, or any other unusual circumstances and had managed to resolve those predicaments, there is now no reason why the rest of the project teams working on similar projects should be put through the same exercise. In other words, the development and dissemination of lessons-learned documents in terms of time, effort, and expense are far more cost effective.

On the project manager side, the information captured in the lessons-learned documents can have a dual effect. First, it can protect the project manager from arbitrary judgments based on the faint memories of the projects in question. Also, the historical data in this documentation can be used in difficult negotiations for future projects and protect the team from imposed estimates.

There are several sources that can be used to obtain the information necessary for the lessons-learned documents. They include:

- Special meetings with the project team members
- Discussions with project customers, sponsors, and other key senior people
- Meeting minutes

When working on the document, it very important to create an atmosphere of trust within a project team and to explain to colleagues that lessons learned is a knowledge transfer tool rather that a compilation of grounds for disciplining company employees. At a minimum, the following information should be included in the document:

- Project scope/goals
- Project time line—estimated versus actual
- Project budget—estimated versus actual

Finally, the document should include a discussion of problems, issues, and risks and their potential solutions to be shared with and used by the project managers of upcoming projects.

15

How Do You Select the Best Projects?

Historical Perspective

The Steppe Winds and the Virgin Lands

In 1953, after the death of dictator Joseph Stalin, the new Soviet leader, Nikita Khrushchev (see Illustration 15.1), became aware of the serious issues in the country's agricultural sector. Because of the prolonged heavy investments in industrial and military growth coupled with a devastating war, the production of wheat, meat, and dairy in the Soviet Union had plummeted to historic levels. Russia, a traditional exporter of grain, was forced to buy it abroad.

Khrushchev, always an energetic and vigorous party leader, came up with what appeared to be a very creative solution to the grain shortage problem. He proposed to open up millions of acres of virgin land in the steppes of Kazakhstan north and east of the Aral Sea.

The overall aim of the Virgin Lands Project was to produce 20 million tons of grain by 1956. The project began with an army of 300,000 volunteers travelling by special trains to northern Kazakhstan and southern Siberia to erect hundreds of tent cities. Another group of several hundred thousand students, soldiers, and agricultural professionals joined them on a temporary basis until the first year's harvest. In addition, 50,000 tractors and more than 6,000 trucks were moved to the area to assist the project team in preparing and ploughing the vast areas of land. As a result of these preparations in the first year of the program, 190,000 km^2 were ploughed; in 1955, an extra 140,000 km^2 were ploughed.

Illustration 15.1 Nikita Khrushchev

The year 1956 was one of great success for the virgin lands; the original target of 20 million tons of wheat was more than tripled. Mr. Khrushchev and the rest of the country rejoiced. The creative idea of investing billions of rubles into the steppes of Kazakhstan looked like a stroke of genius. Thick books were written and large canvases were painted describing the heroic efforts of the people. The project was a great success.

Unfortunately, around the end of 1956, major problems started to emerge amid all of the celebrations and festivities. First, it was discovered that the government was not prepared for a harvest of such proportions. The lack of storage barns and harvesting equipment lead to immense losses and the transportation ministry had not reserved enough freight trains to move all of the grain to major cities. As a result of this waste, the Soviet Union was forced to buy 20 million tons of grain from Canada to meet its needs and to avoid famine. This was a humbling and humiliating experience for a country whose leadership boasted of soon outpacing U.S. agricultural production.

The state also discovered that the cost of Kazakh wheat was three times that of grain grown in the Ukraine due to additional investments, increased demand for fertilizers, and the need to support several hundred thousand workers in the middle of nowhere. In addition, there was only a 40 percent chance of favorable weather conditions in Kazakhstan in any given year. This was well known to meteorologists and Khrushchev's economic advisers, but they conveniently chose to ignore it.

Finally, one very horrendous effect of this endeavour was that, in 1954, the pioneers made the mistake of digging into a saline layer while ploughing the thin fertile surfaces of the steppes. As a result, due to a lack of any measures to prevent erosion, much of that soil was simply blown away by 95-mile-an-hour winds, which covered many nearby towns with dirt and dust to a depth of up to six feet.

An on-the-spot lessons-learned exercise for this case study would show that if there was a project manager of the Virgin Lands endeavor, what mistakes and miscalculations did he make? The goal of the project in question, as worded by the Soviet Gosplan (State Planning Committee), was to "harvest 20 million tons of grain by ploughing at least 43 million hectares of virgin lands in several areas of the country including Kazakhstan." According to this definition, the manager (real or imaginary) of the project did not commit any major mistakes; indeed, even though only 33 million hectares were ploughed, and more than 60 million tons of wheat were harvested. Who can blame the project manager who had been told in no uncertain terms, "take these resources, move them to Kazakh steppes, plough a lot of land, and harvest even more grain"?

Subsequent transportation was the responsibility of other government bodies, namely the Ministry of Transportation. Calculation of economic feasibility of such a venture was definitely not in the scope of the project manager's responsibilities, and even if he had known about the ecological impact of his project, he wouldn't have had enough authority to go against Nikita Khrushchev.

So, who is to blame for this fiasco? Who should have forecasted the high cost of the final product? Who should have initiated several other parallel projects including silo buildings and preparations of additional freight trains? Who should have studied the historical meteorological data and made proper conclusions? Who should have foreseen the ecological impact of the Virgin Land Project? Who should have assessed the overall value of the project as well as the balance of the auxiliary projects required for support and then calculated the strategic impacts? In the context of the Soviet Union, it was obviously the government—the executives of the country, if you will. The purpose of this case study, however, is not to lay blame on a specific group of people, but to ask a more interesting question:

> If these were not project management mistakes, what kind of mistakes were they?

The answer to this question lies in the area of portfolio management—the art and science of assessment, selection, and management of the projects in order to maximize their benefit to the organization or, in this case, the country.

The Story of Two Project Requests

To bring the portfolio management concept closer to home, consider the following account of an actual event: a project management consultant was working for a very large retail company and was approached by a representative of an accounting department. The following conversation took place between the accountant and the project manager (PM):

> ACCOUNTANT: We have discovered a problem with our accounting system. Because of the glitch in the software, a certain percentage of transactions was lost. These orphaned transactions have to be posted manually, which requires a lot of time and effort. According to our estimates, we lose approximately $60,000 annually on manual corrections. Can you help us with that?
>
> PM: Yes, we have been informed about this issue and have done some homework. It looks like a $50,000 project.
>
> ACCOUNTANT: Hmm . . . unfortunately, we have exhausted our budget for this year. I guess we will have to revisit this issue in the next quarter.

On the same day, the project manager was approached by a representative of the marketing department who also wanted to discuss a project idea.

> MARKETING REPRESENTATIVE: We need to update our website; we have a fairly long list of modifications to implement and need you to help us with that.
>
> PM: OK, no problem. So, what is it that you want to change?
>
> MARKETING REPRESENTATIVE: We need to change bullets on this page from small black ones to larger red ones. Also, the font size should increase from 9 to 11, and we need to modify this area so we can insert photos here . . . [she continued with a very long list of purely cosmetic requirements].
>
> PM: No problem. I think we can do it. If you don't mind me asking, who uses this website?
>
> MARKETING REPRESENTATIVE: It is a section of our company's intranet. It is targeted at our store sales associates. They use this website to learn about updates in HR policy, read company news, and so on.
>
> PM: So, are there any direct financial benefits you expect to realize from this project? I have to warn you, the total cost of all these improvements will be around $50,000.
>
> MARKETING REPRESENTATIVE: No benefits I can think of. We just have approximately $50,000 remaining in our budget and our director decided to improve this site.

What happened in these two conversations that took place a couple of hours apart? Two project requests generated by different departments of the same company were presented. The first project, which had a very positive return on investment, was rejected because the department in question did not have enough money in their budget. One does not need complicated financial formulas to understand that a deal involving a $50,000 investment that results in $60,000 annual savings is a very lucrative venture.

The second project was a purely cosmetic uplift to an internal website infrequently used by the most junior members of the corporation. Also, it was not expected to generate any additional financial (or any other) benefit whatsoever.

If one takes off the project manager's hat and puts on the CEO's hat, what do these two stories say about the health of the company's project mix? Obviously, the amount of money involved was negligible in comparison with the rest of the company's portfolio, but still, if a part of the vast machinery has malfunctioned, wasn't it a symptom of much bigger problems?

The explanations for this situation as well as for the failure of Virgin Lands Project lie in improper portfolio management—the art and science of selecting and managing the right projects for one's organization.

Some Statistics

Is improper or a complete lack of project portfolio management an issue in today's corporate world? Revisit some of the statistics from Chapter 1:

- Based on data released by the Bureau of Economic Analysis, the U.S. public and private sectors combined spend approximately $2.3 trillion on projects every year
- This number accounts for a quarter of U.S. GDP. When this figure is extrapolated to the global level, the result is a staggering $10 trillion worldwide being spent on projects
- Eighty-four percent of companies either do not conduct business cases for their projects or perform them on select key projects
- Eighty-nine percent of companies are flying blind with no metrics in place except for financial data
- Eighty-four percent of companies are unable to adjust and realign their budgets with their business needs
- End result? Close to $1 trillion in underperforming projects in the U.S. and $4 trillion worldwide

These numbers clearly demonstrate that modern businesses are not exactly what one would call methodical or systematic when it comes to proper assessment and selection of their project mixes.

What Executives Want

Senior executives obviously do not go to meetings to brag about the skilled group of project managers in their company. Their mission is to make more money or (in a nonprofit sector) to achieve their specific goals. Gone are the days, however, when senior executives' interests in their organizations' projects were limited to when will they be finished and what will they cost. Now, particularly in the commercial areas, they want to know if the mix of their projects will maximize continuing growth and return on investment for the firm, how these projects support strategic plans, and how they will affect the value of the company's shares.

Despite this change, the average senior executive lacks a clear understanding of the differences and relationships between project management and project portfolio management. Based on numerous interviews with executives, the following quote is a common complaint aimed at project management.

> We implemented a project management methodology at our organization several years ago. There have been some improvements such as our projects are better controlled, most of them are on time and on budget, and the quality has improved considerably. There is, however, something missing, something we hoped would be addressed by project management. A considerable percentage of the products we deliver to the marketplace turned out to be less successful than we expected. In addition, my people still complain that they are overworked, and project managers constantly demand more resources. We claim to be the market leader in innovation, but I have recently discovered that only five percent of our projects can be qualified as R&D ventures. What are we doing wrong?

Project Portfolio Management

This section begins with a fictional example that demonstrates a common behavior that exists in many organizations—an impromptu conversation between Bob, director of mobile devices and Michael, senior vice president of product development.

> MICHAEL: What's new in mobile phones?
>
> BOB: Nothing much on our front; we are preparing for the release of our notebook product with advanced word editing, spreadsheet, and e-mail capabilities. But I read in a press release that our competitor, Mokia, is introducing a new cell phone with a 15-megapixel camera and 1000 gigabyte storage for media files.
>
> MICHAEL: Oh my God! They have beaten us again! We can't let this happen. I want you to concentrate on the improved camera and storage capabilities. There is an industry exhibit in January, and I want us to showcase a product that would outperform their device. Get the design and engineering teams to work on it with you. This is a top priority from now on!

Table 15.1 Questions that had to be asked

Questions	Explanation
What is the opinion of the technical experts (engineers and marketing people)?	• Is it technologically possible to build a mobile phone that could outperform the device with a 15-megapixel camera and 1000-gigabyte storage? • Is there a market for such a device?
How important is this project to the goals of the company?	• How would this project fit into the existing project mix of the company?
How well is it aligned with company strategy?	• The company seems to be concentrating on office communications mobile devices involving word processors and spreadsheets. Would the shift into entertainment-type cell phones even be feasible for them?
How good is the project?	• What are the potential revenues of this venture? • What would this project cost? • Do they have enough in-house expertise with respect to entertainment-type mobile devices? • Are there any risks associated with commercialization of the product in question? • Can this project be finished on time for the exhibition? • Are there any other risks?
Where will the project's resources come from?	• Does the company have enough free resources to throw at this project?
What projects should be bumped?	• If the resources are not currently available, what projects should be cancelled or postponed in order to provide resources for this one?

How many times—regardless of industry—has a similar situation occurred in the business world? How many times have projects been initiated based on an on-the-spot decision by a superior?

So, what mistakes (if any) were made by Michael in this story? Table 15.1 lists some of the problems with his decision to concentrate on camera and storage capabilities for the new cell phone.

Project Portfolio Management Explained

Project portfolio management is defined as a methodology for analyzing, selecting, and collectively managing a group of current or proposed projects based on numerous key characteristics while honoring constraints imposed by management or external real-world factors.

The key three requirements that portfolio management professionals should impose on every candidate are:

- Each project as well as the portfolio of projects should maximize the value for the company
- The candidate project should preserve the desired balance in the portfolio mix
- The final portfolio of projects should be strategically aligned and should reflect the business's strategy

Each one of these criteria will be discussed in detail in subsequent chapters of the book. However, it would be worthwhile to explain, at least briefly, what hides behind each one of these somewhat nebulous descriptions.

The definition of *value* can vary from company to company and even from project to project, but it includes certain economic measures (e.g., return on investment, net present value, and payback), competitive advantage, market attractiveness, expected sales, probability of success, and so on.

The balance requirement ensures that the following situations are successfully avoided:

- Too many small projects and not enough breakthrough; too many visionary projects
- Too many short-term and not enough long-term strategic projects
- A disproportionate amount of resources devoted to a few business areas while other important areas are in need
- Poor risk management (all eggs in one basket)

Finally, the fit to the strategic goals requirement makes certain that company finances and other resources are not wasted on ventures outside of the organization's sphere of strategic interests. This particular topic of strategic blunders has been discussed in numerous strategic management textbooks: Harley Davidson's decision to create Harley Davidson perfumes; French pen maker Bic's idea to produce women's underwear, salty snack maker Frito Lay's plan to market a Frito Lay lemonade product, and Xerox's decision to move into the software business, to name a few.

Project Portfolio Management Process Overview

The project portfolio management process can be subdivided into two separate steps:

- Prioritization and selection of candidate projects for the portfolio
- Maintaining the pipeline: continuing, delaying, or terminating approved projects

The first phase happens before project initiation. It starts with the preparation of the business case and a subsequent evaluation of the projects' values, benefits, and risks that might modify the benefits (see Figure 15.1). Then, the overall fit

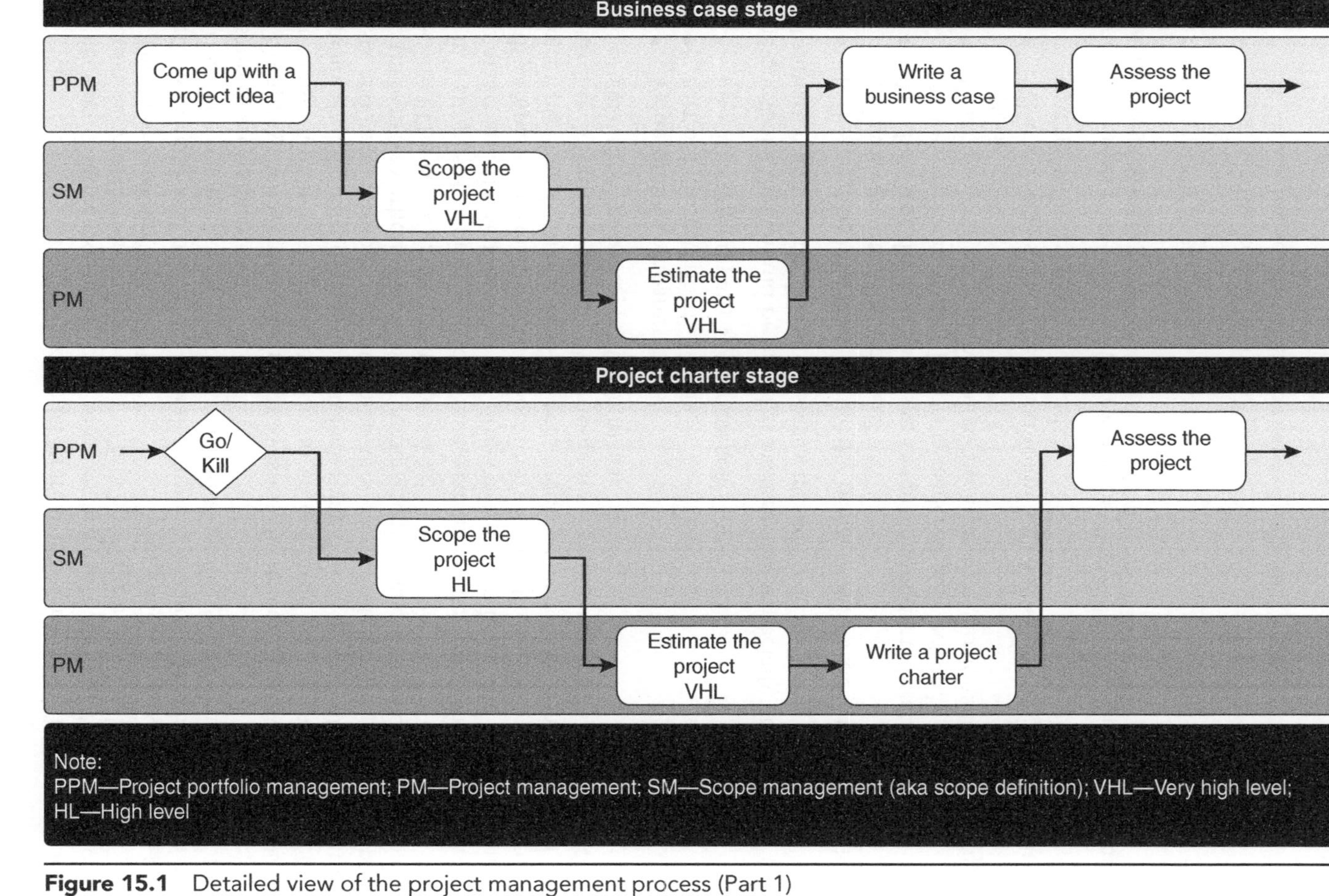

Figure 15.1 Detailed view of the project management process (Part 1)

of each project into the organizational strategy is determined. The balance of the project portfolio is examined next in order to ensure that no department or direction has received insufficient or too much weight in the final portfolio.

The next step is to rank all of the successful candidates according to a selections criteria and assess the overall company resources available for the next period. The resources start getting assigned to projects on the list until all of the resources are exhausted.

Company management also needs to assess the inventory of available resources (including human resources), decide on an optimum or acceptable size for the pipeline (while considering non-project–related work), and estimate durations, costs, and human resource requirements for each candidate project. Accomplishing these tasks without sound project management and scope definition capabilities would be very challenging tasks indeed.

In a simplistic project portfolio management model, once the final selections are made, and the sequence of the projects are established and properly aligned with company's resources, the process moves into the second phase where the project pipeline is maintained by traditional project initiation, execution, and control techniques as well as by periodic reviews of each project with respect to the original three pillars of portfolio management:

- Value to the company
- Part of balanced portfolio mix
- Fit with the company's strategic goals

The questions that should be asked at each review, especially at the end of project initiation and project planning stages, include:

- Is the original business case for the project with respect to value, balance, and strategic fit still supported?
- Are there any drastic changes to the project budget, duration, revenue projections, or to any other factors considered at selection?
- What projects should be killed because they no longer fit the original criteria?
- What projects should be added to the mix because of changed conditions, new ideas, and market demands?

Once the projects move into the execution phase, the following questions are added (see Figure 15.2):

- Is the project on time?
- Is it on budget?
- What are the key milestones?
- What are the technical and design issues?

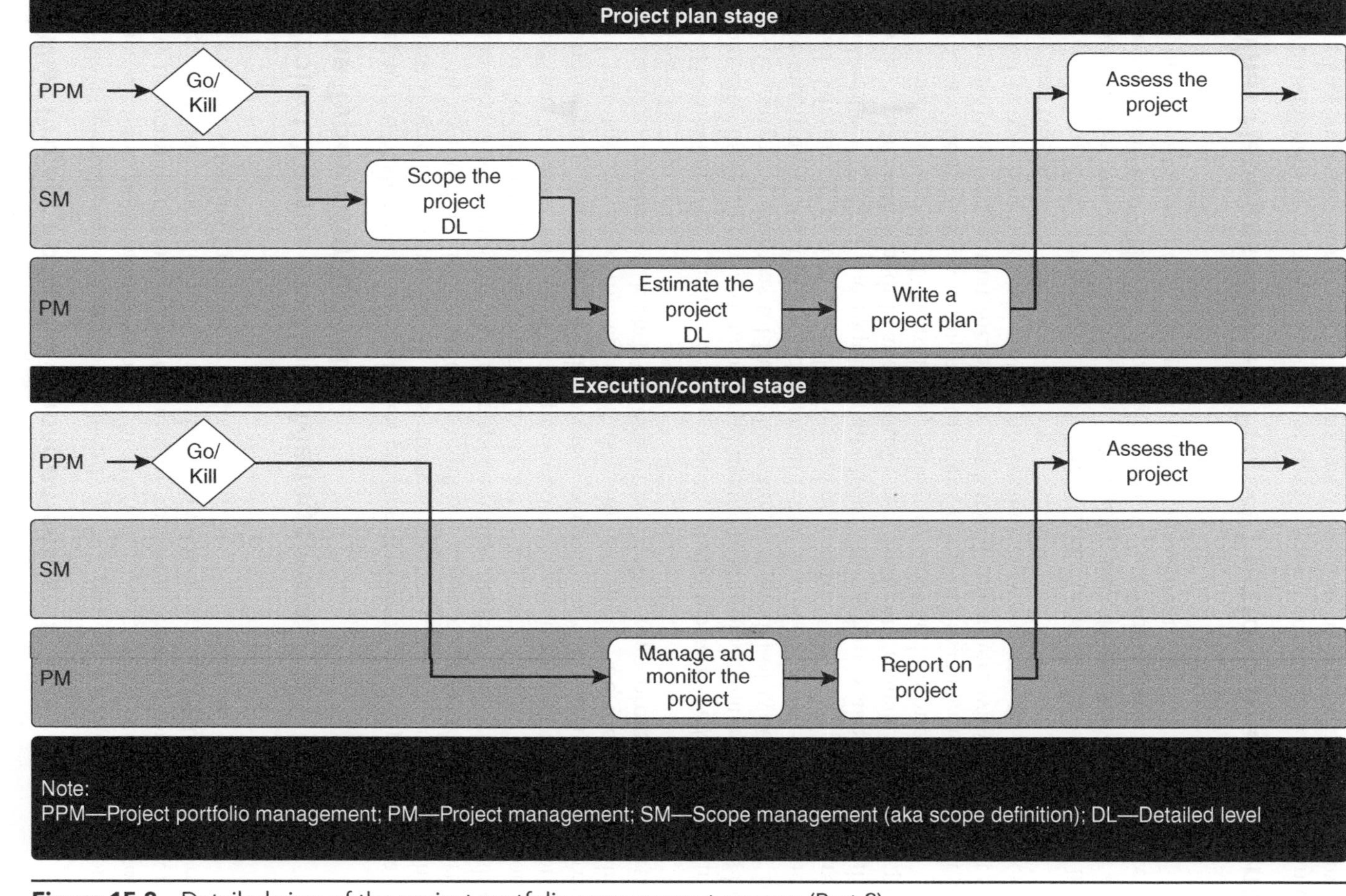

Figure 15.2 Detailed view of the project portfolio management process (Part 2)

What Project Portfolio Management Isn't

Project portfolio management frequently gets confused with enterprise project management, professional services automation, management of multiple projects, and program management. All of these are variances or expansions of project management since they do not address the alignment of projects with strategies or the science of selecting the right projects.

Project Versus Portfolio Management: The Typewriter Effect

Try to establish a boundary between project management and portfolio management. There is a group of activities often attributed to project managers when in fact they should be attributed to a completely different group known as portfolio managers. Identifying needs and opportunities, deciding which projects should be undertaken and which ones should be killed, establishing project priorities, assessing revenue and cash flow projections, aligning project mix with organizational goals, and balancing the project portfolio are all activities that correctly fall into the portfolio management domain and should be the responsibility of portfolio managers or high-level executives rather than project managers (see Figure 15.3).

The phenomenon mentioned previously as the *typewriter effect* will aid in further establishing a desired boundary. Imagine that project manager Bob was hired by Company *X* and was told to deliver the best model of typewriter ever built. He might have questioned the financial feasibility of such a venture, but he was told definitively to stop complaining and concentrate on the project. As a result, Bob collected all of the requirements from appropriate stakeholders, built the project plan with schedule and resource requirements, managed the team properly, and successfully delivered the product on time and on budget.

Once the product was shipped to stores, company management (to their great surprise) discovered that there were no lines of consumers willing to buy it since most people had been using word processing software instead of typewriters for the last twenty years.

Is Bob to blame for the product failure? Could he really have continued insisting that the project was a bad idea? Would he have been able to keep his job if he had done that? This example, albeit a bit simplistic, clearly demonstrates the boundary between portfolio and project management.

What Happens Without Project Portfolio Management?

What happens if a company does not have a sound portfolio management methodology in place? Some of the symptoms attributed to organizations that are not properly analyzing, selecting, and managing its projects are:

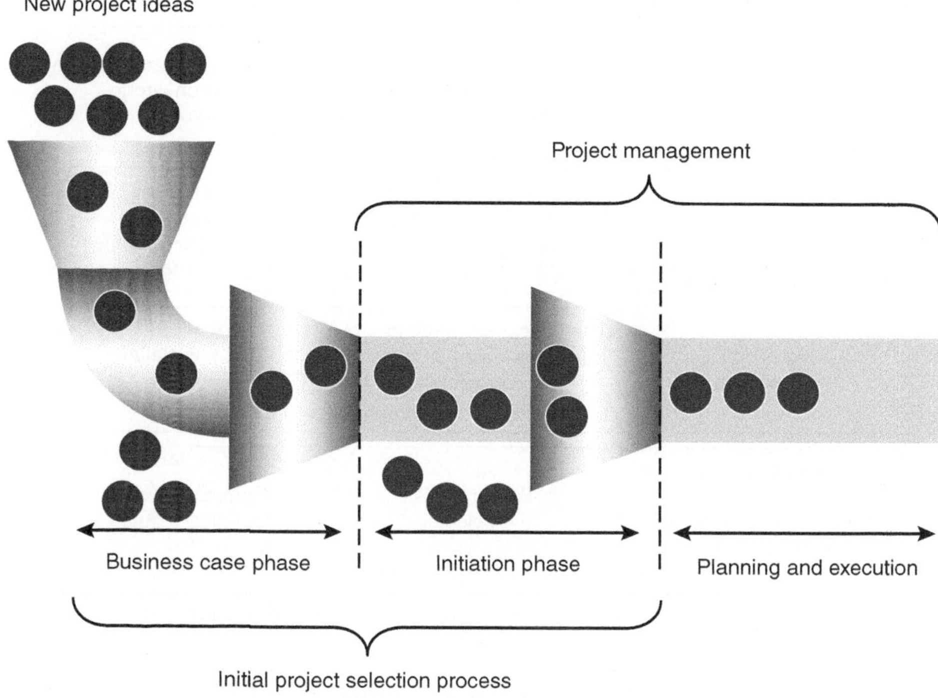

Figure 15.3 Project versus portfolio management

- Project and functional managers often clash over resources
- Priorities of projects frequently change, with resources constantly reassigned
- Senior managers have authority to single-handedly approve and release projects
- Projects begin as soon as approved by senior managers, irrespective of resource availability
- Senior managers regularly complain about how long the projects take or how expensive they are
- Even if the strategic proposal is implemented, the organization frequently does not achieve the desired improvement
- No comprehensive document links all of the company's undertakings to the strategic plan
- Significant turnover occurs at the senior management level, even up to the executive level
- The strategic plan is created as a list of projects; the cause-effect logic tying those projects to the strategic organizational goals is missing

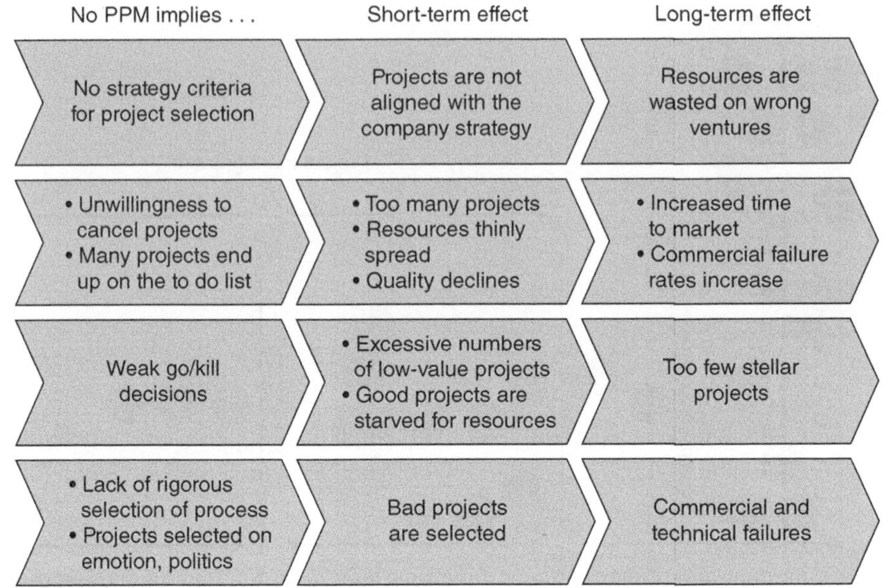

Figure 15.4 Consequences of not having project portfolio management

- The list of projects is not properly prioritized, and it is, therefore, presumed that all ideas should be implemented simultaneously

Do any of these symptoms seem familiar? Read these 10 symptoms again and try to determine how many of them apply to one's own organization.

The Cause and Effect Matrix

The symptoms associated with a lack of portfolio management described in the last section unfortunately represent only the half of the story. The end result is even more depressing (see Figure 15.4).

A reluctance to kill projects and the maintenance of an ever-widening project pipeline leads to a chronic lack of resources, poor quality of products, missed deadlines, and most importantly, high commercial failure rates of products or services created as a result of these projects. A logical by-product of such an approach is the apparent lack of real product winners that capture the customers' hearts and generate considerable revenues for companies.

Finally, if there are no strategic-fit criteria present in the selection mix, many of company's projects might, and most often do, end up being secondary, unimportant, and wasteful ventures that do not benefit the organization.

What Is Needed for Project Portfolio Management?

The obvious question to ask at this point would be: what kind of capabilities should an organization have in order to implement a successful portfolio management program? As demonstrated in previous sections, running proper portfolio management processes implies having in place well-developed and centralized project management capabilities, especially project scoping and estimation.

Scoping and estimation play an especially important role during the business case, project charter, and project plan phases when an organization's executives have to assess the economic feasibility and resource requirements of the proposed projects in order to come up with the prioritized project list (see Figure 15.5). Also, there must be a desire to develop a structured approach to project selection going all the way to the upper echelons of the organization. Since the selection processes should be handled by the most senior people in the company, implementation of portfolio management must be accompanied by their explicit approval and participation.

Finally, depending on how far a company is along the project management path, new roles might need to be created to support these processes. These roles might include project and program managers, a portfolio director, project management office roles, and others. The detailed discussion of the practical aspects of implementing project portfolio management and associated risks, problems, and tips shall be discussed in Chapter 19.

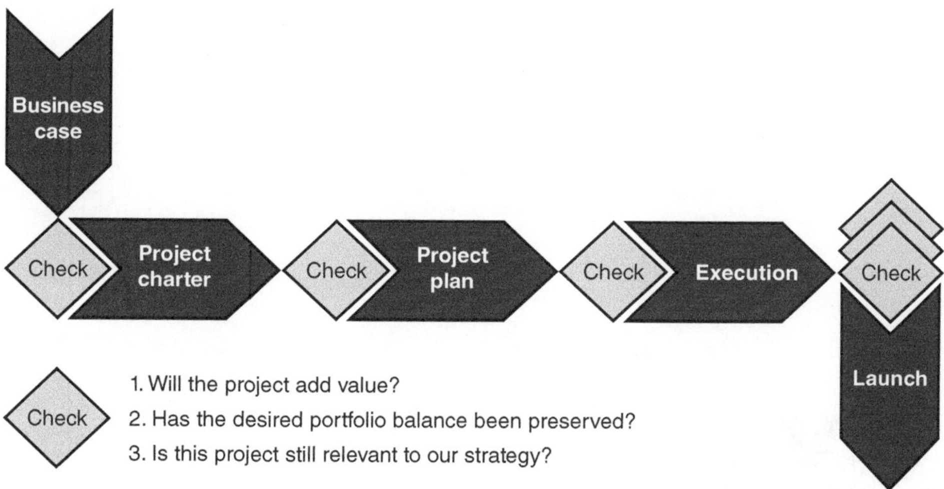

Figure 15.5 High-level view of the project portfolio management process

Summary

Most companies today are struggling when it comes to proper and systematic analysis, assessment, and selection of the right projects. The executives of many organizations are shifting their focus from tactical project management aspects of their ventures to more strategic, portfolio management facets of their entire project mix. Their interests lie more in the domain of the value of their portfolios, their proper balance, and their alignment with organizational strategic goals.

Project portfolio management is a systemic approach for analyzing, selecting, and collectively managing a company's projects based on three key characteristics: project value, portfolio balance, and alignment with strategy, which are all subject to resource, fiscal, and other relevant constraints.

The portfolio management process consists of two sequential phases: selection and prioritization of candidate projects and maintaining the pipeline by continuing, delaying, or terminating approved projects.

Absence of a systemic approach to portfolio management can result in high project failure rates (either technical or commercial), too few stellar product winners, increased times to market, and wasted resources.

While project and portfolio management are two distinct domains, established and centralized project management capabilities, especially project scoping and estimation, are paramount to a successful portfolio management methodology implementation.

This book has free material available for download from the Web Added Value™ resource center at *www.jrosspub.com*

16

How and Why Do You Need to Maximize Portfolio Value?

Historical Perspective

The South Sea Bubble

In the sixteenth century, Spain's investment in the New World had started paying fabulous dividends in the form of galleons from Mexico and Peru loaded with gold and silver. England, with a formidable empire of its own, was quite interested in tapping into these Spanish gold assets.

In the year 1713, the War of the Spanish Succession ended with the Treaty of Utrecht which, among other things, included an Asiento Contract that allowed one British ship a year to trade with Mexico, Peru, and Chile. To make matters even more humiliating for the English, the Spaniards demanded that the ship owners pay a 25 percent tax on all profits to the king of Spain.

Not deterred by these constraints, the British government proceeded to create a South Sea Company, which, with the support of the Bank of England, was supposed to—hold on to your seats—pay off the debt incurred by Britain during the war by raising £2 million through the initial public offering (see Illustration 16.1).

On February 2, 1720, the South Sea Company went public and, despite the warnings from Whig politician Robert Warpole about the dangers of *stock jobbing,* its shares tripled in value in just one day.

Illustration 16.1 *South Sea Bubble* by Edward Matthew Ward

The executives of the company, unsatisfied by such slow growth of their fortunes, proceeded to spread various outrageous rumors including:

- Imminent handover of the Potosi silver mine in Peru to the South Sea Company
- Great demand for English cotton and wool in Mexico
- Spain preparing to exchange parts of South America for Gibraltar

As a result of this PR campaign, in August of that same year the company's stock stood at 10 times more than when the speculation began in February.

In the fall of 1720, however, the rumors started spreading that Sir John Blunt, the governor of the South Sea Company, and his directors started secretly dumping their shares. The stock started its downward spiral precisely at that moment, ruining the lives of several thousand people. The company directors were attacked by angry mobs whenever they appeared on the streets, and the government started to get concerned that the collapse of the company would lead to mass riots in London. King George, whose own son had previously cheated trusting investors out of £40,000 in one of the South Sea Company-related ventures, had to return from vacation in Hannover in order to summon the Parliament to address the crisis.

Consequently, five of the company directors were arrested, but unfortunately, the treasurer, Mr. Knight, managed to escape to France. The Chancellor of Exchequer, Mr. Aislabie, who was instrumental in the South Sea bubble, was jailed while the people of London jeered, hooted, and burned his effigy.

Robert Warpole, now elevated to the status of national hero, spearheaded efforts to help out the South Sea Company creditors, but despite his best efforts, they were only able to regain one-third of their losses.

What happened with the South Sea Company project? Something very common throughout history: people were overly optimistic in assessing the future value of the endeavour despite all logical evidence to the contrary. Interestingly enough, the same mistake is made on many modern megaprojects. The most famous examples include:

- Channel Tunnel for which financing costs were 140 percent higher than those forecasted and revenues were less than half of those projected
- Denver's $5 billion new international airport that was close to 200 percent over budget and passenger traffic in the opening year was only half of that projected
- Japan's $268 million Ibaraki airport that opened for business in March 2010, yet neither Japan Airlines nor All Nippon Airways, which operate 90 percent of the flights in the country, plan to use it

Since the determination of project value is one of the three pillars of project portfolio management, this chapter will describe and analyze the various models available for organizations seeking the worth of the projects in their portfolio mixes.

Determining the Project Value: Financial Models

Net Present Value

Net present value (NPV) and internal rate of return (IRR) are probably the most famous project assessment methodologies. NPV is calculated by taking all future forecasted incremental cash flows the company expects the project to generate, discounting them to their present value and subtracting the original investment (i.e., the cost of the project):

$$NPV = -Inv + \frac{CF_1}{(1+r)} + \frac{CF_2}{(1+r)^2} + \frac{CF_3}{(1+r)^3} + \ldots + \frac{CF_n}{(1+r)^n}$$

where CF_n is cash flow in year n and r is the discount rate.

The decision criterion for the NPV approach is fairly simple: if NPV turns out to be positive, accept the project and if NPV < 0, reject it.

Bang-for-the-Buck Index

The bang-for-the-buck index (BBI) takes the NPV concept further by adjusting it for the resource requirements of a given project:

$$\textit{Bang-for-the-Buck Index} = \frac{NPV}{\textit{Total Resources Remaining To Be Spent on the Project}}$$

For example; here is how the BBI can be used in making project selection decisions at a product company that has only $25 million remaining in resources. First, all of the proposed projects are listed in a table containing their estimated NPVs along with resource requirements for each project and calculated BBIs (see Table 16.1).

Next the projects are ranked in descending order according to their respective BBI (see Table 16.2). An additional column for cumulative resource requirements is appended to the table. The portfolio cut-off point is placed where the cumulative requirements are equal (or less) than the resources remaining in the company. In this particular case, projects D, B, F, and A were added to the portfolio, while projects E and C were dropped.

Assessment of Purely Financial Models

Purely financial models, especially the BBI, possess many attractive aspects. They instill discipline and financial rigor since the champion of every candidate project knows to include estimates for future cash flows, project costs, and the resource requirements. In addition, facing financial realities is a great leap forward for many companies.

Table 16.1 Sample bang-for-the-buck calculation

Project	NPV ($M)	Resource requirements ($M)	BBI
Product A	50	10	**5**
Product B	35	4	**8.75**
Product C	42	24	**1.75**
Product D	10	1	**10**
Product E	14	3	**4.67**
Product F	73	10	**7.3**

Table 16.2 Sample bang-for-the-buck calculation (ranked projects)

Project	NPV ($M)	Resource requirements ($M)	BBI	Cumulative resource requirements ($M)
Product D	10	1	10	1
Product B	35	4	8.75	5
Product F	73	10	7.3	15
Product A	50	10	5	25
~~Product E~~	~~14~~	~~3~~	~~4.67~~	~~28~~
~~Product C~~	~~42~~	~~24~~	~~1.75~~	~~52~~

Because of their concentration on fiscal feasibility and time value of money, these methods are supposed to yield the most economically attractive projects, thus maximizing the future revenues and share prices of the company. In addition, the system favors projects that are closer to completion and penalizes the ones that are years away from conclusion.

However, there are several deficiencies inherent in this methodology. The first one is that financial forecasts with respect to future revenues are wildly inaccurate. The ability to predict project costs does not fare much better. Although the Tunnel Channel and the Denver and Ibaraki airports are extreme examples of this, the same is true of the majority of large projects. Considering the +300 to −75 percent historical range for software development projects and +75 to −25 percent Project Management Institute (PMI®) guidelines for traditional projects, this shouldn't come as a great surprise.

Another deficiency attributed to such methods is that they tend to consider financial goals only, while ignoring some other key aspects that could be of importance to the not-for-profit firms. Also, a significant disadvantage of the purely financial models is that they fail to consider two of the more important ingredients in project success—technical and commercial risks.

Expected Commercial Value

The expected commercial value (ECV) formula attempts to address some of the deficiencies of these purely financial models by introducing probabilities (for technical and commercial success) into the mix:

$$ECV = [(PV \times P_{CS} - C) \times P_{TS}] - D$$

where PV is the value of future earnings, P_{CS} is the probability of commercial success, C is the commercialization cost, P_{TS} is the probability of technical success, and D is the development cost.

The ECV index can be used in the portfolio selection process in the following manner: assume that company X has five candidate projects for next year's portfolio and is constrained by a development budget cap of $10 million. The data for present value, probability of technical success, probability of commercial success, commercialization cost, and development cost (see Table 16.3) has been obtained or, to be more precise, estimated by the company's employees.

In the next step, the ECV value for each project is calculated, and the projects are ranked in descending order according to their scores (see Table 16.4).

The cumulative-development-costs column is added to the table to calculate the total development cost forecast as each project is added to the portfolio. Once the threshold of the total budget is reached ($10 million in this example), all the remaining candidates are removed from the portfolio mix. In the example, projects Alpha, Delta, and Epsilon were added to the portfolio whereas projects Beta and Gamma were cancelled or killed.

Table 16.3 Sample expected commercial value calculation

Project name	***PV* ($)**	**P_{TS} (%)**	**P_{CS} (%)**	***D* ($)**	***C* ($)**	***ECV***
Project Alpha	55	0.9	0.85	6	4	**32.48**
Project Beta	67	0.5	0.5	8	5	**6.25**
Project Gamma	4	0.95	0.8	0.5	0.5	**2.07**
Project Delta	23	0.75	0.8	3	2	**9.30**
Project Epsilon	15	0.85	0.75	1	1	**7.71**

Table 16.4 Sample expected commercial value calculation (ranked projects)

Project name	**ECV**	***D* ($)**	***Cum. D* ($)**
Project Alpha	**32.48**	6	6
Project Delta	**9.30**	3	9
Project Epsilon	**7.71**	1	10
~~Project Beta~~	~~**6.25**~~	~~8~~	~~18~~
~~Project Gamma~~	~~**2.07**~~	~~0.5~~	~~18.5~~

Assessment of the ECV Model

What are the advantages of the ECV model? The main difference between this formula and the purely financial methods is the introduction of probabilities; the outcome is assessed not just on the estimate of future revenues but on the probability of generating planned cash flows. This model also preserves all of the positive attributes of the financial models: introduction of financial rigor, recognition of the time value of money, and acknowledgment of constrained resources.

However, the ECV approach still suffers from the same maladies as the methods described earlier. First, the reliance on future financial forecasts including revenues, costs savings, project budget, and commercialization costs is a definite weak link. Accuracy already has been discussed when it comes to projects estimation; suffice it to say that +300 percent is legitimate from the estimation point of view. A shift in project costs can inflict some serious damage on the formulas described so far.

While the introduction of probabilities into the formulas was a positive step, one must also remember that probabilities are still numbers forecasted by people and are prone to mistakes, as are future cash flow forecasts.

Limitations of Financial Approaches

As was mentioned previously, one of the weakest links in all of the financial approaches to portfolio evaluation is the reliance on financial forecasts, on both the revenue and project costs sides. Examine a very simplistic, if not primitive example. Assume that a real estate development company is contemplating doing a project. The forecasted one-time revenue from the sale of a condo high-rise is $100 million; the estimated cost of the project (both technical and marketing) is $70 million. The return on investment (ROI) of such a venture would be:

$$ROI = \frac{\$100 - \$70}{\$70} = 42.86\%$$

A project that generates a 43 percent ROI would be a very respectable venture, indeed. But it's already known that initial project-cost estimates are subject to a +75 to -25 percent range of accuracy. What happens if the project budget balloons to, say, $110 million, and the forecasted revenues drop to $80 million? This is, by the way, a completely plausible scenario, especially in light of the recent real estate crisis. The ROI formula would be:

$$ROI = \frac{\$80 - \$110}{\$110} = -27.27\%$$

The project in question just went from having a 43 percent ROI to a -27 percent ROI.

It is no surprise that empirical data supports the conclusions arrived at by logical analysis. One study of a company's ability to estimate expected new product sales revenues showed that there were orders-of-magnitude errors. Another research project determined that the sum of NPVs across 30 projects showed a marked decline as the projects progressed from predevelopment to post launch. And yet another research project discovered that of all the methods studied in a large sample, financial methods yielded the poorest results on almost every portfolio performance metric. In addition, larger and potentially breakthrough projects are penalized by financial valuation methods because the expected outcomes are harder to quantify and prove, especially without the time and a budget for proper feasibility studies.

Finally, financial methods are not very useful for nonprofit organizations, including all government agencies. Furthermore, their validity is also greatly diminished when employing them to assess not-for-profit projects such as, for example, investments in the infrastructure or public relations initiatives that might have significant strategic importance for the organization.

Determining the Project Value Using Scoring Models

Scoring models attempt to address the issues encountered in the financial models by trying to balance several key factors influencing the portfolio value.

DuPont Scoring Model

The scoring model developed by the American chemical giant DuPont is based on the following seven criteria:

- Strategy alignment
- Value
- Competitive advantage
- Market attractiveness
- Fit to existing supply chain
- Time to break even
- NPV

Each category can receive a score of 1, 5, or 15 based on their fit to the organizational demands for project value (see Table 16.5). Once every candidate project is assessed and scored, the total points for each proposed venture are summed up, and all of the projects are sorted in descending order according to their total scores (ranging anywhere from eight points to 120 points).

EXFO Scoring Model

EXFO Engineering, a relatively small player in the fiber optics industry, developed a slightly more straightforward approach to the project value determination. Its motto was: there are too many projects to assess and therefore the model must be simple.

Table 16.5 DuPont scoring model

Rating scale	**15**	**5**	**1**
Alignment with strategy	Fits strategy perfectly	Supports strategy	Irrelevant to strategy
Value	Significant differentiation	Moderate differentiation	Slight differentiation
Competitive advantage	Strong	Moderate	Slight
Market profitability	Very profitable	Somewhat profitable	Low profitability
Fit to existing supply chain	Fits current channels	Some insignificant changes required	Significant changes required
Payback period	< 4 years	4-6 years	> 6 years
NPV	> \$20 M	\$4-\$20 M	< \$5 M

Source: Adapted from R. G. Cooper, S. J. Edgett, E. J. Kleinschmidt, *Portfolio Management for New Products* (Basic Books, 2002).

There are only four variables at play, all expressed in the form of questions:

- Does the project fit company strategy? How well?
- What is the market potential? How large is the market?
- Are the financial estimates positive?
- Do we have the R&D know-how? Can we do the project?

The financial estimate EXFO employs is also a fairly simplistic financial index:

$$FI = \frac{S \times P_{CS}}{[D \times (1 - P_{TS})]}$$

where S is the expected annual sales for the product ($000), P_{CS} is the probability of commercial success, D is the development cost ($000), and P_{TS} is the probability of technical success.

Each project is scored based on the previously mentioned criteria, and all the projects are ranked according to the score they received.

Best-Practices Model

The best-practices model was developed by the famous portfolio management expert Robert Cooper. The model relies on six major factors with several subitems (see Table 16.6):

- Strategic alignment and importance
- Product and competitive advantage
- Market attractiveness
- Leverage of core competencies
- Technical feasibility
- Financial reward

The senior management of a company met with the project team to discuss each one of the projects in the portfolio and then rated each one of them in all six categories. The maximum score a project could get was 60, if the organization chose to follow the point system described in Table 16.6. Another scoring mechanism allowing for a total score of 100 was also possible and was used by some companies.

For the purposes of this book, the 60-point model will be used. The minimum score a project can get is zero if it receives no points in all six categories. As can be seen from the table, however, projects also should be killed if they receive a zero score in any of the six categories (except competitive advantage). In other words, if the candidate project receives a rating of zero in the technical feasibility section, it should be canceled right away even if it had received straight 10s across all other categories.

Table 16.6 Best practices model

Key items	0	4	7	10
1. Strategic alignment and importance • Strategic fit and importance • Fits our strategy • Important to do • High impact on our business	• Not in alignment • Not important • Low impact **KILL**	• Somewhat in alignment • Not too important • Modest impact	• Supports business strategy • Important • Good impact	• Aligns very well • Project very important to strategy • High impact
2. Competitive advantage • Unique customer benefits • Value for money • Customer feedback	• None • Poor value • Negative or neutral customer feedback	• Limited • Okay value • Fairly neutral customer feedback	• Some new benefits • Superior value • Positive customer feedback	• Major new benefits • Great value • Excellent customer feedback
3. Market attractiveness • Market size and growth • Margins • Competitive situation	• Small or non-existent • Low growth and low margins • Tough competition **KILL**	• Modest markets • Fair margins • Competitive	• Significant markets • Good margins • Modest competition	• Large growing attractive market • Good margins • Great value
4. Leverages core competencies • Technology • Production • Sales and marketing	• No opportunities to leverage core competencies **KILL**	• Some opportunities to leverage core competencies	• Considerable leverage is possible • Skills required are easily found in the company	• Excellent leverage of our strengths and competencies • Excellent fit between project needs and our skills
5. Technical feasibility • Size of technical gap • How complex technically? • Uses in-house technology	• Big gap • Very complex • New technology to company **KILL**	• Fairly large gap • Difficult • Most of the technology is new to company	• Modest gap • Not too difficult • Most of technology is know to company	• Small or no gap • Easy • We have technology in-house

Table 16.6 continued

Key items	0	4	7	10
6. Financial rewards vs. risk • Payback, NPV, IRR, etc. • Certainty of estimates • Risk and difficulty	• NPV—negative; payback > 5 years • Very wide range of estimates • Very risky **KILL**	• NPV-positive payback = 4 years • Somewhat wide range of estimates • Somewhat risky	• MPV-positive and good; payback = 2 years • Fairly narrow range of estimates • Little risk	• NPV-positive and high; payback < 1 year • Very narrow range of estimates • Very little risk

Source: Adapted from R. G. Cooper, S. J. Edgett, E. J. Kleinschmidt, *Portfolio Management for New Products* (Basic Books, 2002).

Projects that pass the first hurdle are assessed based on their total scores. Many companies use a cutoff point of 30 or 36 points—50 percent and 60 percent respectively—and drop all projects that score lower.

Assessment of Scoring Models

What are the advantages of scoring models? First, unlike financial models, they do not place too much emphasis on financial criteria and they manage to capture multiple goals. This is especially important for not-for-profit organizations and even for-profit companies needing to assess long-term strategic projects. They also manage to reduce a very complex and sensitive problem of go/kill decision making to a small number of reasonably simple questions. Furthermore, these models literally force detailed and deep discussions about the merits and drawbacks of each project based on structured criteria rather than ad hoc debates. These methodologies also yield a final single score for each project, which greatly improves management's ability to rank, pass, or fail each one of the proposed ventures.

There are, unfortunately, several drawbacks to the scoring models that are, luckily, manageable with proper attention and effort. Sometimes a company's management attributes imaginary precision to the scores arrived at via the scoring models. They forget that each ingredient in the total project score was not based on hard data but rather on human assessment of the current situation. Hence, one must always remember that a score of 50.1 percent does not necessarily mean that the project should be promoted to the portfolio. By the same token, a rating of 49.9 percent does not directly imply that the project should be killed right away.

The halo effect is another issue frequently attributed to the scoring model methodology. If the criteria against which the projects are scored are fairly similar (e.g., probability of commercial success and product marketability), high marks in one category will inevitably lead to higher marks in other categories as well. Statisticians refer to this phenomenon as *autocorrelation*—the cross-correlation of independent variables used to predict or explain the behavior of the dependent variable. The only way to avoid this problem is to ensure that the criteria selected are strictly independent of one another.

Finally, another deficiency of scoring models is a complete lack of resource factor. This implies that, theoretically, two projects, a $1 million venture and a $100 million venture, can receive identical scores and hence be treated equally from the portfolio management perspective. This leads to larger projects rising to the top of the portfolio list. Replacing the total score with a total-score-divided-by-project-budget to adjust for the project size is recommended.

Developing Scoring Models

When developing scoring models for an organization, there are a few important tips to remember. These are outlined in Table 16.7.

Table 16.7 Aspects to consider when developing scoring models

Advice	Explanation
Keep the list of questions short	Remember that senior management will be participating in these meetings. Thus, considering that candidate projects can number in hundreds for a larger organization, six to ten questions should be sufficient.
Some factors should be knockouts	A zero score on at least some of the criteria should lead to a kill decision. For example if the project is rated as *irrelevant to our strategic goals*, it should be removed from the list right away.
Try to avoid variable weights	Employing different criteria or different weights to value the projects can complicate the exercise and lead to project attractiveness scores not being directly comparable. The organization might end up comparing apples to oranges.
Try to avoid discussions of the scores awarded to each candidate	Awarding points in each category is a cumbersome and sometimes very politically charged process. The discussion of the merits and deficiencies of each venture is absolutely essential, however, lengthy arguments about what score the project should receive in a given category are not. Use the Delphi technique to obtain the scores efficiently.

Summary

Historically, humankind has been notoriously inept when given the task of forecasting the costs and the future revenue of projects. There are a multitude of examples of such ineptitude in recent history including the Channel Tunnel and the Denver and Ibaraki airports, to name a few. Since the assessment of project value is one of the three key pillars of portfolio management, it is important to understand various methodologies available to organizations for assessing the worth of each candidate project.

There are two broad groups of value assessment methodologies: financial models and scoring approaches. Financial approaches possess several positive characteristics including an introduction of fiscal discipline and a generation of the most economically attractive projects This maximizes the future revenues and share prices of the company.

However, the inherent flaw of these methods is that every input is generated by humans, who are notoriously bad at economic forecasts. Hence, numerous studies have confirmed that purely financial methods are the worst performers among project assessment methodologies.

Scoring models, on the other hand, allow for consideration of several important variables at a time including, for example, market attractiveness and technical feasibility that allow for a more balanced assessment of the candidate projects. While they possess several minor flaws (imaginary precision, halo effect, and a lack of the resource factor), these deficiencies can be easily addressed by fine-tuning the special approach chosen.

This book has free material available for download from the Web Added Value™ resource center at *www.jrosspub.com*

17

How and Why Do You Need to Balance Your Project Mix?

Historical Perspective

Battle of Crécy—The Optimal Balance

On August 26, 1346, the English army led by King Edward III and French forces under the command of King Philip VI met south of Calais near the village of Crécy-en-Ponthieu (see Illustration 17.1). Both armies were quite formidable by fourteenth-century standards; however the French side outnumbered the English by a healthy ratio of at least three to one. The English force of between 10,000 and 16,000 combatants had to face a French army of between 35,000 and 100,000 combatants, depending on which sources one chooses to believe. French forces were also supported by 6000 Genovese crossbowmen led by Carlo Grimaldi, an ancestor of Monaco's current ruling Grimaldi dynasty.

Furthermore, France, at the time, was a powerful and prosperous nation in Europe with a population of 20 million and countless generations of nobility bred almost exclusively for the purposes of warfare. By comparison, England only had a population of 4 million, very few warrior nobles and virtually no recognition in Europe in terms of military skill or might. To makes matters even worse for the English, the French army had close to 12,000 heavy cavalrymen in their ranks. At the time, heavy cavalry was considered to be the ultimate weapon; countering heavily armed horsemen with men-at-arms was akin to sending infantry to fight heavy armored tank divisions—a suicide mission to say the least. According to some historians, the English had only a few knights to go up against the formidable French cavalry.

Illustration 17.1 Battle of Crécy

So far, the description of the situation sounds like a very raw deal for the English. However, the battle ended by dusk with a complete English victory. The French had lost close to 15,000 men and several of their highest-ranking members of nobility including King John of Bohemia; Rudolph, Duke of Lorraine; the Count of Flanders; the Count of Alençon; the Count of Blois; the Viscount Rohan; the Lord of Laval; the Lord of Chateaubriant; the Lord of Dinan; and the Lord of Redon.

What were the English losses? Two knights and approximately 200 men-at-arms had perished in that battle.

What was at the heart of the English success? Was it superior hand-to-hand combat skills, ultimate bravery, or the superior strategic skills of the English commanders?

It turns out that the answer to this question is a bit more complicated. First, the English were able to accumulate a lot of battle experience from the Scottish Wars. Second, the English soldiers, hardened by several highland campaigns, were more professional and disciplined than their French counterparts—a factor of immense importance in the military conflicts of medieval times.

Finally, and most importantly, the English leaders were able to come up with the most efficient mix of pikemen, regular infantry, and famed bowmen. The relatively small English force at the Battle of Crécy consisted of 8000 archers and 4000 infantry and pikemen. Knowing that the French battle strategy was to unleash a couple of volleys from crossbows followed by a charge of heavy cavalry, the English commanders used an ingenious strategy that was supported by the resources available. Mixed infantry and bowmen were placed on relatively high ground and waited for the French—Genovese, to be more precise—crossbowmen to approach. Since the range and the rate of fire of the crossbows were lower than that of the English bows, the 6000 Genovese mercenaries presented no problem whatsoever. The French knights, angered by the crossbowmen's hesitance to die valiantly for France, blocked their path to retreat when the Italians started to pullback from the front lines. King Philip's reaction to the behavior of the Genovese was even more interesting: "Kill me those scoundrels, for they block our advance and serve no purpose!"

Later when the French cavalry mounted several attacks (fifteen in total), the English bowmen unleashed volley after volley of deadly three-yard arrows on them. With up to a 15-arrows-per-minute firing rate and 8000 archers at work, one can appreciate the ferocity of the English assault.

Pikemen also played an important role by being the next line of defense against the French riders who survived the hail of arrows. The English resurrected the deadly pikemen-weapon idea borrowed from their Scottish neighbors. Remember the conversation William Wallace had with his peers in *Braveheart*? "We'll make spears, hundreds of long spears, twice as long as a man." And, finally, the English foot soldiers, armed with swords and axes, finished off what was remaining of the French knights.

What is the main project management lesson of the battle of Crécy? It is that the proper balance of projects is as important as other factors at play. In this chapter the second pillar of project portfolio management will be discussed—the proper balance of projects in the portfolio mix.

Why Seek Balanced Portfolios?

According to many leading project portfolio management researchers, most companies' portfolio mixes are unbalanced. Out of the six criteria identified by Robert Cooper[1] for measuring portfolio performance across multiple companies, poor portfolio balance was the second weakest element; the *we have too many projects in our portfolio* element was the weakest.

What are the most typical imbalances in modern project portfolios? According to leading research groups, there is a definitive prevalence of smaller projects—fixes, minor improvements, and small modifications requested by customers—over larger strategic ventures that should be responsible for generating future revenues and sustaining organizational growth. Frequently some areas of a business receive disproportionally large investments despite the fact that both common and business sense tells management that these resources should be used elsewhere.

A haphazard approach to portfolio balancing can lead to serious risk exposure for a company; the lack of what finance people call diversification can lead to an *all the eggs in one basket* effect. For example, a company may invest a vast percentage of its resources in one particular product but neglect all other product families. The demand for the product might suddenly drop or disappear completely (not an unheard-of phenomenon in today's world) leaving the organization without alternative sources of revenue. Therefore, achieving the proper balance of projects in a given portfolio is the second pillar of portfolio management in general and of project selection in particular.

What Dimensions Should Be Considered?

Companies that try to analyze and assess the balance of proposed projects in their portfolios typically employ bubble charts as visual aids for evaluation of their ventures. Bubble diagrams are basically two-dimensional *XY* plots with circles or other shapes representing projects. The dimensions can vary from industry to industry and even from company to company, although some are more popular than others. Some of the dimensions to be considered by a company are:

- Fit with business strategy (high, medium, low)
- Inventive merit
- Financial value ($)
- Strategic importance to the business (high, medium, low)
- Durability of competitive advantage (short, medium, long-term)
- Competitive impact of technologies (high, medium, low)
- Probability of success (%)
- Cost to completion ($)
- Time to completion (weeks, months, quarters, years)

One might notice that some of the dimensions described for bubble diagrams were also used as ingredients in the assessing-the-portfolio-value exercise described in Chapter 15. It could be worthwhile for some organizations to consider additional dimensions in order to broaden their portfolio insight. For example, markets, market segments, product categories, or technology/platform types could represent one of the dimensions. Another approach would be to break down the projects according to their types:

- New products
- Product improvements, extensions, and enhancements
- Maintenance and fixes
- Cost reductions
- Fundamental R&D

Bubble Charts

Risk-Reward Bubble Diagram

Figure 17.1 demonstrates a very popular risk-reward type of bubble chart. The probability of technical success is assigned to the vertical axis and the projects'

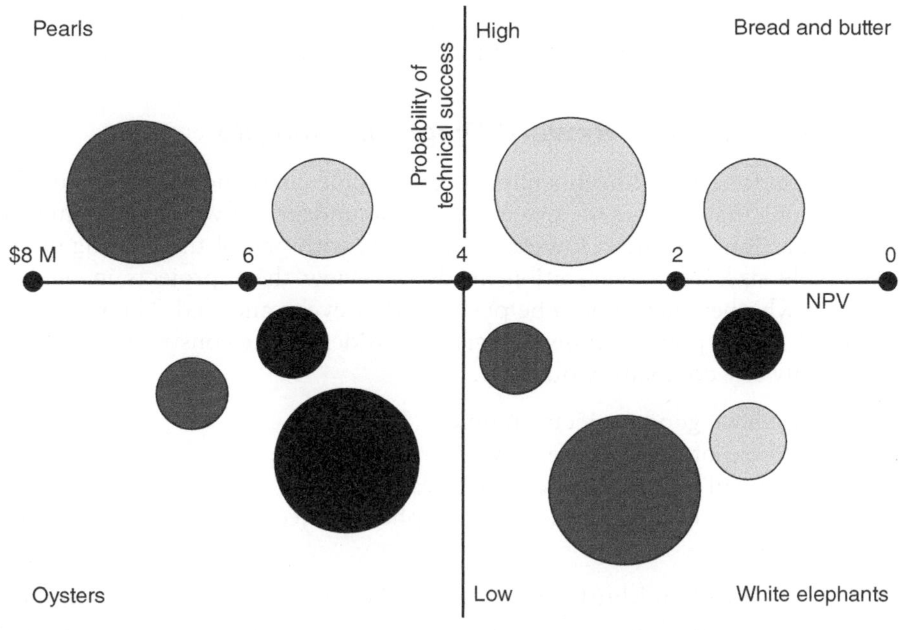

Figure 17.1 Risk-reward bubble diagram

net present values are assigned to the horizontal axis. Circles represent projects and their area is proportional to the project size. Finally, the color of each circle denotes the product group in which it belongs. The net present value (NPV)-risk approach naturally breaks the chart into four quadrants:

- Low-value and high-risk projects are called *white elephants*
- Low-value and low-risk ventures are called *bread and butter*
- High-value and high-risk projects are called *oysters*
- High-value and low risk endeavors are called *pearls*

The most attractive projects in the mix are obviously the pearls—potential star products that might generate large revenues for their companies. Products like iPod, iPhone, Microsoft Office, the first Xerox photocopying machine, and Viagra all fall into that category.

Oysters also have the potential for great success, but the probability of technical delivery is relatively low. Bread and butter ventures are typically smaller, simpler projects with high probability of success but low reward.

The worst projects are the white elephants—low-success, low-reward ventures—that are very difficult to kill. Personal experience has shown that many of the projects initially perceived to be pearls or oysters ended up in the white elephant category the closer they got to the execution and close-out stages.

Analysis of the Risk-Reward Diagram Example

What can be determined from analyzing the bubble chart shown in Figure 17.1? The first thing that catches the eye is the over-abundance of white elephants. The company has four high-risk, low-payoff projects with one of them being of very considerable size. The organization needs to review these projects in order to determine whether they should be postponed or even cancelled. The right questions to ask at this point in time, especially considering the constrained resources of practically any company, would be:

- Do we have good projects on hold?
- What kind of projects are they?
- Do they fall into pearl or oyster categories?
- Can we cancel some of the white elephant projects and kick-start the good ones instead?

As far as the bread and butter projects go, the situation is slightly more complicated. If one is dealing with a fairly conservative company (e.g., bank, insurance corporation), then the two low-payoff, low-risk projects are probably fine. If, however, the organization is a player in an aggressive industry (e.g., telecommunications, software), then one could argue that there are too many resources tied up in bread and butter projects. In this situation, cutting some of the scope on such projects could be a possible solution to the problem.

It is only natural for company executives to want to move the oyster ventures to the pearls sector of the chart. There is only one way to accomplish this feat: the probability of technical success of these projects needs to be increased. One of the ways to do that is to move the resources that were freed up from the postponement or cancellation of the white elephant or bread and butter projects to the oyster projects.

3M Risk-Reward Bubble Diagram

The 3M risk reward diagram is slightly different (see Figure 17.2). It uses NPV as one of the dimensions, but the probability of technical success is replaced by the probability of overall technical and commercial success. Also, the areas of the shapes no longer represent project size; the circles are replaced with ellipses to account for the uncertainty of the estimates. A vertical ellipse means that the company is fairly confident about the NPV of the project in question but expects a considerable amount of variability in the probability of success. A horizontal ellipse implies fuzzy NPV but a fairly accurate estimate with respect to the probability of success. Logically, the large circles are the worst thing an executive can see on such charts—fuzzy or loose projects with considerable uncertainty on both financial and probability of success sides. And by the same token, small tight circles stand for highly certain estimates.

Analysis of the 3M Risk-Reward Diagram Example

What can be said about Figure 17.2? Projects *A* and *E* seem to be in good shape with Project *A* being a high-payoff, low-risk venture that all executives love and Project *E* seemingly falling into the bread and butter category. Project *D* looks like the most troublesome of all: the probability of success is accurate and fairly high (60 to 80 percent), but the payoff range on one end ventures into the negative NPV area. As such, this project would, at a minimum, require very tight monitoring over its life cycle and would, at a maximum, become a candidate for postponement or cancellation. Project C is also fairly problematic because it possesses a fairly low probability of success (30 to 60 percent) along with a wide range of probabilities. The payoff situation is slightly better, but again, the estimate range is fairly wide. Project *B* is definitely in the desirable territory as far as the financial attributes go, but the company is highly uncertain about its overall realization. The probability of success is distributed between 30 percent and 80 percent.

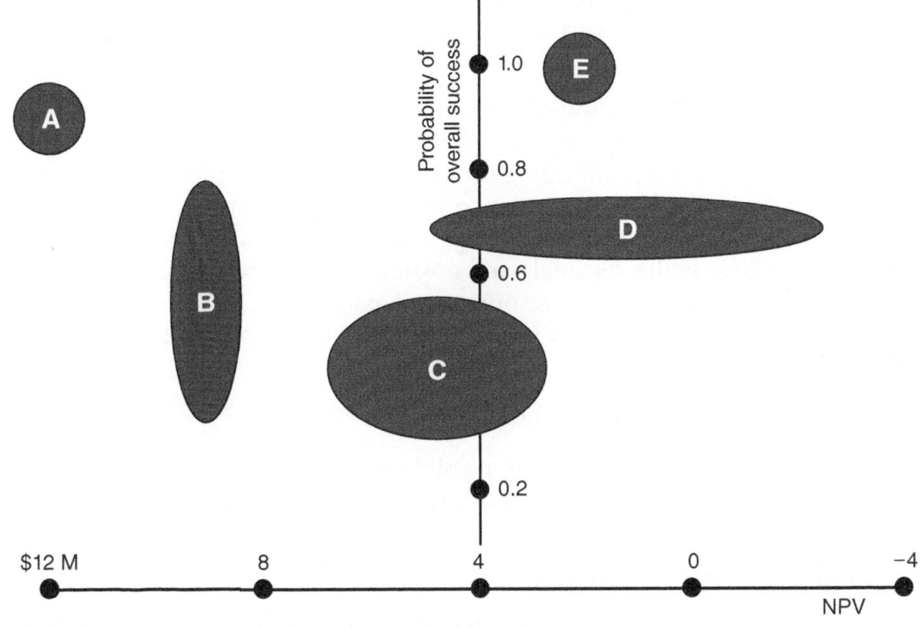

Figure 17.2 3M risk-reward bubble diagram

What are some of the options available for the company executives in this particular scenario? Assuming full resource utilization by the company at the time this snapshot was taken, it could be worthwhile to consider postponing or cancelling Project *D* altogether and reallocating the freed resources to Projects *A* and C to improve the odds of success for these two ventures.

Simple Risk-Reward Diagram

The simpler version of the risk-reward diagram contains NPV on the vertical axis and probability of overall success on the horizontal axis. The projects are plotted as different geometric shapes and colors to account for different project types. In this particular example (see Figure 17.3) solid squares stand for infrastructure projects, solid circles indicate new products within existing product families, and white rectangles symbolize new products in brand new product groups.

Analysis of the Simple Risk-Reward Diagram Example

A careful review of Figure 17.3 can lead one to the following observations:

- The new product, new product family projects, while all with high NPVs, have fairly low probabilities of success
- New product, existing product family ventures are all in the fairly high payoff and reasonable probability area
- Infrastructure projects are in the lower-payoff and high probability of success cluster

There are several possible action scenarios for this particular portfolio. If the company belongs to an aggressive industry, they may consider cutting some of the infrastructure projects and reallocating the freed up resources to the new product, new product family projects in order to boost their probabilities of success. If, on the other hand, the organization is in a fairly conservative industry, cutting some of the riskiest white rectangle and possibly solid circle ventures might be a good alternative to free up some resources and assign them to the remaining new product, new product family and new product, existing product family projects.

Popular Dimensions

Table 17.1 demonstrates some of the possible dimension pairings for the bubble charts used by organizations conducting portfolio balance analysis.

Several Words of Caution

Some of the bubble diagrams may suffer from the same issues that affect the financial valuation models described in Chapter 16. This refers, of course, to

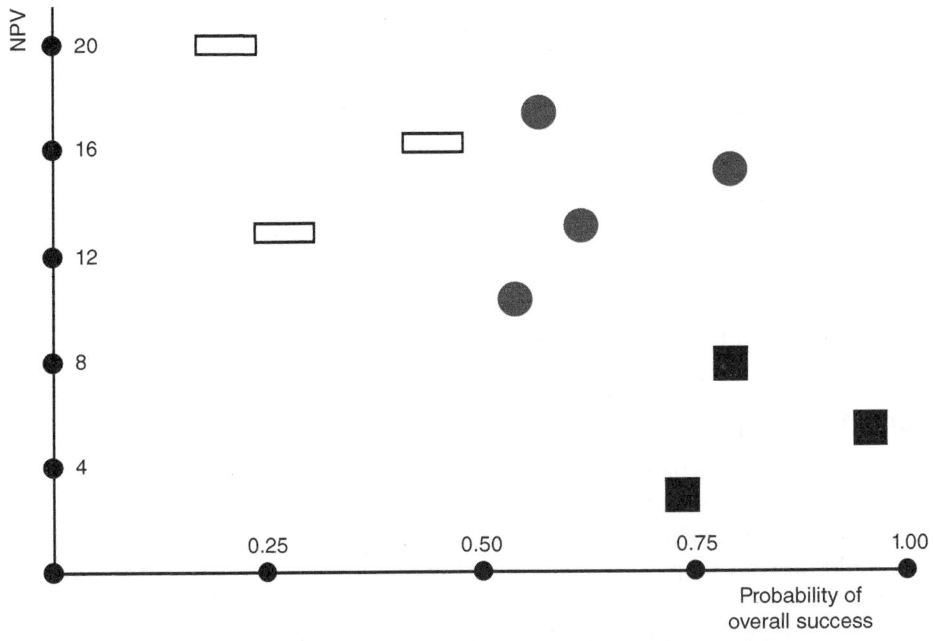

Figure 17.3 Simple risk-reward diagram

Table 17.1 Popular bubble diagram dimensions

Type of chart	Axis	By	Axis
Risk v. reward	Probability of success	X	NPV, IRR, etc.
Newness	Technical newness	X	Market newness
Ease v. attractiveness	Technical feasibility	X	Market attractiveness
Strength v. attractiveness	Competitive position	X	Market attractiveness
Cost v. timing	Cost to implement	X	Time to completion
Strategic v. benefit	Strategic fit	X	NPV, attractiveness, etc.
Cost v. benefit	Cumulative reward	X	Cumulative costs

Source: Adapted from R. G. Cooper, S. J. Edgett, E. J. Kleinschmidt, *Portfolio Management for New Products*. (Basic Books, 2002).

the financial forecasts that typically play a prominent role in bubble charts. It is, therefore, essential to be conservative with revenue and cost projections and to conduct portfolio reviews on a regular basis as projects progress from initiation to close out stages. As mentioned previously, the revenue-to-cost ratio can shrink dramatically especially on groundbreaking research and development-type ventures.

Substantially increasing the number of bubble charts in an attempt to cover all possible dimensions can, and probably will, backfire as company executives are very likely to start suffering from information overload. Data from industry research suggest that two or three different bubble charts per portfolio should be sufficient for most companies.

Unlike the portfolio valuation methods described in the previous chapter, bubble charts do not produce a list of ranked projects. Therefore, they should be viewed primarily as displays of information rather than decision models. Unfortunately, the decision making responsibility falls on the shoulders of the executives who should analyze, discuss, and choose the right combination of projects in order to maintain the desired balance in the company's portfolio.

Summary

Achieving the proper balance in a company's portfolio is the second pillar of project portfolio management. It is essential to avoid situations where certain business areas, projects, or product groups receive a disproportionate amount of resources that could possibly jeopardize company growth and increase its risk exposure.

There is a multitude of dimensions available for bubble charts (e.g., fit with business strategy, inventive merit, financial value, strategic importance, project groups). Which ones should be used depends heavily on the industry in which the company operates, the economic outlook, and the preferences of the executives.

As a result, organizations that are willing to analyze and assess their portfolio balance have a large number of bubble charts to choose from. The most popular chart seems to be various versions of the risk-reward diagrams, several examples of which were discussed in this chapter.

When conducting portfolio balance reviews, remember to consider the uncertainty of financial forecasts, both with respect to revenue projections and cost estimates. Also, limit the number of bubble diagrams to two or three because presenting executives with a large number of these charts might lead to unnecessary confusion and possible abandonment of the exercise altogether.

Finally, remember that the charts are not graphic decision tools; they simply paint an as-is picture that should be analyzed and acted upon by senior management.

References

1. Cooper, R. G., Edgett, S. J. Kleinschmidt, E. J. *Portfolio Management for New Products* (Basic Books, 2002).

18

How and Why Do You Need to Link Portfolio to Strategy?

Historical Perspective

Strategic Blunders of the British Admiralty

The survival of Britain has for centuries depended on the strength of its navy. The British navy has known a lot of glorious moments over the course of its history including the battles with the Spanish Armada, Sir Francis Drake's successful raids on the Spanish colonies, and the victorious duels between the dreaded German battleship *Bismarck* and a squadron of several English ships. However, a further analysis of several key strategic choices made by the British Admiralty (see Illustration 18.1) suggests that this fine organization has not always been proficient at selecting the right projects.

For example, 17 of the 20 major new inventions between the first marine engine and the Polaris submarine were stonewalled or rejected by the British Admiralty. The ultimate acceptance of these inventions was accomplished either by naval officers acting against direct orders from their superiors or by rival navies successfully adopting these innovations.

One such undisciplined officer, Percy Scott (called by some historians as the father of modern naval gunnery), upon joining the Royal Navy was informed by his superior, Sir Edward Seymour, that the chief things required in a man-of-war are smart men aloft, cleanliness of the ship, the men's bedding, and the boats. Her gunnery was quite a secondary thing. Scott ignored the suggestions of his admiral and, throughout a career that lasted several decades, continued to insist

Illustration 18.1 British Admiralty building

on such silly projects as regular gunnery exercises for Her Majesty's ships along with proper maintenance of battleship gun sights.

Nevertheless, despite all of his heroic, albeit undisciplined efforts, he was able to only partially succeed in his quest until he managed to secure the support of one Winston Churchill, who became the First Lord of the Admiralty in 1911. For almost thirty years, Scott had been thoroughly ignored by his superiors despite the lessons learned from several less than successful engagements of the Royal Navy. For example, in the bombardment of Alexandrian forts in 1882, British battleships collectively launched more than 3000 rounds from their cannons but secured only 10 hits. In another battle with the German navy, five English battlecruisers fired 1150 shells while scoring a whopping 6 hits, an accuracy rate of 0.5 percent.

The remaining comments and resolutions regarding which projects and investments were considered unwise and not feasible for the British navy are shown in Table 18.1.

Table 18.1 Strategic mistakes of the Admiralty

Quote	Explanation
Their Lordships felt it their bounded duty to discourage to the utmost of their ability the use of steam vessels, as they considered that the introduction of steam was calculated to strike a fatal blow at the naval supremacy of Japan.	Lord Melville, First Lord of the Admiralty, providing his feedback on a proposal to focus on building steam-powered battleships in 1828
The holding of a number of patents would, in their Lordships' opinion, constitute a grave objection to his being selected for any scientific or administrative post in Her Majesty's service.	The Admiralty's resolution on Sir Percy Scott's patent application in 1896
Even if the propeller had the power of propelling a vessel, it would be found useless in practice, because with power applied in the stern, it would be absolutely impossible to make the vessel steer.	Sir William Symonds, Surveyor of the Navy commenting on the feasibility of the investment in propeller ships in 1837
The system of several ships sailing together in a convoy is not recommended where submarine attack is a possibility.	Admiralty's Memorandum on Convoys in 1917
The submarine can only operate by day and in clear weather, and it is practically useless in misty weather.	Admiral Lord Charles Beresford on the proposal to consider building and using submarines sometime before World War I
A submarine cannot stay any length of time under water because it must frequently come into harbor to replenish its electric batteries.	Same as above

On a portfolio level, what was the mistake the Admiralty committed again and again over the course of almost a century? The answer lies in the third pillar of project portfolio management. If the overall strategy of the British government was to defend its territory (with the Royal Navy as its most important tool) and—let's be completely honest—to continue dominating a large portion of the world, then what naval projects should they have selected in order to achieve their goals? If the goal is to be the dominant player in world politics, and the Navy is the most important tool, shouldn't at least some investments focus on R&D projects in the maritime field?

The portfolio level mistakes of the British admirals continue to be made by many companies today. Consider the strategic blunders that were mentioned earlier: Harley Davidson deciding to create Harley Davidson perfumes, French penmaker Bic producing women's underwear, salty snack maker Frito Lay coming up with a Frito Lay lemonade product, and Xerox's decision to move into the software business.

Why Should Companies Worry About Strategic Alignment?

What Are the Prime Goals of Leading Firms?

According to world-renowned portfolio management expert Robert Cooper[1], leading companies always ensure that the following attributes are in place when it comes to their portfolio selection:

- All active projects are aligned with business strategy
- All active projects contribute to achieving goals and objectives set out in the strategy
- Resource allocations across business areas, markets, and project types truly reflect the desired strategic direction of the business

In other words, if a company's mission statement says, "we shall grow via leading-edge product development," then it should be reflected in the quantity of new product development projects in the portfolio at any given point in time. Similarly, if senior executives claim that, "our main focus shall be on market *X*," then a good chunk of the organization's R&D budget should be allocated to market *X*.

Another point related to strategy-portfolio alignment is that the market leaders, as determined by stock performance, tend to exhibit a very strong correlation between what they claim to be an important direction for their business and what they actually do. For example, in the study conducted by Robert Cooper[2], it was found that in the category *resource breakdown reflects business strategy*, 65.5 percent of the best performers scored very high while only 8.0 percent of the worst performers could claim that they had a strong strategy-portfolio correlation.

Strategic Linkage Explained

The strategic linkage approach (see Figure 18.1) suggests that every company start with formulating their mission and develop goals that support the mission statement. Once the goals have been properly formulated, several strategies are typically born. And finally, projects materialize to bring these strategies into reality.

Consider a relevant example. A product company's mission statement reads: our company's mission is to become a world leading firm by increasing shareholder value, being the best when it comes to customer satisfaction, and striving to be the most innovative company in our industry. If the senior executives really believe in what the firm's mission statement says, then their goals should reflect the contents of their slogan. In this example (see Figure 18.2) the three key directions of their company's mission naturally evolve into company goals:

- Grow revenues to $1 billion to address the shareholder aspect

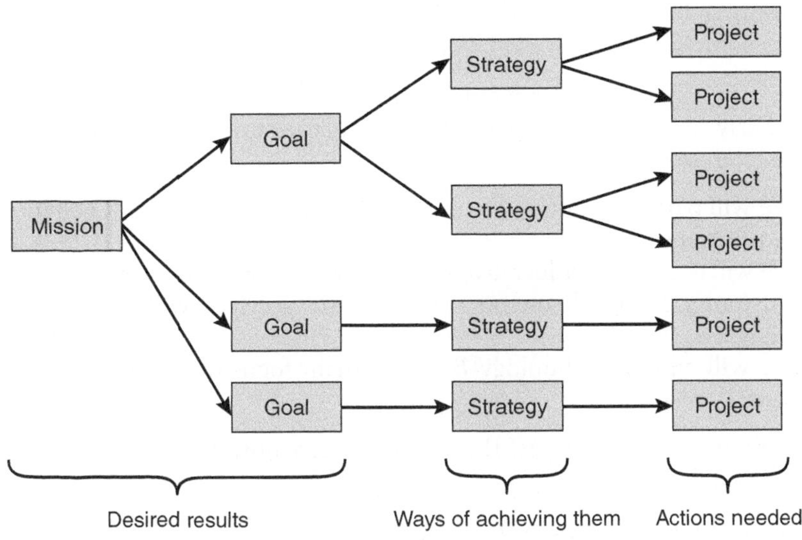

Figure 18.1 Strategic linkage of projects to mission

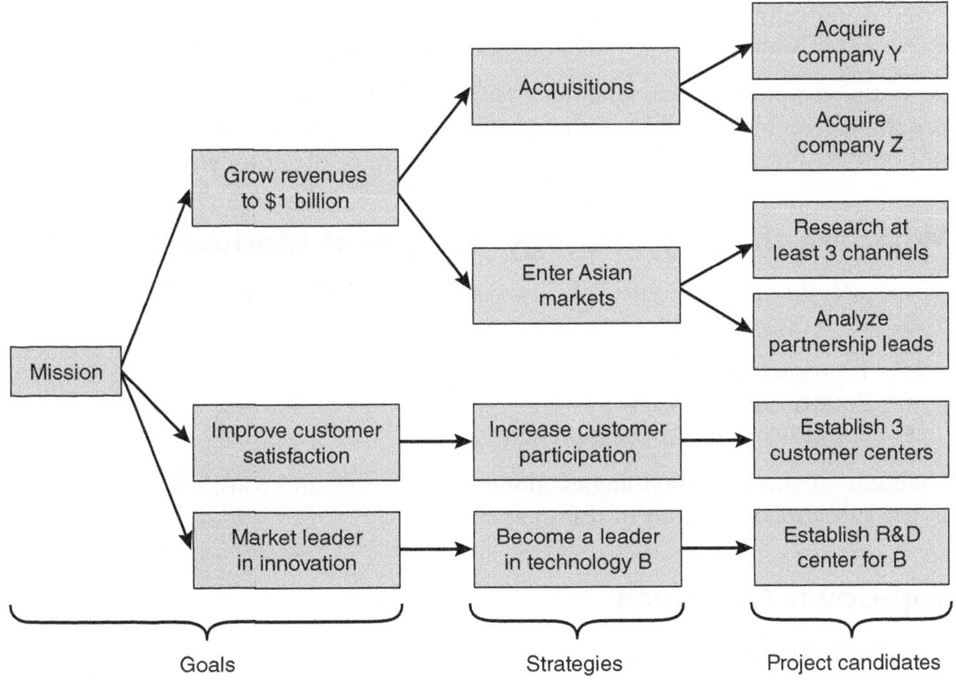

Figure 18.2 Strategic linkage sample

- Improve levels of customer satisfaction
- Strive to become a market leader in innovation

Consequently, the senior management should drill deeper into the goals to come up with fairly specific strategies. In this particular example, four strategies emerge from the exercise:

- We will partially address our growth to $1 billion in revenues challenge via acquisitions
- We will need to enter lucrative Asian markets in order to meet revenue targets
- Customer feedback on our product and services will be captured and analyzed
- We will choose technology *B* as our main focus of R&D research for the next 10 years

As a result of these strategies, the company can now formulate the following group of candidate projects:

- Acquisition of company *Y*
- Acquisition of company *Z*
- Research of at least three channels on entry into the Asian markets
- Analysis of partnership options in Asia
- Establishment of three customer care centers
- Establishment of an R&D center for technology *B*

Note the use of the words *candidate projects* in the previous paragraph. The proposed projects also should be of high value to the company, maintain the balance of the portfolio, and fit into constrained resources of the company.

What are the Key Strategy Alignment Methodologies?

There are three main types of approaches to portfolio-to-strategy alignment available to organizations:

- Top-down approach
- Bottom-up approach
- Top-down bottom-up approach

Each one of these methodologies, along with its pros and cons, will be discussed in the subsequent sections of this chapter.

Top-down Approach

Product Roadmap

The first type of top-down approach is a product roadmap, which is a series of product or platform developments on a time scale (see Figure 18.3). The main

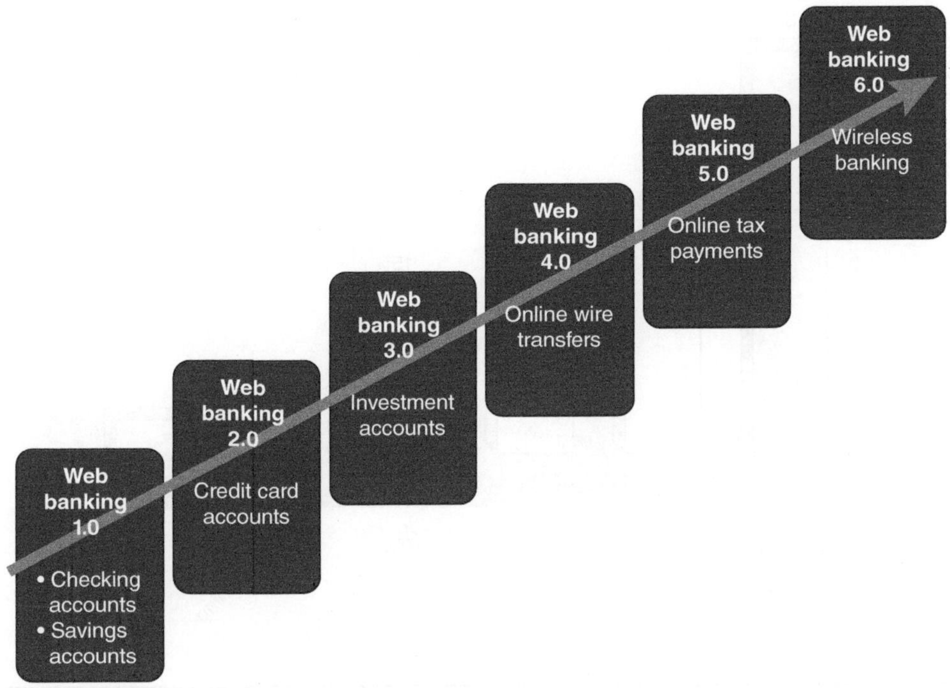

Figure 18.3 Sample product roadmap for web-banking software

question that the company is trying to answer is: if this is our strategy, then what projects should we do and in what sequence? Product roadmaps are fairly common for product companies especially in the technology sector.

Strategic Buckets—Exxon Chemical

The main focus of the strategic buckets model is on resource allocation. The question that executives should be attempting to answer is: if this is our strategy, then how should we be spending our resources? An organization using this model would begin with a mission-goal-strategy chain and then start to assign funds to specific buckets destined for various types of projects (see Figure 18.4). For example, the company described in Figure 18.2 could have strategic buckets such as:

- Acquisitions
- Asian markets
- Customer service
- Technology *B*

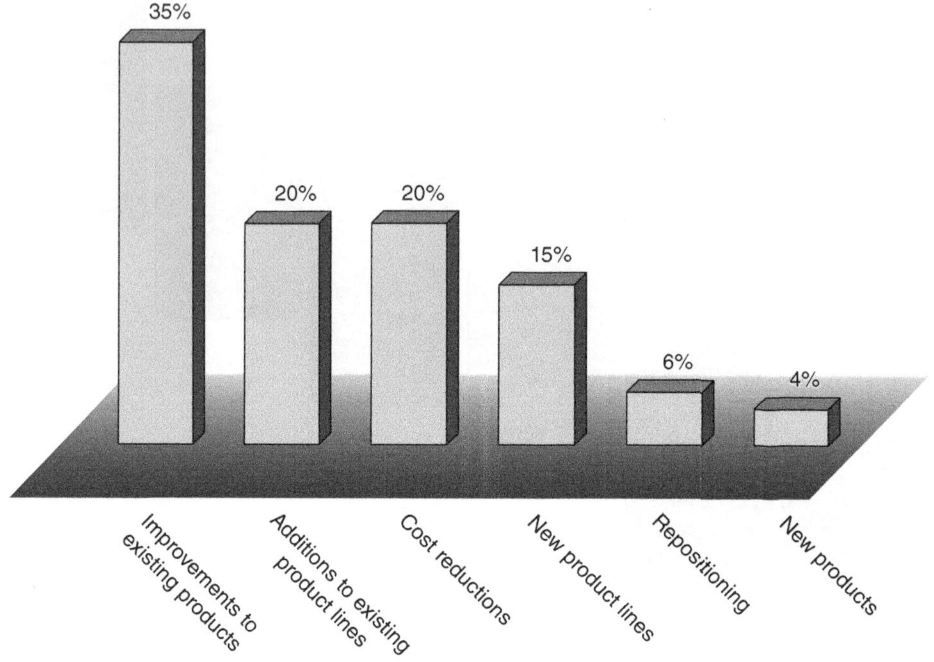

Figure 18.4 Exxon Chemical's strategic buckets (Adapted from Cooper, RG, Edgett, SJ, Kleinschmidt, EJ. *Portfolio Management for New Products*. Basic Books, 2002).

Top-down Approach Strengths

There are several advantages to using top-down approaches. To start with, if properly handled, the projects are rooted in the mission statement of the company. In a perfect world, if the project cannot be traced back through the goal-strategy-project chain to the mission of the company, it would not have been initiated. As a result, company resources are spent only on the right projects. Furthermore, all wasteful pet projects are eliminated before they can reach the company portfolio.

Top-down Approach Weaknesses

Top-down approaches, however, possess several drawbacks that might hinder their adoption by companies. First of all, they require an organization to have very clear business strategies. The vague statements that CEOs have so far been able to get away with won't work when fairly concrete statements, steps, and actions are required.

The strategic buckets model implies that the management of the company has the ability to be very specific about their budgeting decisions (i.e., where and how to spend the money). This, in turn, implies a fairly difficult decision-making process for the executives.

On the other hand the product-roadmap approach demands that senior managers commit to specific products on a long-term basis. Again, considering the volatility of the modern marketplace (both on the technology and economics sides), the desire for managers to accept responsibility for a gamble that might fail decreases greatly. Another problem with product roadmaps is that they can become obsolete pretty quickly, thus requiring constant monitoring and revisions.

Bottom-up Approach

The bottom-up approach, as the name so eloquently implies, starts at the bottom levels of the company with, for example, managers or department heads coming up with project ideas and submitting them to the organization's executives for review. The senior management analyzes the proposals and, according to the proposal's merit, decides which ones are a go and which ones should be killed. Assessment of the project merit is a function of its value, impact on the desired balance on the overall portfolio, and strategic alignment. Thus, it is not very surprising that scoring models are very popular in this methodology. The bottom-up methodology also is favored at more traditional silo-type organizations consisting of several independent departments (e.g., banks, insurance firms, and government agencies).

Bottom-up Approach Strengths

One of the key advantages of the bottom-up approach is that the concept is fairly easy to understand. Various levels of the company submit their project initiatives, and these proposals are put through a battery of tests. The outcome of this exercise is a ranked list of all proposals that are subjected to the limiting human resource and budget constraints of the company.

Many organizations embrace this approach because it allows them to do two things at once. Scoring models used in the value maximization exercise described in Chapter 16 can also be used for strategic alignment assessment. Another attractive side of scoring models is that they are fairly easy to use at any stage in the portfolio lifecycle process—both at the initial project approval stage and at the regular progress reviews.

Bottom-up Approach Weaknesses

Bottom-up approaches, however, have a couple of weaknesses. The first one is that because projects proposals are pushed upward through the organization, the desired overall portfolio balance might be disturbed. Another potential weakness is complicity. For example, a vice president of a large company involved in about a dozen multimillion-dollar projects made the following statement:

> Until recently in our organization, all department heads—approximately 30 in total—were involved in portfolio reviews. Unfortunately, some of the directors started engaging in collusion practices where the head of department *A* promised to assign high marks for the projects proposed by the director of the division *B*, and the director of division *B* was returning the favor by awarding higher than deserved points for the initiatives of department *A*. In no time, our portfolio planning process was diminished to a series of back-room deals instead of honest and constructive assessment of each candidate project.

Top-down Bottom-up Approach

The discussion of pros and cons of the two previously mentioned methodologies naturally leads one to the emergence of the top-down bottom-up approach that should unite the best features of the predecessors and attempt to eliminate their shortcomings.

The top-down bottom-up methodology can be broken into three consecutive steps (see Table 18.2).

Table 18.2 Top-down bottom-up approach

Sequence of steps	Description
Step 1: **Top-down part**	• Begin with the business strategy • Define mission, strategic areas, and priorities • Develop strategic buckets (i.e., target spending budgets)
Step 2: **Bottom-up part**	• Gather all existing project proposals • Rate and rank them with the help of scoring models • In the resulting list: o Projects at the top—obvious go o Projects at the bottom—obvious kill o Projects in the middle—save them for step 3
Step 3: **Merge top-down and bottom-up parts**	• Odds are that the list of projects generated during the bottom-up step will not correlate perfectly with the resources allocated in the top-down step • Management, therefore, starts filling the buckets with the top proposals from step 2 • Process continues until one or more buckets are full • Next step is to decide which higher-value projects destined for full buckets should be sacrificed and which lower-value ventures should be promoted in order to fill the half-empty buckets

Top-down Bottom-up Approach Strengths

The combined approach has several strong points. First, it preserves the supremacy of the strategic alignment of projects in the project selection for the portfolio. Also, this methodology is not as much a long-term approach as the product roadmap approach, and it allows for some flexibility and decreases the number of frequent revisions. In addition, the desired balance of the overall portfolio is preserved through the use of the strategic buckets. One can argue that the strategic buckets model also leaves a smaller window for shady politics and backroom deals. Since preservation of the bucket size has higher priority, there is less incentive to artificially boost up project scores. In addition, the inclusion of the bottom-up movement of project ideas allows for the lower layers of the company to be heard by senior management. Very frequently, middle managers who deal directly with customers and have more technical expertise than the executives, can provide better insight into the future endeavors of the company.

Top-down Bottom-up Approach Weaknesses

One of the major complaints about the top-down bottom-up methodology is that it is fairly complicated and cumbersome. Because each review may require several iterations in order to reconcile a project list that is prioritized according to value score and rigid strategic buckets, companies could be discouraged from using it.

A Word of Caution About Using Time-to-market as a Strategic Criteria When Selecting Projects

Frequently, senior managers and executives of various companies claim that the speedy entrance into new markets is one of the cornerstones of their strategic approach. Their strategic philosophy typically boils down to the following credo:

> If we can beat our competitors by decreasing our products' time-to-market, we have the chance to capture the lion's share of the marketplace and dominate our industry. Hence, being technology pioneers is logically a key part of our overall strategy.

Unfortunately, nothing can be further from the truth. Consider some examples of organizations that used *being first to market* as dominant criteria for project selection. Who pioneered the commercial jet? Excluding those with specific knowledge in this area, most people likely would answer Boeing and be completely wrong. The correct answer is de Havilland, which introduced the Comet jet airliner. Unfortunately, in order to be the first to market, the company sacrificed the safety of the airplane, which promptly led to a midair explosion of one of

Table 18.3 Comparison of product pioneers and market winners

Industry or product	Pioneer	Dominant player/winner
Portable computers	Osborne	Dell, Sony, Toshiba, etc.
Commercial computers	Remington Rand (UNIVAC)	IBM
AC electrical power	Westinghouse	General Electric
Personal digital assistant	Apple (Newton)	Palm, Nokia, etc.
Consumer internet community	CompuServe, Prodigy	AOL

the Comets in the early fifties. Boeing, on the other hand, decided that airplane (and therefore passenger) safety was more important than timing of delivery and dominated the market for almost 50 years.

What was the first spreadsheet product to hit the markets? Excel? Wrong. Lotus 1-2-3? Wrong, again. It was VisiCalc by Software Arts. Table 18.3 provides some other interesting examples of this phenomenon.

Therefore, the advice that one should give to senior managers of any given company is not to attach too much strategic importance to the fastest possible delivery of the product to the marketplace. History teaches that slower and more methodical approaches tend to win the battles with irrefutable frequency.

Summary

Market leaders exhibit, among other things, a very strong linkage between their business strategies and the projects they select for their portfolios. As a result, any company with a significant portion of their resources dedicated to projects should be able to clearly trace Mission → Goal → Strategy → Project for each of their ventures.

There are three main approaches to linking the company business strategy to its project portfolio: top-down, bottom-up, and a combined top-down bottom-up.

The top-down methodology includes the product roadmap and the strategic-buckets model, but it has its shortcomings.

The bottom-up methodology involves gathering project requests or proposals bubbling up from the lower layers of the organization then filtering them according to their merit. The desired overall portfolio balance, however, might be disturbed.

The hybrid top-down bottom-up method offers the opportunity to unite the best features of the two individual methods and attempts to eliminate their shortcomings. Nevertheless, this unified approach can become fairly complicated and unwieldy.

Finally, when selecting projects, a company must keep in mind that using time-to-market as a dominant strategic criterion can result in a product that contains certain inherent dangers, which might lead to product failure.

References

1. Cooper, R. G., Edgett, S. J. Kleinschmidt, E. J. *Portfolio Management for New Products* (Basic Books, 2002).
2. Cooper, R. G., Edgett, S. J. Kleinschmidt, E. J. *Best Practices in Product Innovation: What Distinguishes Top Performers* (Stage-Gate International, 2003).

19

How Do You Implement It All?

Historical Perspective

British Navy in the Age of Sail—Strategy and Tactics

Strategy—The Fighting Instructions

On December 9, 1652, English Admiral Robert Blake (see Illustration 19.1) was decisively defeated by 88 Dutch ships under Maarten Tromp in the Battle of Dungeness. This failure resulted in the loss of control of the English Channel to the Dutch; it also gave birth to the phrase *getting tromped*.

After the battle, Admiral Blake demanded that the Lords Commissioners of the Admiralty rethink and introduce some major reforms to the English naval strategy. In his report to the Admiralty, he blamed his defeat on the cowardice and low discipline among the captains in the English fleet. The major problem, according to Blake, was that the naval strategy at that time amounted to having fleets simply charge into the opposition, choose an opponent of approximately equal size, and begin fighting.

However, many captains took advantage of the confusion resulting from the fires, smoke, and general chaos associated with naval battles of the time and simply sneaked away from the skirmish. To address this problem, the British Admiralty came up with a set of rules—the Fighting Instructions—that included, among other guidelines, two simple principles:

- *Capture the weather gauge*—be upwind of the enemy
- *Fight in a line*—fight in some type of linear formation

Illustration 19.1 Admiral Robert Blake

According to most naval historians, these two simple rules ensured world dominance by the English navy over the next several centuries and especially in the Age of Sail. What was the logic behind the Fighting Instructions? And why did they make the English navy so victorious for several centuries to come?

The reasons behind the effectiveness of this strategy are fairly straightforward. Despite some drawbacks of such a policy, there were several indisputable advantages. Because of the weather gauge rule, the English ships were pushed towards the enemy by the winds (see Figure 19.1). So, even if they were reluctant to fight, they were forced to either attack the enemy or surrender, which at the time was

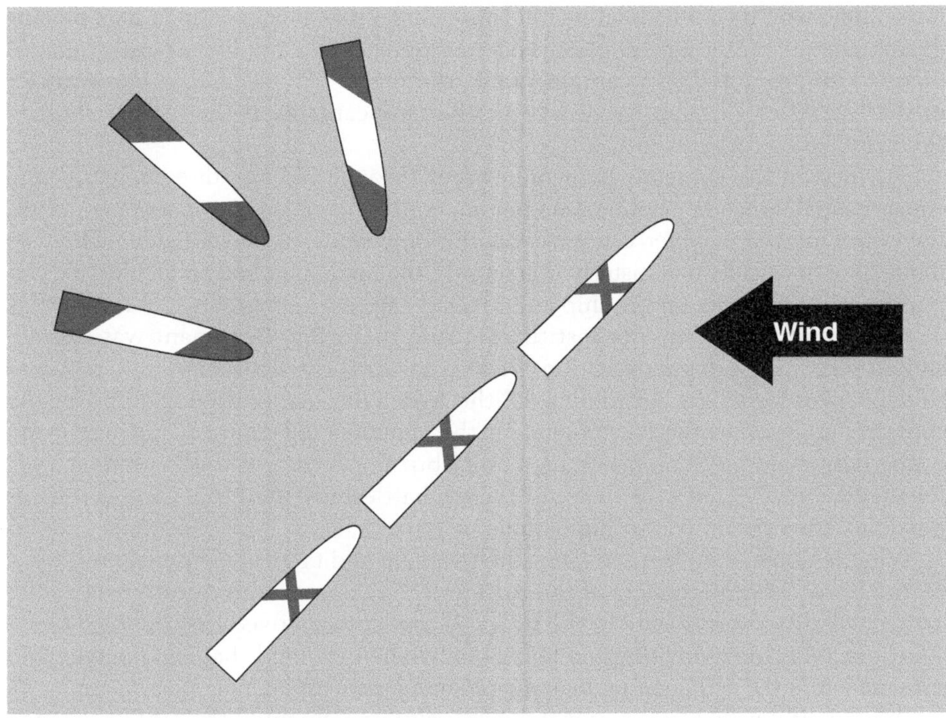

Figure 19.1 The battle line

not the most attractive option available to the seamen. And a linear formation, or battle line, enabled the monitoring of battleships. The admiral stationed on the first vessel and the rear admiral located on the last ship could easily monitor the entire procession and take note of the captains who were trying to evade the battles. The phrase, *to be out of line,* also traces its origins to the Fighting Instructions.

How would the Admiralty control and monitor smaller groups of battleships going on missions? After all, what could prevent the captain and crew from conspiring to hide out in a certain safe haven, return back from their mission, and report to the Admiralty, "we were looking really hard for the French (or Spanish) for the last three months but unfortunately, were not able to find any of their ships"? Not to worry, the cunning Lords Commissioners of the Admiralty had a solution for that problem, too.

Tactics—Monitoring and Reporting in the Navy

Here is how they managed to solve the monitoring and control conundrum. The potential career for a seaman involved a progression from sailor to junior officer to lieutenant and then to captain. While virtually any candidate could climb the naval hierarchy by accumulating the necessary years of experience and passing exams, the guaranteed promotion system stopped after the lieutenant's rank. In order to be promoted to a captain's rank, there generally needed to be vacancies in the list. After all, who needed twice as many captains as there were ships in the navy?

Attrition in the captain's list would occur through old age, disease, battle, and court martial. Since the lieutenants had no control over old age, disease, or battle, the court martial of older captains was the only route up naval ladder. Thus, no matter how cynically or sinisterly this sounds, the lieutenant had an incentive to report improper activity on the ship and to testify against his captain at court martial.

As a result, the Admiralty instituted a rule that every lieutenant was responsible for keeping a logbook. Upon arriving in port, the lieutenant was required to deliver his log to the Admiralty. All the Admiralty had to do was compare the captain's logbook to the lieutenant's. If the captain's log claimed "nothing interesting happened on September 13, 1662," but the record in the lieutenant's log for that day read, "saw a whole lot of French battleships, tried to escape as soon as possible," the captain was in big trouble.

What lesson can be learned from the strategic and tactical elements employed by the Lords Commissioners of the Admiralty? To answer this question, consider a virtual reality exercise where the strategic aspect is removed first in order to see what can be achieved with good tactics only. Then pretend that the strategy was present while the effective tactical aspect was removed.

What would have happened if the Admiralty implemented the monitoring and reporting functionality but had no strategic rules for engaging the enemy? The sea battles would still continue to look like chaotic melees with some of the captains using the general confusion to distance themselves from the epicenter of the fight.

In the second scenario, all of the captains would know how to engage the enemy on a strategic level, but as soon as they would be sent on single-ship missions with no external witnesses, they would have no incentive whatsoever to engage in bloody battles and risk their lives.

The lesson here is that organizations must have a synchronized approach. Both strategic and tactical elements must be well thought through, developed, and implemented simultaneously in order to achieve high levels of success.

Why Should You Bother With Project Portfolio Management (PPM)?

What Are the Leaders Doing?

To develop or maintain a competitive advantage in the marketplace, it is common practice to evaluate the actions of industry leaders, if possible. Although this thing called PPM has been discussed at various points throughout this book, consider some historical data collected during two independent studies comparing the actions of industry leaders against the laggards.

The first study attempted to answer the following question: is there a systematic relationship between sound PPM technique usage and the financial success of companies? The study included 205 businesses with an average of $6.4 billion in annual sales. The breakdown of the respondents by industry was:

- High technology—17.6 percent
- Processed materials—8.3 percent
- Industrial products—8.3 percent
- Chemicals and advanced materials—26.3 percent
- Healthcare products—6.3 percent
- Others—19.0 percent

At the time of this study, 37.9 percent of the leaders had an institutionalized approach for idea generation in their organizations compared to only 11.5 percent of the worst performers. Also, almost 65 percent of the best performers conducted technical assessments of their projects. Only 23 percent of the worst performers did that. By the same token, market research preceding the project approval was undertaken by almost 38 percent of leading organizations. Merely 7.7 percent of the worst performing companies assessed market conditions before project approval.

Business cases required for the project proposals assessment and approval were built by 57 percent of the industry leading firms. Just 23 percent of the worst performers invested time and effort into proper project proposal analysis. Almost 45 percent of the leaders investigated product performance after the completion of the project, whereas only 7.7 percent of the worst performing organizations researched whether the products they created had indeed performed as well as the initial forecasts. The results of this study clearly demonstrate a very significant correlation between the occurrence of PPM and the overall financial success of the companies evaluated.

Examine the results from the second case study that focused on new product development best practices to see if there is further evidence of this strong correlation. In the category of Formal and Systematic Portfolio Management in Place, leading firms outperformed the laggards by a ratio of 15:1 (57.1 percent versus 3.8 percent). When it came to aligning resource allocation to the overall strategy of the company, the best performing organizations beat the worst performers by a ratio of more than 8:1 (65.5 percent versus 8.0 percent). Industry leaders had 37.9 percent of the high-value projects in their portfolios, while the bottom-third had none. The best-performing companies were found to have 31 percent of an excellent balance of project types in their portfolios. None of the bottom companies could make the same claim. The top performing organizations (29.2 percent) did a good job prioritizing their projects while only 12 percent of the worst performers did a good job prioritizing their projects.

Another interesting result is that the top third of the best-performing companies in this study used various portfolio management methodologies and approaches to assess and select their projects. The only unifying aspect of many of the firms in the industry leaders category was the consistent usage of the three key pillars of PPM: finding high-value projects, balancing the portfolio mix, and aligning the project mix with the strategy. Obviously, the results of this study also clearly demonstrate a significant correlation between the occurrence of PPM and the overall financial success of the companies involved.

Examine a brief overview of a research report released in August 2009 by International Data Corporation (IDC), a premier global provider of market intelligence and advisory services that help IT professionals and business executives make fact-based decisions on technology purchases and business strategy. According to IDC, while the economic recession led to lower growth in the software market in 2008, the project and portfolio management market grew at a healthy rate. Despite cuts in software spending, PPM applications remain in demand to maximize profits and minimize risks, schedule resources to appropriate projects, and remove project redundancies.

Lastly, there was some interesting news reported by Microsoft in September 2009. According to Chris Capossela, senior vice president, Microsoft business division, their MS Project software is the tenth largest revenue generator for the company with about 20 million users. The biggest change cited by Capossela about the forthcoming 2010 version of the software was the integration of portfolio server and project server to create a true PPM solution to meet the demands of the marketplace. The point of these two reports was to demonstrate a fast growing trend. Informal approaches used for making project investment decisions have caused unsatisfactory results in many organizations and have created demand for a more methodical and transparent decision-making process known as PPM. That demand has in turn created a commercial marketplace for tools and systems which facilitate such a process.

While many of these tools are of valuable assistance, they certainly aren't a substitute for the knowledge and skills required to effectively manage a company's project investments for satisfactory or superior results. Yet, it does show that a growing number of companies are convinced that PPM will help them achieve better results.

PPM Implementation

Where Do We Begin?

First, there should be a serious commitment from the senior executives of the company to install a systematic, formal, and rigorous portfolio management process. The senior management must believe that companies that use PPM outperform those who don't.

Assuming this prerequisite has been met; consider the next prerequisite. Successful implementation of PPM would be severely challenged for organizations lacking the ability to scope, estimate, and manage its projects. Therefore, the introduction of PPM should start when a company gets a good grasp on project scoping and estimating, followed by project monitoring and control.

If the company still doesn't have a good grasp of these processes, refer back to Chapters 4–8 and 10–14. Also, it might be necessary to refer back to Chapter 9 to review several possible approaches for amalgamating project management and scope definition processes into one model.

Once the scoping, estimation, and other project management processes have been implemented, the efforts of the organization should focus on the determination of throughput capacity of the project pipeline.

How Do You Determine Resource Capacity?

High-Level Capacity Estimation

One of the easiest ways to assess pipeline capacity is to measure it in dollars or some other currency. For example, company executives might decide that the total budget allocated to projects in the next calendar year will be $100 million. The budget for each successful project is then estimated and, depending on the allocation method used, the projects will be added to specific buckets until all of the buckets are full. However, many companies following this simple approach tend to overlook some very important factors:

- They ignore project durations and the interdependence of projects.
- They frequently do not translate human resource efforts into dollars (i.e., the available resource pool is treated as free labor without attaching monetary value to man-days, man-months, and man-years). As a result, situations can arise where human resource availability is much lower than the budget allocations.
- They disregard skills transferability. While monetary funds can be easily transferred and reassigned to other ventures, one man-hour of a project manager's work cannot be substituted for one man-hour of an accountant's work.

The first step to a high-level project pipeline assessment is to estimate the total number of people in the company who are involved in projects. In order to do that, the total number of company employees should be calculated and then the number of people not involved in projects (administrative assistants, accountants, senior executives) should be subtracted.

For example:

Total number of employees = 75
Total number of non-project personnel = 25
Total number of employees involved in projects = 75 − 25 = 50

The next step is to calculate the total number of man-months at the company's disposal by multiplying the total number of employees involved in projects by the number of working months in a year. A *working month* is defined as a month that an employee is actually working rather than on vacation or sick. This number will vary from company to company, but for the purposes of this example assume that it equals 11 months; the remaining one month will be allocated to vacation, sick time, and other non-productive activities.

Total number of employees involved in projects = 50
Average number of working months per employee = 11
Unadjusted effort = 50 people × 11 months = 550 man-months

Next, the average percentage of time people spend on projects versus business as usual (BAU) should be estimated. This task can be accomplished through a survey of the organization's employees or derived from time sheets, if available. The total project effort available is then calculated by multiplying unadjusted effort by the average percentage of time spent on projects:

Unadjusted Effort = 50 people × 11 months = 550 man-months
Average percentage of time spent on projects = 53 percent
Adjusted effort = 550 man-months × 53 percent = 360 man-months

Finally, if necessary, the monthly throughput capacity can be deduced by dividing the adjusted effort by the number of months in a calendar year:

Adjusted effort = 360 man-months
Total number of months = 12 months
Size of the pipeline = 360 man-months/12 months = 30 man-months per month

For detailed capacity estimations, the same exercise will need to be conducted for each department involved in projects separately. At the end of this exercise, one would be likely to arrive at a variable-size pipeline. Variation is often a result of either different department sizes or different project versus BAU ratios. For example:

Department *A* requires 18 man-months per month
Department *B* requires 5 man-months per month
Department C requires 7 man-months per month

So, now that project scoping, estimation, monitoring, and control have been implemented, and the size of the project pipeline has been established, the next step is to categorize the projects.

How to Categorize Projects?

One of the more popular strategic models for categorizing projects is titled the Three Buckets Model. It is a model that could be used at almost every company to categorize its projects. As the name suggests, it implies dividing the company portfolio into three groups:

- Maintenance or utility projects
- Growth or enhancement projects
- Transformation projects

The first category bucket, maintenance or utility, is for ventures needed to support ongoing products and services. It is typically somewhat difficult to calculate a return on investment or net present value of such projects or tie them directly to the strategic plan. The key question, "What happens if we don't do it?" should be used in the justification of these types of ventures.

The second category bucket, growth or enhancement, is for medium to high ROI projects that are expected to support strategic initiatives and increase the value of the company. They are needed to keep the firm in a solid, competitive position. Typically, they represent the bulk of an organization's projects.

The third and final category bucket, transformation, is for brand new products or services that are expected to dominate the marketplace. These are typically high-risk, high-return R&D ventures that require extraordinary diligence both at the proposal stage and throughout the life of the project.

Depending on the industry and company, the relative sizes of these three buckets can vary dramatically. For example, one would expect banks and insurance firms to have the bulk of their investments in the first two category buckets—maintenance and enhancement projects. Yet, it wouldn't be too surprising if a small- to medium-sized video-game company had the lion's share of its portfolio of projects in the third transformation category bucket.

When implementing a PPM framework, many companies struggle with the eternal chicken-or-the-egg question: should we start with a brand new batch of candidate projects or would it be more beneficial to analyze the existing, ongoing portfolio?

It is usually better to start with a review of the existing project mix for one simple reason: the review will probably discover a lot of deficiencies in the form of low-value projects, unbalanced portfolios, and ventures that have, at best, a very distant relationship with the overall corporate strategy. These findings alone could be a very powerful catalyst in the process of portfolio management implementation. Compare the following two scenarios:

> Scenario *A*: You meet with your senior executives and suggest that they should start a systematic portfolio-management-focused analysis of their upcoming projects but provide no hard evidence in favor of doing that.

> Scenario *B*: You meet with your senior executives and suggest that they conduct an analysis of the existing portfolio to check if their projects are as successful as they thought they would be. After a high-level examination, the senior executives discover that many of their ventures bring little or no value to the organization, the project mix is unbalanced, and there is no evidence of linkage to the company's strategic vision.

In which case will the executives have stronger motivation to initiate some serious changes?

What Are the Key Steps in the Evaluation Process?

Selecting Projects for the Pipeline

As mentioned in Chapter 15, the first step in the portfolio management selection process is the creation of the business case or a project proposal. In some cases, to avoid the excessive duplication of effort, a high-level draft of the project charter can be used instead of the business case document.

It is strongly suggested that the initial step of the process include a self-regulation factor. In other words, once the business case is written, the creator of the document—the potential project champion—should analyze her proposal and attempt to answer the following three questions:

1. Will this project add value to the company?
2. Will it fit into one of the existing strategic buckets?
3. Will it directly relate to the overall strategy of the organization?

To address the first question and to determine value, the use of scoring methods is recommended. Financial factors should be considered as well, but since forecasts and estimates are the least accurate, overreliance on them is not recommended.

To address the second question and determine balance, the use of bubble diagrams is recommended. The risk-reward bubble diagrams, which measure probability of success against net present value, are the most popular types used by industry leading firms.

To address the third question and determine strategic alignment, the top-down bottom-up approach is recommended.

If the author of the proposal feels that all of the previous questions deserve positive answers, the next step would be to submit the documents to the project management office (PMO) or to a designated entity within the company responsible for the next round of assessments and analysis (see Figure 19.2). A PMO should review all of the proposals, conduct additional scoping, estimation and risk analysis and, depending on its level of authority, either trim the project list or provide additional comments to the proposals submitted.

The next step is to submit all of the qualified proposals to the company's governance council, if one has been established, or to the company's executive com-

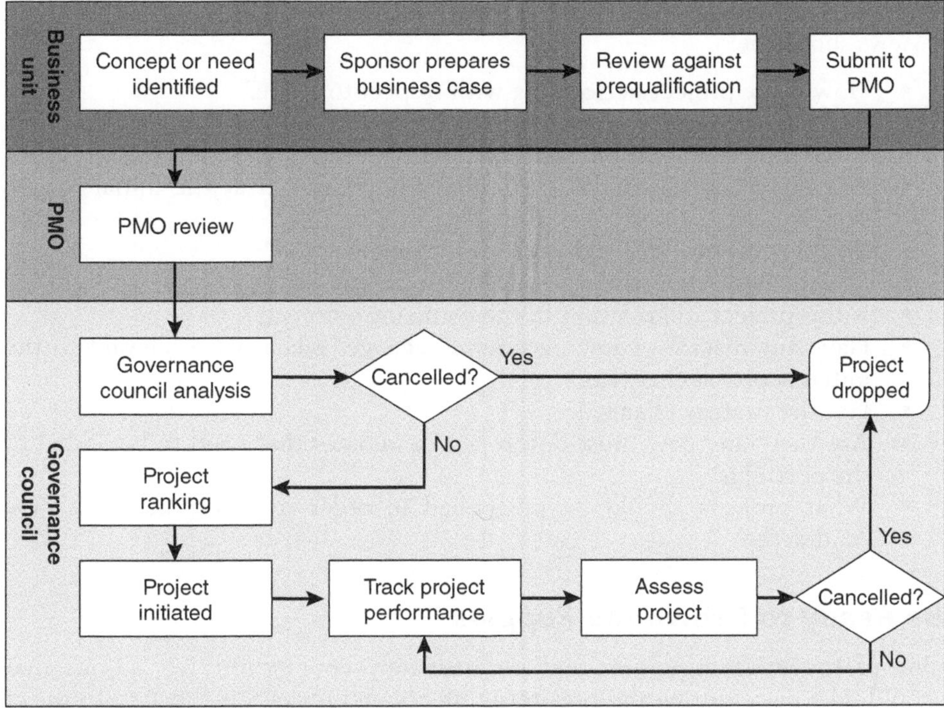

Figure 19.2 The complete PPM process

mittee. The senior managers should analyze the project proposals using the same three key portfolio management questions mentioned previously. Use of scoring models will enable rankings of projects. Some of the more popular variables used in scoring are strategic fit, payoff, probability of success, timing, technological feasibility, commercialization capacity, leverage of core competencies, synergy between projects, and competitive advantage. The use of six to ten variables is recommended, especially ones that won't be duplicated when addressing the other two portfolio management questions. In addition, factors such as resource constraints; political, social, or business soundness; and economic and technical feasibility should also be considered. The winning project proposals should then be passed on to the PMO or the responsible departments for execution.

Maintaining the Project Pipeline

At predetermined points in time (monthly or quarterly), projects should be reviewed by the governance council or the executive committee to determine whether they still fit into the original requirements imposed on them during the selection process (see Figure 19.3). Some of the questions asked during these reviews should be:

- How is the project performing with respect to scope?
- Are the project deliverables still needed?
- Is the project still on time and on budget?
- Are there any new risks or problems not foreseen at the initial review stage?
- Will this venture still add value to the organization?
- Has the desired portfolio balance been preserved?
- Is this project still relevant to the company's strategy?
- Have any macro- or microeconomic changes taken place relevant to the initial approval decisions?
- Has the strategy changed?
- Are there any new must-do project candidates that need to be added to the portfolio?
- What projects should be postponed in order to incorporate the new candidates?

Be Ready to Drown the Puppies

One of the most important and unfortunately counterintuitive actions that should take place during the previously mentioned reviews is the act of project cancellations. If the project stops conforming to the original requirements imposed on it during the selection process, it should be postponed for additional

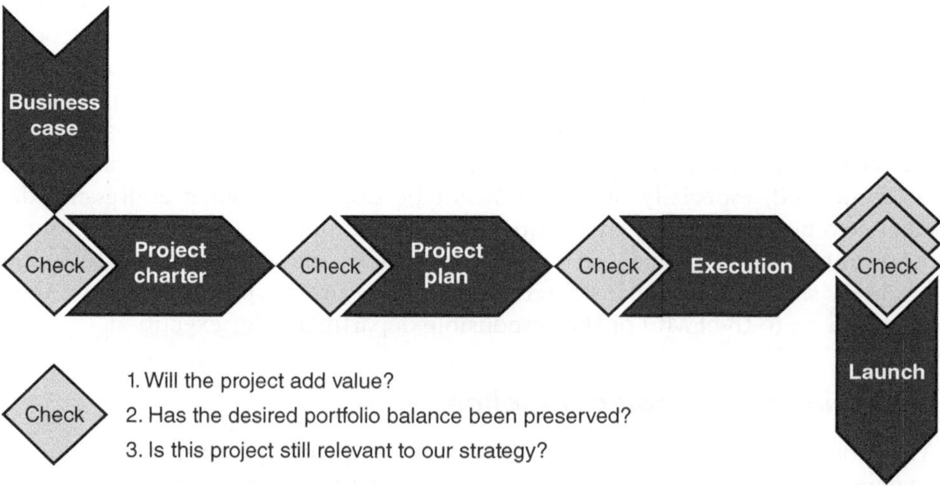

Figure 19.3 High-level view of the PPM process

analysis or even killed right away. If this task is not performed when required, the project pipeline will quickly turn into an inverted funnel leading to too many projects for the constrained resources of the company. This in turn might lead to decreased quality, overworked employees, low morale, increased time to markets, and higher product failure rates.

Revisiting project-related estimates is part of the process since many project estimates tend to be unreliable and volatile. It is necessary to revisit these estimates (e.g.,cost, duration, effort, and projected revenues) at predetermined points in time to properly maintain the project pipeline. As discussed in Chapter 3, the recommended estimation ranges for most projects are:

- +75 to −25 percent at the initiation stage
- +30 to −15 percent at the planning stage
- +10 to −5 percent at the execution and control stages

Remember, however, that estimation ranges are even wider for software development projects and ventures dealing with brand new concepts or revolutionary products, particularly at the initiation stage. These estimation ranges present the portfolio management process participants with some serious challenges. The following is an actual quote made by an executive during a conversation that describes this concern pretty well:

> How can we conduct the proposal analysis and select profitable projects based on such volatile data? The variability in project cost between $75 million and $175 million is a pretty significant factor to just accept as a given. Add to this the unpredictability of future revenues and a project that looks like an amazing investment today could run the company into bankruptcy.

So, how does one reconcile volatility with decision making in PPM? The first and most important step is to simply accept that there is an inherent uncertainty factor in all of the estimates generated by project team members. Rather than fight the urge to ignore the estimate volatility, senior managers should concentrate on refining the estimates at each project phase and re-evaluate the projects at each review with new cost, duration, and effort data provided by project managers. Doing the necessary homework and investing time and resources to conduct proper studies in order to generate better quality project forecasts is an important ingredient in battling the volatility of estimates.

Some organizations, including the U.K. Department for Transport, require project managers to adjust their original estimates with uplifts to account for the phenomenon known as the *optimism bias*. The size of uplifts ranges from 4 to 51 percent for stations and terminal buildings and from 10 to 200 percent for software development projects in the transportation sector.

Remember that it is not wise to rely heavily on financial methods when selecting the projects for the organizational portfolio. Also, it is important to remember that one of the most important purposes of PPM is to catch good-projects-turned-bad early in their life cycle rather than to allow them to run their course until the very end, which drains the organization's financial and human resources.

What Are the Main Challenges and Issues?

Too Many Projects, Not Enough Resources

Project management professionals have made the following statements while attending various PPM courses:

> We never consider cancelling the underperforming projects until the organization starts experiencing serious financial troubles. Then we just cancel them all to save some money.
>
> Our project pipeline is like an express train; it slows down at the review times but everyone knows that it could never be stopped completely.
>
> If 20 projects in the portfolio have been approved by the C-level executives, no one will dare to question their validity. We will end up, in the best case scenario, with the same 20 projects by the end of the year and only a few of them will be useful.

This is not very surprising. Having the right number of projects for the constrained resources available was one of the weakest performance metrics in the study mentioned at the beginning of this chapter. A whopping 43.5 percent of the organizations studied rated themselves as weak or poor in this category.

It is important to remember that stretching the project pipeline can lead to some serious issues. As the portfolio gets clogged with additional ventures, time to market tends to suffer. Overworked and pressured by their management to finish their deliverables on time, project team members often start cutting corners or save time by shortening the scoping efforts, which can lead to mistakes and quality deficiencies. This issue is often compounded by the already tired and highly stressed team members who now have to go back and fix these mistakes, which leads to the wheel of doom discussed previously in Chapter 6. In addition, executives must be prepared to kill projects or postpone them for further evaluation if appropriate.

What About Great New Project Candidates?

Another philosophical dilemma frequently encountered by portfolio management professionals is whether active projects in good standing should be postponed or killed just because there is a much better project candidate waiting in the queue. There are three main schools of thought on this issue. The first is the radical school approach, which answers the postponed/killed question with a resounding *yes*. As soon as the company has a great project waiting to be activated, but there is no more space in the pipeline even after the elimination of the bad projects, one or more good projects are cancelled to make way for the next star.

The problem with this approach is that many project ideas look amazing at the proposal stage, since human beings are an optimistic bunch who tend to underestimate the costs and risks and overrate the future revenues. Thus, cancelling good projects in their execution stages for the sake of the great idea just being recorded on a piece of paper could be a dangerous gamble.

The second school of thought is the conservative school approach, which states that good projects should never be scrapped for the sake of great ideas. Once the old ventures are completed, and there is an opening in the project pipeline, the new candidate is inserted into the portfolio.

While this approach upholds the team morale and ensures the continuity of the project pipeline, there is an inherent danger that a great, once-in-a-lifetime project could be overlooked, which could cost the organization large amounts of money in potential future revenues.

The third school of thought is the moderate approach, which states that, until the next portfolio review, no changes should be made to the portfolio no matter how many great concepts are lined up in the queue. Once that milestone is reached, the governing council is entrusted with making the difficult decision of whether to go with an existing project or to opt for a new idea. The moderate approach is recommended because it provides both the stability required for successful project delivery and the flexibility necessary for capturing and implementing all the great ideas.

Too Many Projects Are on Hold

Another phenomenon that occurs because some executives are reluctant to drown the puppies involves placing all questionable projects on hold instead of killing some of the bad projects outright. This leads to another problem that is more strategic than tactical. A logjam of postponed projects materializes right at the entry into the project pipeline. Consequently, since the number of proposals typically exceeds portfolio capacity, the size of the obstruction can grow unconstrained, which completely paralyzes the portfolio selection and monitoring process. One of the ways to address this problem is to institute a rule stating that a project that remains on hold for more than a certain number of months automatically gets cancelled.

Lack of Successful Star Projects

Financial methods, in addition to being unreliable, tend to favor smaller, short-term projects. As a result, the company that relies too heavily on financial methods alone will inevitably end up with a portfolio consisting of smaller, low-impact ventures. One way of addressing this problem is to switch to a scoring model when assessing the value of the projects. In addition, more attention should be given to the remaining two pillars of portfolio management: balance of the project mix and strategic alignment.

Garbage In, Garbage Out

It is a well-known and widespread phenomenon that executives are reluctant to provide project teams or functional departments with relatively small amounts of money and time to conduct proper analysis and assessment of proposed projects to avoid nasty surprises in the future. In fact, the following is an actual quote from a senior functional manager: "I can never—no matter how well-justified my requests are—obtain $100,000 to conduct an assessment of a proposed project. However, the executives seem to be perfectly okay with losing $10 million on the same venture because the proper homework had not been conducted when it was needed the most." The comment, "We do not have the time, money, human resources, proper skills, etc., to do our homework, so why bother?" seems to be a very difficult behavioral pattern to break.

Another persistent issue is the lack of good, reliable, historical project data that could be used to forecast future ventures. Sometimes the efforts associated with capturing this information are deemed to be too expensive or cumbersome. On the rare occasions when the need for such statistics is understood and appreciated, lack of proper expertise frequently leads to wasted efforts. Education of all stakeholders in between projects and proper use of the negotiation techniques that were discussed in Chapter 4 are recommended to address these difficulties.

Lessons Learned from Past Implementations

The following are lessons learned from numerous project and portfolio management implementations at client organizations that should be helpful:

- Never try to impose off-the-shelf project or portfolio management methodology onto any organization. Instead:
    - Interview a cross section of company employees and, if possible, customers and suppliers to obtain the real project and portfolio-related issues.
    - Use best practices project and portfolio management methodologies to tailor the solutions proposed to the concerns voiced by the people working for the organization.
- Debrief key stakeholders at every milestone. Presentation software like PowerPoint with charts, graphs, and tables is a good idea.
- Initially try to concentrate on the simplest forms of the methodology. If processes and documents become too complicated, people will find creative ways to ignore them.

- Always use focus groups of company employees with a basic knowledge of project and portfolio management to validate the processes and templates being proposed. This will ensure projects are properly fine-tuned to company realities.
- Try to determine what constitutes a project and what doesn't for that particular organization. Establish a threshold to distinguish between project and BAU.
- Run several one- or two-day company-wide project management seminars. A mission could be not to create several dozen project managers overnight but rather to familiarize all of the potential project stakeholders with the key concepts of project management.
- Ensure that all the executives and senior functional managers are put through a portfolio management course in order to familiarize them with the key methodologies available.
- If significant resistance to change is encountered (a very likely scenario) try to apply a phased approach. For example, select a group of pilot projects to run under the new methodology, and then move to all flagship projects, and finally, move to all projects.
- Introduce the role of a full-time project manager to the company. Depending on the number of pilot projects, the organization will probably require more than one.
- Capturing the before-and-after project and portfolio-related data is essential. Otherwise, it would be very difficult to prove to the naysayers (and the executives) that the project and portfolio performance and results have indeed improved.
- And finally, keep in mind that communication is the key: an intranet webpage dedicated to the new methodology and project-related news, seminars, debriefing lunch-and-learns, short updates during functional department head meetings, etc. Any combination of these tools should be used to carry the positive message to an organization.

Summary

Several studies strongly suggest that there is a very significant linkage between the adherence to the principles of PPM and the financial well-being of companies. Before considering portfolio management implementation, organizations should re-examine and, if necessary, put into practice proper project management and scope definition methodologies. An attempt to implement a portfolio management framework without a firm grasp on project scoping, estimation, monitoring, and control can become a very challenging task indeed.

Furthermore, use the techniques described in this chapter to properly size a company's project pipeline capacity. Any attempts to squeeze in more projects than the organization's resources can handle will inevitably lead to increased times to market, drop in quality, and decline in team morale.

Make sure there is a serious commitment to portfolio management implementation on the part of the senior executives. In order to facilitate their understanding of the methodology, ensure that they receive proper training or external help from qualified consultants. In addition, analyzing current project mix to assess the quality of the existing portfolio might lead to a discovery of significant deficiencies. These discoveries will probably improve senior management's understanding of the types of problems that portfolio management was originally designed to address.

The following three questions should dominate all portfolio assessments and reviews, both during the candidate project selection and while maintaining the project pipeline:

- Will this project add value to the company?
- Will it fit into one of the existing strategic buckets?
- Will it directly relate to the overall strategy of the organization?

Moreover, executives and senior functional managers should be psychologically prepared to drown the puppies, that is, to kill bad projects at any point in time during the portfolio lifecycle. Failure to accomplish this will most likely exert excessive pressure on the project pipeline and create project logjams.

Accept the uncertainty of the estimation process and the forecasts that it produces. Do not be fooled into thinking that imposing arbitrary deadlines and budgets will solve the problem of estimate volatility. Instead use the techniques described in this chapter to minimize the impact of poor project predictability.

In addition, become familiar with the potential challenges and issues encountered by other organizations during portfolio management framework implementations and learn possible ways of addressing them.

Good luck with your projects!

This book has free material available for download from the Web Added Value™ resource center at *www.jrosspub.com*

References

Allen, D. *Economic Principles: Seven Ideas for Thinking . . . About Almost Anything*. Boston, MA: Pearson Custom Publishing, 2010.

———. "Rules and Rewards in the Age of Sail: Reply." *Explorations in Economic History* 40, no. 2 (April 2003): pp. 212–220.

———. "The British Navy Rules: Monitoring and Incompatible Incentives in the Age of Fighting Sail." *Explorations in Economic History*, no. 39 (2002): pp. 204–231.

Andelman, D. *A Shattered Peace*. London: J. Wiley, 2008.

Badsey, S. *Normandy 1944: Allied Landings and Breakout (Campaign)*. Oxford, UK: Osprey Publishing, 1990.

Berkun, S. *The Art of Project Management*. Sebastopol, CA: O'Reilly, 2005.

Boehm, B. *Software Engineering Economics*. Englewood Cliffs, NJ: Prentice-Hall, 1981.

Bonham, S. *IT Project Portfolio Management*. Norwood, MA: Artech House Publishers, 2004.

Bushkov, A. *Ekaterina II: Alzmaznaya Zolushka (Catherine the Second: The Diamond Cinderella)*. Saint Petersburg, Russia: Neva, 2005.

By department, "Gunning for Sergeant York." *Time* (April 15th 1985): http://www.time.com/time/magazine/article/0,9171,1050466,00.html (accessed on Aug. 3, 2010).

Carpenter, C. *The Wars of the Roses: Politics and the Constitution in England, c. 1437–1509*. New York: Cambridge University Press, 2002.

Carswell, J. *The South Sea Bubble*. London: Cresset Press, 1960.

Central Intelligence Agency. *The CIA World Factbook 2008*. New York, NY: Skyhorse Publishing, 2007.

Collins, J. *Good to Great: Why Some Companies Make the Leap . . . and Others Don't*. New York, NY: HarperBusiness, 2001.

Cooper, R. G. "Winning at New Products: Pathways to Profitable Innovation." *PMI Research Conference 2006 Proceedings—Montreal* (July 16–19, 2006).

Cooper, R. G., Edgett, S. J., Kleinschmidt, E. J. "Best Practices for Managing R&D Portfolios." *Research Technology Management* 41, no. 4 (1998): pp. 20–33.

———. *Best Practices in Product Innovation: What Distinguishes Top Performers*. Ancaster, ON: Stage-Gate International, 2003.

———. "New Product Portfolio Management: Practices and Performance." *Journal of Product Innovation Management* 16, no. 4 (1999): pp. 333–351.

———. "Portfolio Management for New Product Development: Results of an Industry Practices Study." *R&D Management* 31, no. 4 (Oct. 2001): pp 361–380.

———. *Portfolio Management for New Products*. New York: Basic Books, 2002.

Cowles, V. *The Great Swindle: The Story of the South Sea Bubble*. New York: Harper, 1960.

Dickie, J. *Cosa Nostra: A History of the Sicilian Mafia*. New York, NY: Palgrave Macmillan, 2005.

Ditton, M. M. "The DIVAD Procurement: A Weapon System Case Study." *The Army Lawyer* (August 1988): pp. 3–9.

Divine, D. *The Blunted Sword*. London: Hutchinson, 1964.

Duffy, C. *Prussia's Glory: Rossbach and Leuthen, 1757*. Chicago: Emperor's Press, 2003.

Eckhardt, C. C. "The Alsace-Lorraine Question." *The Scientific Monthly* 6, no. 5 (May 1918): pp. 431–443.

Eggen, D., Witte, G. "The FBI's Upgrade That Wasn't." *The Washington Post* (August 18, 2006).

Esposito, V.J. *A Concise History of World War II*. London: Pall Mall, 1964.

Fisher, R., Ury, W. L., Patton, B. *Getting to Yes: Negotiating Agreement Without Giving In*. London: Penguin (Non-Classics), 1991.

Flyvbjerg, B., COWI, *Procedures for Dealing with Optimism Bias in Transport Planning: Guidance Document*. London: UK Department for Transport, 2004.

Flyvbjerg, B. "From Nobel Prize to Project Management: Getting Risks Right." *Project Management Journal* 37, no. 3 (August 2006): pp. 5–15.

Flyvbjerg, B., Bruzelius, N., Rothengatter, W. *Megaprojects and Risk: An Anatomy of Ambition*. Cambridge, UK: Cambridge University Press, 2003.

Gause, D. C., Weinberg, G. M. *Exploring Requirements: Quality Before Design*. New York, NY: Dorset House Publishing Company,1989.

Goldstein, H. "Who Killed the Virtual Case File?" *IEEE Spectrum* Vol. 42, no. 9. (September 6, 2005), pp. 24–35.

Golley, J. *Genesis of the Jet: Frank Whittle and the Invention of the Jet Engine*. Wiltshire, UK: The Crowood Press, 1997.

Gottesdiener, E. *Requirements by Collaboration: Workshops for Defining Needs*. Reading, MA: Addison-Wesley Professional, 2002.

Haig, M. *Brand Failures: The Truth About the 100 Biggest Branding Mistakes of All Time*. Philadelphia, PA: Kogan Page, 2003.

Haley, G., Goldberg, S. "Net Present Value Techniques and Their Effects on New Product Research." *Industrial Marketing Management* 24 (1995): pp. 177–190.

Hattendorf, J. *England in the War of the Spanish Succession*. New York: Garland, 1987.

Hawthorne, R. "The Franco-German Boundary of 1871." *World Politics* (January 1950): pp. 209–250.

Howard, M. *The Franco-Prussian War: The German Invasion of France 1870–1871*. New York: Routledge, 2001.

Hymowitz, C. "Diversity in a Global Economy—Ways Some Firms Get It Right." *Wall Street Journal Online* (November 16, 2005): http://www.wallstreetjournal.com.

Iakovlev, A. *Tsel Zhizni: Zapiski Aviakonstruktora (The Purpose of Life—Memoirs of the Airplane Designer)*. Moscow, Russia: Izdatelstvo Respublika, 2000.

Jewkes, J. *Sources of Invention*. New York: W.W. Norton and Company, 1971.

Jones, S. *Estimating Software Costs: Bringing Realism to Estimating.* New York: McGraw-Hill Osborne Media, 2007.

Keegan, J. *Six Armies in Normandy*. London: Penguin, 1994.

———. *The Second World War*. London: Hutchinson, 1989.

Kendall, G., Rollins, S. *Advanced Project Portfolio Management and the PMO: Multiplying ROI at Warp Speed*. Fort Lauderdale, FL: J. Ross Publishing, 2003.

Kim, S. *Essence of Creativity: A Guide to Tackling Difficult Problems*. United States: Oxford University Press, 1990.

Letavec, C. *The Program Management Office: Establishing, Managing and Growing the Value of a PMO*. Fort Lauderdale, FL: J. Ross Publishing, 2006.

Levine, H. *Project Portfolio Management: A Practical Guide To Selecting Projects, Managing Portfolios and Maximizing Benefits*. Hoboken, NJ: Jossey-Bass, 2005.

Lewis, N. *The Honoured Society: The Sicilian Mafia Observed*. London, UK: Eland Publishing, 2003.

MacDonald, C. *The Mighty Endeavor: American Armed Forces in the European Theater in World War II*. Cambridge, MA: Da Capo Press, 1992.

Mackay, C. *Extraordinary Popular Delusions and the Madness of Crowds*. Petersfield, UK: Harriman House Classics, 2003.

Maizlish, B., Handler, R. *IT Portfolio Management Step-By-Step: Unlocking the Business Value of Technology*. New York: Wiley, 2005.

Malhotra, D., Bazerman, M. *Negotiation Genius: How to Overcome Obstacles and Achieve Brilliant Results at the Bargaining Table and Beyond*. New York: Bantam, 2006.

McConnell, S. *Software Estimation: Demystifying the Black Art*. Redmond, WA: Microsoft Press, 2006.

More, R., Little, B. "The Application of Discriminant Analysis to the Prediction of Sales Forecast Uncertainty in New Product Situations." *Journal of Operations Research Society* Vol 31, (1980): 71–77.

Moustafaev, J. "Are We Supposed to Negotiate on Projects?" *Project Times* (September 2, 2009): http://www.projecttimes.com.

———. "Defining the Detailed Scope: How and Where Do You Find Requirements?" *Project Times* (July 22, 2009): http://www.projecttimes.com.

———. "Harnessing the Chaos: Are Portfolio, Project and Requirements Management Interrelated?" *Project Times* (May 13, 2009): http://www.projecttimes.com.

———. "How And Why Do We Write Project Charters?" *Project Times* (July 08, 2009): http://www.projecttimes.com.

———. "Integrating Project Management and Business Analysis." *Canadian West Coast Chapter PMI*. http://www.pmi.bc.ca/LinkClick.aspx?link=Articles%2fIntegrating+Project+Management+and+Business+Analysis.pdf&tabid=155.

———. "Kick-Starting Your Projects: What You Should Know About Defining Scope." *Project Times* (June 03, 2009): http://www.projecttimes.com.

———. "PMO A La Carte: Advantages and Challenges." *Canadian West Coast Chapter PMI*. http://www.pmi.bc.ca/LinkClick.aspx?link=Articles%2fPMO_A_La_Carte_-_Advantages_and_Challenges.pdf&tabid=148.

———. "Who Needs Walk-throughs, Inspections and Peer Reviews?" *Project Times* (August 12, 2009): http://www.projecttimes.com.

———. "Why Should You Manage Scope and Customer Expectations?" *Project Times* (October 7, 2009): http://www.projecttimes.com.

Nahum, A. *Frank Whittle: Invention of the Jet*. London, UK: Icon Books, 2004.

Neufeld, J., Watson, G. M., Chenoweth, D. *Technology and the Air Force: A Retrospective Assessment*. Honolulu, Hawaii: University Press of the Pacific, 2002.

Newark, T. *Mafia Allies: The True Story of America's Secret Alliance with the Mob in World War II*. Minneapolis, MN: Zenith Press, 2007.

Nicolle, D. *Crécy 1346: Triumph of the Longbow*. PUBLISHER CITY: Osprey Publishing, 2000.

"No time for Sergeant." *The Nation* (September 1985).

O'Farrell, J. *An Utterly Impartial History of Britain—Or 2000 Years of Upper Class Idiots in Charge*. New York: Doubleday, 2007.

Pollard, A. *The Wars of the Roses. Problems in Focus*. London: MacMillan Press, 1995.

Pournelle, J. *Blood and Iron: There Will Be War*. New York: Tom Doherty Associates, 1984.

Powell, J. R. *Robert Blake: General-At-Sea*. London: Collins, 1972.

Project Management Institute. *The PMI® Project Management Fact Book, 2nd ed*. Newtown Square, PA: Project Management Institute, 2001.

———. *A Guide to the Project Management Body of Knowledge*. Newtown Square, PA: Project Management Institute, 2001.

Reagan, G. *Guinness Book of Historical Blunders*. Enfield, UK: Guinness Publishing, 1994.

———. *Histrionics: A Treasury of Historical Anecdotes*. London: Robson Books, 1996.

Regan, G. *Battles That Changed History*. London: Carlton Books, 2006.

———. *Brassey's Book of Naval Blunders*. Dulles, VA: Potomac Books, 2000.

Robertson, S., Robertson, J. C. *Mastering the Requirements Process*. Reading, MA: Addison-Wesley Professional, 2006.

Ross, C. *Richard III. Yale English Monarchs*. Yale University Press, 1999.

Shell, R. G. *Bargaining for Advantage: Negotiation Strategies for Reasonable People* 2nd ed. London: Penguin, 2006.

Skarzynski, P., Gibson, R. *Innovation to the Core: A Blueprint for Transforming the Way Your Company Innovates*. Harvard Business School Press, 2008.

Standish Group. *CHAOS Report 2006*. Boston, MA: Standish Group International, 2006.

Suvorov, V., Beattie, T. *Icebreaker: Who Started the Second World War?* PUBLISHER CITY: Viking Press, 1990.

Tagliabue, J. "Villalba Journal: How Don Calo (and Patton) Won the War in Sicily." *The New York Times* (May 24, 1994): http://www.nytimes.com/1994/05/24/world/villalba-journal-how-don-calo-and-patton-won-the-war-in-sicily.html (accessed on Aug 3, 2010).

Tunstall, B., Tracy, N. *Naval Warfare in the Age of Sail. The Evolution of Fighting Tactics, 1650-1815*. Edison, NJ: Wellfleet Press, 2001.

Tzu, S. *Art of War*, PUBLISHER CITY: Filiquarian, 2007.

von Hippel, E. *The Sources Of Innovation*. Oxford: Oxford University Press, 1985.

Wawro, G. *The Franco-Prussian War: The German Conquest of France in 1870-1871*. Cambridge: Cambridge University Press, 2003.

Webb, D. *Inflation: The Value of the Pound 1750–2005*. London: House of Commons Library, 2006.

Weiss, J., Wysocki, R. *Five-phase Project Management: A Practical Planning and Implementation Guide*. New York: Basic Books, 1992.

Wideman, M. *A Management Framework for Project, Program and Portfolio Integration*. Bloomington, IN: Trafford Publishing, 2006.

Wiegers, K. E. *Software Requirements*, 2nd ed. Redmond, WA: Microsoft Press, 2003.

Young, R. R. *Effective Requirements Practices*. Reading, MA: Addison-Wesley Professional, 2001.

Zetterling, N. *Normandy 1944, German Military Organisation, Combat Power and Organizational Effectiveness*. Winnipeg, MB: J. J. Fedorowicz Publishing, 2000.

Index